**Sylvia Loring.** With her go[...] eyes, she's tougher than sh[...] vulnerable than she'd like to believe. Right now she's struggling for success and the story that could make her name a household word—if she lives to see it in print ...

⭐

**Colette Daniels.** A gossip columnist as inventive as she is seductive, she set her stakes high, both in her career and her love life. But sometimes gambles have a way of putting everything at risk ...

⭐

**Ben Fincastle.** This North Carolina senator's front-running position in the next presidential election is almost guaranteed—unless certain details of his private life make national news. And Ben will do anything to protect his public image ...

⭐

**Hale Gardiner.** A brilliant scion of one of Virginia's First Families, she became the youngest-ever editor of the *Washington Tribune* at the age of thirty-one. Now her connections to the power elite are about to play havoc with her conscience ...

⭐

**Max Ridgway.** Sylvia Loring had broken his heart once. Then she came back, asking for a purely professional association. But Max has other ideas ...

⭐

# Official Secrets

## LINDSEY MITCHELL

**WARNER BOOKS**

A Warner Communications Company

WARNER BOOKS EDITION

Cover design by Anne Twomey
Cover photo by Anthony Lowe

Warner Books, Inc.
666 Fifth Avenue
New York, N.Y. 10103

 A Warner Communications Company

Printed in the United States of America

First Printing: May, 1990

10 9 8 7 6 5 4 3 2 1

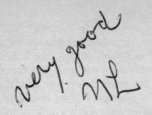

*very good*
*ML*

# CHAPTER
## 1

Sylvia Loring swung her dusty white Chevy Nova into the glittering procession of limos, Rolls-Royces, and standard-issue, Embassy Row Mercedes-Benzes. When the guard appeared at her window, Sylvia produced a gilded invitation: "L'Ambassadeur de France et Madame Alain de Saint-Phalle prient Miss Colette Daniels de le Washington Tribune de leur faire l'honneur"—here the invitation broke into English—"to attend a reception on Sunday, the 24th of November . . ."

"Merci, Mademoiselle Daniels," he said, extending his hand for the key.

Sylvia smiled. She was not the famous Colette Daniels, nor would she want to be. In fact, she disdained society writing, seeing it as closer to publicity than journalism. Yet she had to admit that ever since Colette handed over the invitation, she'd been excited. In her week-long stint substituting for Colette, this was to be the premier event, a party honoring the French Olympic team, which was gearing up for the 1992 games. It wasn't so much the prospect of mingling with A-list guests that stirred her, but rather a hunch —or was it a wish?—that she would meet someone tonight.

Sylvia checked herself in the mirror. She had strong, Slavic cheekbones and the blue-gray eyes her college boyfriend had called "ocean eyes" because they were the clear blue of the ocean's depths. Cascading blond locks spilled onto her little black dress. Sylvia kept her hair long even when all the other women reporters had defected to the power cut. It was almost platinum, but unlike some natural blondes, Sylvia had lush brown eyelashes and brows, and in summer her tall, slim body took on a glorious tan. At twenty-seven, she could walk into any party and turn heads.

Just inside the turreted, flagstoned mansion, two white-wigged trumpeteers announced Sylvia's arrival with a resounding flourish.

Helene de Saint-Phalle, the ambassador's svelte, silver-headed wife, was there to greet her, wearing a rose-colored, floor-length silk. Tashi, the ambassadorial lhasa apso—dressed for the occasion in a sapphire-studded collar—was perched on her arm. "Hello," said the great lady, extending her hand.

"Sylvia Loring. *Washington Tribune*."

"Yes, of course," said Madame Saint-Phalle, smiling politely. "Colette did say she wasn't working tonight. You must be the assistant she spoke of. But you know Colette," she said with an appreciative giggle. "At the last minute, the phone rings and she has decided to come after all."

Colette's assistant! Sylvia thought to herself. That woman would say anything to enhance her status, even if it was patently false. Before Sylvia had a chance to correct Madame's false impression, the trumpets sounded once more, heralding the arrival of a new guest.

"Oh!" exclaimed the French ambassador's wife, leaving Sylvia for a network anchor who'd once had words with the current President on prime-time TV.

Hale Gardiner had instructed her reporters, especially those in the all-important features department, to become more aggressive rather than less so, to step up their coverage of attention-grabbing stories, even gossipy stuff. Hale called for items that would make all of Capitol Hill turn to the *Tribune* during lunch hour, stories that would revive the paper's flagging circulation.

Just two months ago, Hale, together with publisher Digby Reeve, had unveiled an ambitious plan to overhaul the paper, doing away with its stuffy image, making it competitive for the nineties. She had introduced a crisp, new masthead, a new typeface, and decided to run color art every day. And she established a bonus-money fund from which to reward reporters who snared major stories.

Sylvia had to admit she was charged by this "new administration," as she jokingly referred to it. Deep down, she was a believer in journalism as the cornerstone of democracy, and America's capital—of all places—needed two strong competitive newspapers, just as Congress needed two strong parties to provide checks and balances. And Sylvia understood the urgency of the situation: There was a certain, unannounced time limit in which this new highly capitalized strategy would have to begin paying off. If it didn't work, the *Tribune* might be gobbled up by some corporate raider or worse: It could follow the fate of so many other second newspapers throughout the country and fold.

Sylvia pulled out her notebook and moved into the reception line, where she met Ray, a *Trib* photographer, who was already snapping shots of celebrities, who seemed to love the attention. Here were the faces that regularly graced the *Washington Tribune* society page, name guests whose presence could make or break an event. In Washington, the ne plus ultra party was one attended by the President. Cabinet members, congressional leaders, and first family members were also prized guests, as was any political celebrity standing trial or under fire. The President was absent from this gathering, but he would have been here, Sylvia overheard one guest assure another, had he been in town.

Helping himself to finger food off an enormous silver platter was the secretary of state, a man with a Texas-size appetite whose closeness to the President made him the next-best party catch. The famous former attorney general, who resigned his post rather than bloody his hands during the Watergate scandal, emptied his highball glass and conversed with the only female jurist on the Supreme Court and the powerful board chairman of the city's other newspaper. Now a fixture on the diplomatic party circuit, he was explaining his work to promote ocean law in a low, slow-voweled, patrician tone.

Then Sylvia spotted Ben Fincastle, the Democrats' great White House hope for next year, having a tête-à-tête with none other than Colette Daniels. They were standing on the veranda, under an enormous heat lamp, bathing their bodies with warmth in November weather that would otherwise feel nippy. Something in their manner suggested they were utterly alone together.

When Colette had reviewed with Sylvia the parties to be covered during her week off, she'd warned her to dress for this one. And Sylvia had plunked down a bundle at Garfinckle's for an understated, black silk jersey dress by Louis Feraud, a stretch on her salary.

Colette certainly heeded her own advice. Wrapped into a strapless, snakeskin, gold-lamé bustier, her ample breasts spilling over, and a matching skintight skirt, Colette was flaunting every voluptuous inch. A brunette, she had large, bewitching features—thick eyeliner accentuated her wide-set hazel eyes—and could carry heavy jewelry and makeup without being overwhelmed by either. That dress, Sylvia realized from her own shopping trip, would have cost a mint. Was there something to the in-house gossip that Colette had wangled a clothing allowance from the tightfisted *Trib*?

It wasn't that Sylvia disliked Colette, she just didn't trust her. It seemed there was nothing Colette wouldn't do to get ahead. They'd both started at the *Tribune* five years ago—two jittery novices overwhelmed by the Big Time they'd just entered. But six months into her job, after Sylvia's first big byline, Colette's true colors emerged. A local TV station called inviting Sylvia to appear on a panel of hot young journalists. Colette intercepted the call, told the producer Sylvia was out for the week, and volunteered to be the guest. Her performance drew plaudits from the editors; the only hitch was that Sylvia had been out for coffee at the time— not out for the week.

Though guests pressed in around him, looking for an opening to meet the future president, Ben Fincastle would not take his eyes off Colette. He removed the handkerchief from his jacket pocket, and with a sly smile, moistened it and dabbed at something on her cheek.

Seeing him for the first time in person—his coal-black hair, graying slightly at the temples, his chiseled jawline, his powerful physique—Sylvia had to grudgingly admit that Colette had once again zeroed in on the most charismatic man at the gathering.

Fincastle's name appeared in Colette's column all the time, along with the occasional catty reference to Ben's "oh-so-plain" wife, Judy. Rumors were flying that Colette and Ben were sleeping together, but Sylvia wouldn't believe it. Not that Colette wasn't capable of it, but no man this close to winning his party's presidential nomination would run the risk. And certainly not after the Democratic front-runner in the last election had self-destructed over a blond model.

Still, it was true that Colette had been a different person these last few weeks, drawing into herself more, detaching herself from life at the paper. Her "mornings" had grown later and later and now started at three P.M., when she would totter in in high heels and sunglasses, pour her Tab into a tall crystal glass, and finish it off with a straw. Then she'd put in an hour or two on the phone, talking in her little-girl voice with publicists and socialites, giving you the impression that she couldn't possibly know how to key into a computer, much less compose a story. But every morning like clockwork, out came these glorious renderings of life in the fast lane: party banter, silly faux pas—almost too real, too blunt to be believed.

There was no disputing Colette's value to the second paper in town. Almost everyone had heard of her and, during an interview, invariably asked Sylvia what Colette was *really* like. They turned to Colette, they said, before reading William Safire, Ellen Goodman, and the news from Moscow. And, usually, before they tackled the formidable *Washington Post*. But Sylvia knew that Colette was more an opportunist than a journalist, employing methods that diminished the honor of their profession.

With the *Trib* photographer Ray in tow, Sylvia wasted no

time shifting into action. This was the period of high intensity, when the celebrities were all here together. Often, they arrived in clusters and stayed only long enough to put in an appearance.

"You're not Colette Daniels," said a tipsy, balding State Department officer, spotting her reporter's notebook. "You're much too pretty to be that cruel." Sylvia had a weakness for oversized, weather-beaten men who were witty and fearless, with miles of experience on them. Besides, she'd learned that you usually get the most from middle-level people. If they're at the bottom, they know nothing; if they're at the top, they'll say nothing. And this one looked interesting. But, unfortunately, the only way to satisfy Hale Gardiner was to pepper the column with "big names"—even if they had nothing more insightful to say than that the lights were low or the champagne was dry. Just so long as you could bold-face the name in the column, run their photo or a stock mug shot, and draw readers. Sylvia regretfully excused herself.

A few paces away, she stumbled onto a bona fide scene.

"Okay, prick!" said a stunning, Oriental-looking woman to a man Sylvia recognized as an important congressman, chairman of some committee. His name was at the tip of her tongue, but just out of reach. Not to worry, she could match up the name with his photo in the Congressional Pictorial Directory.

The woman's voice carried over the din of the party. "If that's the way you do business," she said, "let me lay this one on you. You made me a promise, and I'm gonna collect!"

"I don't know who you are or what you want," the congressman said hotly, and turned to go.

The woman seized the congressman's tuxedo sleeve with a violent grip. "Not so fast, Bob."

That was it, Sylvia thought to herself, Bob Rossen, chairman of the powerful Judiciary Committee.

Just as Ray's camera flashed, the woman "accidentally" jostled a drink on Rossen, some of it landing on her own bodice.

"Damn it!" Rossen roared. Then, realizing that his picture

had just been taken, he addressed Sylvia and Ray. "You're not going to use this," he said, as if he were giving orders.

"What's going on here, Congressman Rossen?" Sylvia said, pleased with herself for coming up with his last name. It always gave you an edge to know someone's name when he or she didn't know yours.

The congressman glared at her and then at Ray. "Nothing is going on here," he said. "And that's how we're going to leave it." He gave her a sharp stare, awaiting her verbal complicity.

"Do you know this woman?" Sylvia persisted, jotting down his last remark, but he stomped off toward the coat-room.

Needing the woman's name for the caption on this delicious shot, Sylvia followed her into the powder room.

The young woman was furious and distraught at the same time, desperately tending her soggy dress. "That son of a bitch," she kept mumbling to herself as she mopped at the spill with one monogrammed hand towel after another. The drink had been tomatoey—probably a Bloody Mary—and would not come out of her lavender and silver chiffon dress.

Her energy was frenetic, off kilter, and she carelessly went through the stack of cloth towels meant to serve an evening's guests, tossing them like used Kleenexes into a pile on the marble counter. It occurred to Sylvia that she might be on something, maybe cocaine.

Despite it all, she was stunning, with lustrous dark hair and long shapely legs. About five-seven or five-eight without heels, she was quite tall for an Oriental. In the brightly lit room, Sylvia could see that under her makeup the girl was very young, perhaps still in her teens.

She grew increasingly agitated at her failure to remove the stain. "This baby set me back two hundred dollars," she said, referring to the dress. "And I won't make a dime to-night."

"Let me run out and get some soda water," Sylvia volunteered. "It's supposed to take out this kind of thing."

For an instant, a look of utter gratitude crossed the girl's face, as if she were in desperate need of mothering. For just a moment, she seemed overwhelmed by Sylvia's offer.

When Sylvia returned with a glass of club soda, the girl went to the door and locked it.

"Let's do it the easy way," she said, yanking her dress off over her head. Even though there was no one else in the powder room, Sylvia was startled by the young woman's readiness to strip down to bra and panties in front of a total stranger. And despite the filmy, transparent dress fabric, she wore no slip.

"I'm Sylvia Loring," she said. "What's your name?"

"Kokoh," said the girl.

Applying the club soda to the dress, together they worked the stain out. Kokoh wriggled into the dress and stooped to pull on her heels.

"Kokoh, I'm a reporter for the *Washington Tribune*."

She glanced up, impressed. "Oh, yeah?"

Sylvia hesitated. She was reluctant to bring out her notebook for fear that Kokoh might clam up. She would have to make mental notes. But she'd passed the first hurdle. Kokoh didn't turn off the minute she identified herself. "I couldn't help but notice the tiff out there. What was going on?"

"With Bob?"

"Bob Rossen."

Kokoh stood up straight, her dark eyes flashing. "One thing I won't take is when someone pulls that shit on me. Like they don't even know me, like I'm some douche bag or something. It'd be one thing if his wife was here, but to act like he doesn't know me from jack shit—that I won't take."

"Do you work with Rossen?"

"Yeah, I work with Rossen," she said with digust. "If you call this work." Kokoh cupped a circle with one of her hands and thrust two fingers into it, in and out.

Kokoh's meaning was clear, but somehow Sylvia couldn't believe what she was hearing. This kid was telling her she was sleeping with the powerful chairman of the Judiciary Committee, a man whom the *Trib* Sunday magazine had featured last Valentine's Day on the cover with his wife of twenty-five years, with the pull quote: "I love her more today than I did yesterday. And I'll love her more tomorrow than I did today."

"How did you meet him?" Sylvia asked.

"How do you meet a dude who pays?" Kokoh laughed. Tossing her long mane, she clattered over to the full-length mirror.

"Are you his mistress?"

"If you're asking does he pay my rent, no way. He's too cheap." Kokoh bent toward the mirror to examine the damp spot on her dress. "I'm just the girl Bob asks for. Spicy, Oriental pussy."

A tentative knock sounded on the door.

"Busy," Kokoh barked. Then, hearing retreating footsteps, she giggled in delight. "I love it!" she crowed. "I don't care if it's the queen of England—she's gonna have to wait."

Sylvia laughed, despite herself. The girl had style. She was also full of herself. "Sounds like you're good at what you do."

"The best."

"Does Bob Rossen think so?"

"It's not just Bob," retorted Kokoh huffily. "They all think I'm the best girl. All those dudes. I could give you names in this town that would blow you away."

In the silence the room seemed to shrink, and Sylvia could feel her heart grow large and clamorous in her chest. For the first time, Sylvia realized that if Kokoh were credible, she may have stumbled onto a major story, a scandal that could shake American politics—and even possibly affect the outcome of next year's election. Rossen was, after all, a Democrat. Uncovering sex scandals was the journalist's equivalent of playing with matches. You could build the perfect fire or you could burn the whole house down. Sylvia started to speak, but Kokoh was ahead of her.

"I've had it with this crap." Kokoh blurted, as if talking to herself. "I'm supposed to be a model, and that sucker owes me."

"Tell me about it," Sylvia said, trying to keep her voice

calm, the way you do in a sudden emergency, trying to drown out the thunder in her chest.

Kokoh told her about it. She told how she worked with other girls who sexually serviced senators and congressmen and lobbyists and "all the big, fat, rich dudes." She told how politicians are cheap and how they usually paid in cash or charged it on their American Express cards.

When it was evident that Kokoh knew what she was saying, Sylvia pulled out her notebook and grilled her. Specifically, what was her beef with Bob Rossen? (He promised to stake her for a modeling portfolio, but now he "forgot.") Did Rossen have relations with any other girls? (No.) Did Kokoh have any proof that he'd paid? (Yes, she had a copy of his charge slip from today.) Who were the other politicians? (Kokoh had been working only a little while and didn't know all their names right off as she did Bob's, but she could find out.)

A series of sharp raps on the door, and a stern French-accented voice announced that the powder room had been occupied for "some time now"; would the occupant "please vacate the room—there are other guests here."

"Buzz off," Kokoh hissed, and then loudly, "One sec!"

"Listen," said Sylvia quickly, handing Kokoh her pen and notebook. "Write down your number. And last name. I'll call you."

"It's spelled K–O–K–O–H," she said, proudly enunciating the last consonant. Kokoh scribbled, not trying to mask her excitement. "Is my picture going to be in the paper?"

"There's a good chance."

"I hope you got me from my good side," Kokoh said. "Could you call me a model in the photo?"

"Sure," said Sylvia, trying to decipher Kokoh's juvenile scrawl. "Kokoh King. 555-2739. Have you ever done any professional modeling?"

"Not really," said Kokoh. "But I did pose in a miniskirt for a mobile-home ad back in Florida."

"What if I call you an 'apprentice model'?"

"Sounds good."

Kokoh unlocked the door, and there, in stiff disapproval, was the French ambassador's wife and her dog. Behind them, visibly annoyed by this breach of etiquette, was a short line of bejeweled women.

"Hi, girls," Kokoh said as she strutted past.

Sylvia hardly saw them. What had transpired in the powder room was giving her a delirious buzz, as if she had just downed two glasses of the finest champagne.

Excited about what could be a huge scoop, Sylvia rushed toward the coatroom to gather her wrap and leave for the *Tribune*. She had enough material for the column—why stick around? She was dying to tell someone about Kokoh. Pam Tursi, her best friend and *Trib* business reporter, would be the first.

A dark, tuxedoed stranger stepped directly into her path, nearly throwing her off balance. Sylvia stopped just short of banging into him. He had the body of a football tackle—thick and dense—and dark curly hair. Like so many Washington faces, his looked familiar.

"B. D. Cole," he said, offering his hand. He spoke his name as if delivering the trump card, as if he need say no more.

A thrill rushed down Sylvia's spine as she realized that Washington's most celebrated consultant and strategist had singled her out. B. D. Cole was the capital's kingmaker, the force behind Ben Fincastle, and one of the town's most eligible bachelors. He was universally credited with masterminding the political strategy that had elevated Fincastle from a field of little-known Democratic contenders to his current front-runner position. B. D. did everything for Ben, from selecting his ties to composing his reading list. "The power to make a president," the *Post* had trumpeted in its most recent profile.

"Sylvia Loring, with the *Tribune*, right?"

"Yes," Sylvia said with a smile, but her insides were churning as she desperately searched for something to say. Her eyes lit on her reporter's notebook, and she pulled it out in relief. "Do you mind if I ask you a question?"

"Fire away," B. D. said.

"How would you rate this party?"

"Fair to middling, with a bang at the end," he said, the play in his eyes telling her that the "bang" was meeting her.

"Come on," she said.

"Well," he quipped, eyeing a middle-aged woman in a significant diamond-and-sapphire necklace, "I'd give my left hand for the mineral rights to this party."

Sylvia had to laugh. That was a good, snappy throwaway quote, she thought, taking it down. This man was media savvy. But she wanted more. Something really good. "I see," she retorted, feigning disappointment. "Zero, zilch."

"OK, here's something for you. You can have it only if you promise not to attribute any of it to me. Not to use my name."

"Fire away," she said.

"Bob Rossen's wife is filing for divorce."

"Rossen. Judiciary?"

"Yeah," he said. "Sally Rossen just finally had enough."

Sylvia hesitated. B. D. was famous, but still she had to check sources. "Where'd you hear this?"

"Trust me. I heard it this afternoon. It's straight up. Colette would jump at that item."

"You're sure about this?"

"Yep," he said with absolute conviction and a touch of curtness, as if no one needed to double-check him. "Just no B. D. Cole. I'd play it this way: 'Rumor has it Sally Rossen is asking for divorce from her husband of whatever years.' "

His words interrupted her scribbling. "So, Sylvia Loring, are you ever a person, not a reporter?"

She looked up at him, disconcerted.

He took hold of her notebook and pen. "WHEN DO I CALL YOU?" he wrote, and without a word returned the notebook for Sylvia to read.

Staring at the words, Sylvia's mind raced. Less than an arm's length away, masculine and burly and smelling faintly of cologne, was a man who could launch a thrilling flight from her earthbound routine. Pam was right: Life was short. *Oh, go for it* rang in her brain. She looked up from the notebook, saw only his eyes smiling, and scribbled an answer beneath his question: "Tomorrow at work."

# CHAPTER
## 2

As she did every morning, Sylvia parked her car in a cheap lot and walked the six blocks to work, stopping by a breakfast stand for a cheese Danish and a cup of coffee to go. She was in a hurry, eager to get a copy of the morning edition and see how her column looked in print, to savor a few minutes alone with her work before the others started trooping in.

She approached the Washington Tribune Building, with its brick-and-sandstone facade, feeling a rush of proprietorial pride. The entire newspaper operation—advertising, editorial, production and printing—was headquartered here in the original building, built in the 1850s by Silas Reeve not long after the Smithsonian Institution was completed.

Sylvia greeted the guard at the front door with a smile and breezed through. The lobby was a breathtaking testament to faded glory. Weathered Oriental rugs covered the solid marble floors, and elaborate wooden carvings climbed the walls to the ceiling. Ringed velvet guardrails hung on ancient brass stands to route pedestrian traffic.

Sylvia flashed back to the first time she'd passed through the *Tribune*'s massive, carved brass revolving door five years before. She'd acted boldly then, coming in without so much as an interview, feeling a dizzying mixture of terror and calling. Fresh out of college with a degree in English, her one and only contact in the real world was Digby Reeve, the *Tribune* publisher whom she'd met at a party the previous spring. At the time, he'd been enough taken with her to volunteer the prospect of employment.

From her mother's house in Silver Spring, Sylvia had called Digby's office repeatedly without a response. Finally, on Jan Loring's advice, Sylvia appeared at his office to drop off her college newspaper clips. Where, as luck would have it, she bumped into him. When, in the course of their conversation, she mentioned that she had recently broken up with her boyfriend, he suddenly warmed to her.

"Reporters should be young and heartbroken when they start out," he said. "They work harder and they work overtime. Does the name Hale Gardiner mean anything to you?"

Digby never actually told Sylvia she had the job. Or mentioned salary. But after forty-five minutes and two cups of coffee in his office, he told her to come back Monday at nine and they'd find her a desk.

Taking the stairs two at a time, Sylvia bounded up into the newsroom, where wire-service machines—drawing from continuous reams of paper—pecked and clacked out the stories one at a time. The desks in the newsroom were arranged in a haphazard layout, the floors uneven and mostly linoleum. Some griped that the building was small and tight, uncomfortable to work in, but Sylvia loved it. The *Washington Post* newsroom, by contrast, was new and impersonal, carpeted and climate-controlled. "Icily regular, splendidly nil," Sylvia pronounced after her first visit. "They could just as well sell insurance there!"

Enormous bundles of the morning edition sat on wide tables, brought up by production and awaiting the close scrutiny that only the newshounds—and three dozen cranky, know-it-all readers—would give it. Sylvia picked up two copies and waved them in the air to an older copy editor, who was scanning a story from under his obsolete visor.

Taking her seat behind a large, metal, circa-1957 desk, Sylvia pulled the Style section out from under the news section. It was still a thrill to see her byline, her creation, in print. Being a reporter had always seemed to Sylvia an honor, a public responsibility: to be able to write and shape public opinion, to take information and through some mysterious creative process distill it and throw it out with a new slant.

And she was always learning. Journalists were paid to ask questions, to be good listeners.

Sylvia turned anxiously to the front cover of the second section, scanning her column for any errors she'd missed last night.

Her eyes landed on the giant photo of Rossen being ingloriously doused with a Bloody Mary, the dark liquid streaming from Kokoh's glass to Rossen's chest. The photo was even better than she expected. Ray had snapped Rossen at precisely the moment in which horror and surprise converged on his face. His nostrils were flared, a shock of hair fell down over his forehead, and his mouth was open with angry dismay. The photos consumed three times the space as the type, with the other celebrities beaming out in lesser poses.

Then the column:

> "Unexpected drama spiced the exclusive party for the French Olympic team at the home of French Ambassador and Madame Alain de Saint-Phalle. It wasn't so much the sumptuous fare—Huitres aux Feuille de Laitues (oysters in lettuce); Feuilletee d'Asperges (asparagus in puff pastry); Petite Salade de Pigeon aux Noix (pigeon salad)—that was flown in from France and heartily welcomed by such gastronomes as the secretary of state, who confided to a fellow traveler between bites, "This is only my second dinner." Nor was it the Parisian artists, imported from the Left Bank for the evening to draw as party favors caricatures of some of the world's most famous faces. As any Francophile knows, the French artist is uncompromising with his art. And certainly, renditions of the proboscis of said secretary and First Pal, the double chins of a female jurist, and the puffed-pastry flesh of a famous Massachusetts senator bore out this maxim.

Rereading it, Sylvia loved this last line! And the next: "The senator's sketch was later found rumpled in a waste can by an enterprising journalist."

Damn it, it suddenly occurred to her—now when it was

too late to do anything about it—why didn't she think to run the rumpled sketch in the paper? How could she have overlooked this last night?

The column continued:

"Despite the heralding welcome by trumpeteers and attendant canine greetings from Tashi, Madame Saint-Phalle's prized dog, one congressman would have been better off had he stayed home. The Party In Town last night honored the promising French Olympic team, gearing up for the Winter Olympics. But little did Bob Rossen, powerful chairman of the House Judiciary Committee, suspect that he would take a medal in the splash-and-spill competition. All eyes were on him when a lovely young lady doused him with what was left of her Bloody Mary.

The congressman implied that the spill was accidental. The young lass, apprentice model Kokoh King, insisted Rossen—with whom she says she has a bone to pick—was the intended target.

"Nothing is going on here," the congressman huffed, "and that's how we're going to leave it." At that, his eminence collected his wrap and exited the party.

Whoever was right, it certainly made for some lively theatrics last night at the party of a country renowned for its high drama.

"But this was only the opening act for Rossen. The second and final act unfolded when he was safely off-stage. The Washington rumor mill was operating in high gear at the bash, with word that Sally Rossen is filing for divorce. One partygoer speculated that another woman was involved. As the French would say: *Cherchez la femme.*"

Sylvia put the column down. Journalism was getting riskier every year. As in every other profession, lawsuits were on the rise. At the *Tribune*, reporters were required to keep their notes for every story for three years after it ran. Sometimes you got sued for the most inconsequential things. One investigative reporter she knew had chased down stories on the Mafia and organized crime, drug-running and corruption in government for years, and had never been taken to task. Not until he wrote a little feature article on a man running for sheriff in Montgomery County, Maryland. He described the sheriff as "a potbellied Pillsbury doughboy of a man." The sheriff had sued and won a judgment against the paper, arguing that being so described damaged his political career.

Sylvia's column was risky, even though she'd steered clear of Kokoh's allegations (which she would follow up later). She really stuck it to Bob Rossen, something Sylvia would have been more reluctant to do had he not patronized her and Ray that way last night. That passing exchange had revealed great arrogance on his part, as well as a contempt-for-the-press attitude. Treating Sylvia like a publicist was the single worst approach anyone could take.

Dennis Berman, Style editor and Sylvia's boss, shuffled in. His eyes, usually sleepy at this hour, crackled with fire.

"You've certainly dispelled one myth this morning," Dennis said, holding the paper. "That only Colette can dish it out." Dennis had a high regard for Sylvia's talents, and he had considered it beneath them for her to take on the stint for Colette. Of course, part of his vehemence had been self-interest: He was reluctant to lose one of his ace reporters for that long. Without Sylvia, he'd have to run more wire copy to fill his hole or use free-lancers. "With a little practice," he continued, "you might even get good at this."

Despite his gruff exterior, Dennis Berman's heart was in the right place. He had started in the business in 1960 as a college reporter covering the Civil Rights movement. As a senior at Amherst College in Massachusetts, he'd finagled a grant from the administration for a trip to Greensboro, North Carolina, to cover the Woolworth lunch counter sit-in; with that, his career was off and running. The sixties had left its mark on him. Even though he tried to dress for success in pastel shirts and ties, the ties were invariably rumpled or off center, the shirt hanging out of the back of his pants.

Dennis had already gotten a bitter call from Rossen's administrative assistant, who was making threatening noises, he said. Possibly a lawsuit.

This was part of the excitement. You put a story out there and waited for the reaction, if any. And Dennis loved confrontations, noble journalist versus corrupt politician (or businessman, bureaucrat, lobbyist, whatever) going to do battle. Instead of retreating when under fire, Dennis advanced.

" 'On what grounds?' I asked him." Dennis could recount conversations verbatim and right down to the accent of the other party.

" 'Defamation of character,' he says.

" 'You gonna tell me Rossen wasn't there? You gonna tell me we pasted his head onto stock art?'

" 'Well no,' he said. 'The innuendo of that girl having a bone to pick. What'd you mean by that? People might jump to conclusions.' The man asked for some kind of retraction, or apology.

"I told him we can't apologize when we haven't made an error. I held firm. He knew and I knew he didn't have a leg to stand on."

"He was probably just calling to let off steam," Sylvia suggested.

"Sylvia, you've really hit a nerve here. Rossen is ripping on this one," Dennis continued. "I find it interesting what he's squawking about. Didn't say a word objecting to the divorce stuff."

Dennis smiled broadly at her. A smile of admiration, congratulations. A smile of good job, kid, you got Rossen on this one! All the gossip columnists in the country would follow the *Tribune*'s lead, most giving credit to the paper for breaking the news. But true to form, Dennis could never leave a compliment alone. He always had to amend it, to bring up some unexplored venue, some way the story could have been improved. "Now, tell me this: When did Sally Rossen file?"

"Take it easy, Berman," Sylvia said. "There's more."

Sylvia told him that Kokoh King had confessed last night

to being a prostitute and identified Rossen as one of her regulars. Not only that, but, Kokoh claimed, so were a number of other Capitol Hill heavyweights.

Dennis Berman whistled through his teeth.

Still in her fox jacket, Colette Daniels emerged from the elevator and made her entrance in the Style section, an entrance pointedly ignored by colleagues. Colette had read Sylvia's column first thing, naturally, and then fielded a frantic call from her friend Sally Rossen. Of course, what Sylvia had written was all true. But what surprised and rankled her most was that she got the information in the first place. Sylvia didn't even know the Rossens. She didn't travel in those circles. When Hale assigned Sylvia to cover parties this week, Colette had been pleased. Pleased at the thought of Sylvia floundering for once, at a loss for what to write. But never had she expected serious muckraking, never had she thought Sylvia—despite her much-vaunted talents—capable of wresting secrets from a town that was notoriously tight-lipped to anyone outside the club, especially to earnest, upright young journalists.

There was Sylvia, smug and self-assured at her desk, apparently enjoying the flap her column had caused. Her pure blue eyes gazed at Colette with a deceptive look of innocence.

"I never got around to asking you whether you had a good time at the party," Sylvia said without a hint of irony in her voice. Sylvia's blasted friendliness was the most irritating thing about her.

"Yeah, you were too busy mucking with dirty laundry."

"What's that supposed to mean?"

Colette would have to set Sylvia straight, before the woman destroyed the capital she'd spent years accumulating: her contacts, her friendships, her little black book of A-list names and numbers. No one on the *Tribune* would have been invited to a party at the Saint-Phalles'—not Sylvia Loring, not anyone—were it not for Colette. When she'd first gotten the society job, she wasn't being invited to anything important. So she'd rented a limousine and driver one afternoon and had made the rounds, calling on the important embassies, leaving her card. And like clockwork, the invitations started rolling in.

"That you don't go smearing other people's dirty laundry all over the society page. At least, not Bob and Sally Rossen's."

"You mean, not if they're personal friends of yours."

"Yeah, as a matter of fact, that's precisely what I mean. At the very least, if you wanted to run with that stuff, you should have checked with me."

"What do you take me for, Colette, your personal assistant? Which, by the way, is the impression that Helene de Saint-Phalle happened to have."

With that, Colette wheeled away. She had made her point. She went to her desk—which was two down from Sylvia's —lifted her telephone receiver, and punched out a number, one she knew by heart.

"Helene," she started. "What a delightful party! Listen, dear, I just called to apologize for the column. I had absolutely nothing to do with it. I hope it didn't bruise too many feelings. The girl's new at this. She didn't know when to quit."

Colette threw Sylvia a withering glance. She knew damn well Sylvia had heard every word, as she had intended. But Sylvia was carrying on as if she hadn't bothered to listen. Then, Colette reminded herself with some satisfaction, Sylvia Loring had nothing going except for this ragtag newspaper. She never protested the encroachment of reporting work on her personal time, was here at all hours of the day and night, hacking away. There were many times when her own flashes of insight more than bested Sylvia's hours of plodding. And didn't her therapist tell her that her intuition was among her most glittering gifts?

Just last week, she'd overheard Sylvia talking with Pam Tursi about some college boyfriend, somebody who was history five years ago. Carrying the torch for a man had always seemed foolish to Colette. How could anyone fail to see that life should be lived right now? That every moment should be grabbed? Every chance? She collected her bulky pocketbook and left the building. She was going to act on her own philosophy.

# CHAPTER
## 3

Dorothy Hale Gardiner let her white, terry-cloth bathrobe drop to the floor as she stepped into her Victorian, ball-and-claw-footed, cast-iron bathtub. She was a woman of medium height and build, with thick auburn hair that rose to an obstinate cowlick at her side part, just above her forehead. She had small breasts, a thick waist, and what a prep-school rival had once referred to as "piano-stool legs" (a slur she'd neither forgotten nor forgiven). Her features were small and regular—a Brahmin nose, sharp, penetrating eyes, and a serious but delicate mouth. If she ever wore makeup she might be considered pretty.

The bath was Hale's morning ritual. Every morning in preparation, she made coffee and stocked the tub basket with the papers: the *Washington Post*, the *New York Times* and the *Times of London*, which she liked to read for an international perspective. When she had a particular interest in one of her reporter's stories, she'd slip the *Tribune* into the basket as well.

Hale turned on the spigots and poured bath salts and oils into the water, running her finger like a wand through the fragrant brew, testing its temperature. She liked bathing in water almost hot enough to poach an egg.

Daylight streamed into the bathroom from the skylight above as Hale eased into the antique porcelain tub her decorator had found in mint condition at auction. It had once belonged to F.T. Frelinghuysen, secretary of state under President Chester A. Arthur, and there were papers of documentation. Watching her skin turn red with the heat, Hale poured herself a large cup of coffee from the thermal carafe, adding Half 'n' Half and a cube of sugar. She set the cup on the tray straddling the tub and punched a button on the wall to activate the whirlpool.

It was Monday, the beginning of a new work week, with its new, unexpected set of problems to go with the perennial ones: editors jousting for the position of their pet stories, or dropping thinly veiled hints about getting one of the coveted parking spots at the executive lot. Everyone was always asking for a raise, and honestly, Hale couldn't conceive of how anyone could live on as little money as some of her staffers made.

She wondered for a moment if, were they all given raises, they would have the sense to spend them wisely, to replace their tacky wardrobes with pieces of dignity and tastefulness. But it was unlikely. The women were the greater offenders. She'd actually seen Pam Tursi come into work one day in a miniskirt on a motorcycle, and some of the city reporters wore jackets and skirts that looked as if they were bought at J. C. Penney seven years ago.

More often than Hale cared to admit, she found herself fantasizing about being editor of not the *Washington Tribune*, but the *Washington Post*, and she reminded herself that someday it could happen. If she stayed her course, if she put the *Tribune* back in the black, back in the race, then she had a fair chance to become just that, the first female editor of the *Washington Post*, the most influential paper in the capital and the second most important paper in the country after the *New York Times*.

It was Monday, though, and there was Colette's column to look forward to. Always a treat. Hale slid a bar of sandalwood soap down her thigh. Colette Daniels was probably her proudest accomplishment. She had recommended Colette for the job as society editor to Digby Reeve a year and a half ago when that post had come open, and for the substantial salary increase that went with the job. Hale would be quite content at the *Tribune* if all her reporters were Colette Danielses, if they all knew exactly what was expected of them in their respective jobs and had the wherewithal to deliver.

She tossed away the outside news section and flipped to the second section. There it was, consuming half the page, the clean, redesigned script reading simply "Society." But wait . . . there was Sylvia Loring's picture, beaming out from Colette's spot on the page. Of course, Sylvia was subbing this week for Colette. How could she forget? Dennis Berman had thrown such a little fit about it—as if it were anything less than an honor for Sylvia to be asked to fill Colette's shoes.

Then, suddenly fuming, Hale wondered who had told Style to play Sylvia so big. Giving Sylvia K. Loring half the page! Any first-year journalism-school student would have the sense to know that when Colette was on vacation, you would play the column down, run it on the inside, not play it up.

Then Hale looked at the column more closely. Reading sentences here and there, she noticed how deftly Sylvia had dished some of the city's heavyweights. When she scanned the photo and caption of Congressman Bob Rossen being doused with a Bloody Mary, something inside her turned.

Hale lifted her wall-mounted phone receiver and punched the digit that was preprogrammed to ring up Colette at home. After a brief but pithy exchange with Colette, who had just returned from the *Trib*, Hale rang up Luanne, her personal secretary.

"I'll be in at eleven," Hale announced, sinking deeper into the hot tub. "Have Sylvia Loring in my office when I get there."

Patricia, the Style section secretary, called out to Sylvia as she walked past. "You haven't picked up your messages." Patricia pulled two pink slips out from Sylvia's message slot and held them in the air. Sylvia glanced at the first as she reached her desk. It had B. D.'s name on it.

Last night, after she'd finished her column, her thoughts kept returning to the party, and the two improbable people she'd met there whom she couldn't seem to shake from her mind. B. D. Cole and Kokoh King.

It was peculiar. She, as the journalist, was supposed to be looking in on people's lives, pinpointing them on the great social canvas and examining their weaknesses in detail, yet she felt just the reverse. As if their very existence threw her own life into question, Sylvia Loring was now being thrown up for inspection, glaringly exposed for what she was—and what she lacked. There was no man in her life.

Max, her college boyfriend, had offered her romance. And he'd waited patiently for her to come around, but she never did. She'd told him she was afraid of hurting him, but she knew it was more than that. She was afraid of sex, scared of letting herself go, of growing so vulnerable with a man. She was fearful that it would take her outside herself and make her irrational, make her lose that fragile sense of control. And so when, after her graduation, Max had pressed her for commitment, she had run the other way.

When Sylvia lost her virginity, she'd made sure it was with a man she cared nothing about, a man whom she couldn't possibly grow to love, whose name she'd almost managed to forget. She'd met him in New York, and was never clear exactly what he did except that he made a lot of money and traded in stocks and bonds. It was a fling that had lasted only as long as she was there that first summer out of college, before she returned to Washington.

The phone at her desk rang, and she almost jumped. "Sylvia," came B. D.'s deep voice on the line. "The column came out great. I already got two calls about it. But how come I didn't get a byline? A little credit here!"

He said this last seriously but had to be kidding, since he'd specifically told her not to mention his name. "All right," Sylvia answered, "I owe you one." The words tumbled out of her mouth almost involuntarily. It was as if she were speaking from a script that someone else had written, powerless to change the words. She was surprised at how effortlessly she spoke them.

"That's right, you owe me one. How about dinner tonight?"

"Tonight?" Sylvia stalled to think it through. She'd already made plans with Pam, to go swimming and get some take-out food together. Pam had gone to some trouble to find a babysitter for her four-year-old. "Let me check on something and get back to you."

"Get back to me?" B. D. responded with a hint of impatience.

"I already made some tentative plans. How about tomorrow night? Or sometime later this week?"

"How about unmaking your tentative plans for tonight?" B. D. asked more gently. "Have you ever been to dinner at the White House?"

The White House! Well, in that case, Sylvia thought to herself, of course she'd go. Pam would understand, but, on principle, she had to clear it with her before she accepted.

"I can let you know in five minutes," she said. "Let me have your number."

"No," B. D. retorted, "Let me call you back. I'll give you ten."

Pam Tursi was five-one and a half, five-two on a good day. She was exactly Sylvia's age—twenty-seven—and they were born in April, both Aries. They made an odd-looking pair, Sylvia towering over Pam, her long blond hair in stark contrast with Pam's dark, kinky curls.

Pam was at her desk in the business section, wading through a pile of mail and must-reads, and copies of *Forbes*, *Fortune*, and *Business Week*.

Hearing Sylvia's distinctive footsteps on the linoleum, Pam looked up. "Great column!" she exclaimed. The two friends made it a point to read each other's every printed word. "You really pulled that story out of the hat. Daniels must be shaking in her booties!"

Sylvia didn't want to talk about the column, or even her cat fight with Colette; B. D.'s call had already displaced them both in her mind. Sylvia motioned Pam toward the glass-walled office of the business editor, where they could talk in private.

"About tonight," Sylvia said. "B. D. Cole has just called inviting me out to dinner." She paused before delivering the coup de grâce. "At the White House!"

"The White House," said Pam as if she couldn't believe it. "Are you kidding me?"

Sylvia stood there looking at Pam, her eyes incredulous but abuzz with the energy of expectation, as if she couldn't quite believe it herself.

"He said, quote, 'Have you ever been to dinner at the White House?' " Sylvia said. "Would you call that an invitation?"

"Unless he's a very strange bird," said Pam. "What are you going to wear?"

"But you and I made plans. I don't think you should cancel plans with your best friend when something comes along."

"Best friends are people you can cancel plans with when something like this comes along."

"Are you sure?" Sylvia stood there almost not wanting to hear this, not wanting to have this last obstacle removed.

"What's wrong?" said Pam. "You look lost all of a sudden."

"It's just that I don't know how I really feel about him."

"You don't have to feel anything for him. You do have to go to dinner."

"Now you sound like my mother," said Sylvia.

"Sylvie, this is a chance of a lifetime. It is a big deal. I've never been invited to the White House. I bet not even Crown Princess Gardiner has eaten there."

"You're right, you're right," said Sylvia. She couldn't say no to this, but she also felt that accepting the invitation meant that she was crossing some hidden boundary line between acquaintance and intimacy, a line that she hadn't crossed in so long. She'd thought there'd be time to think things through, get used to the idea, but now there was no such time. Dinner was less than ten hours away.

Back at her desk, Sylvia glanced down at the other message. Hale Gardiner wanted to see her in her office at 11 A.M.

# CHAPTER
## 4

Sylvia walked the length of the newsroom into Hale's large office. Her digital watch read 10:58. She had already gotten clearance from Dennis to take the rest of the day off. It was a request she made so rarely—and she never used any sick days—that he wouldn't even accept one of her vacation days in return. "Just go. You deserve two days for this column," he said, quickly adding, "but you're getting only one."

Sylvia had toyed with the idea of telling Dennis why she wanted the day, but then dismissed it. It seemed too much like bragging to tell him she was dining at the White House, and if she did tell him, she'd never hear the end of it. Dennis had become Colette's number-one sniper ever since she'd dropped her journalist peers to move in loftier circles.

In Hale's glass-walled office, Sylvia eased into the thick leather swivel armchair opposite her desk under the curious gaze of the staff. Who came and went was a subject of constant scrutiny by the busybodies in the newsroom, and already they must have figured that she'd been summoned by the boss. There was an unwritten code about who could walk into Hale's office and who needed an appointment. The managing editor, editorial-page editor, and city and national editors could waltz in any time they pleased. Dennis, the Style editor, had to choose his moments, as did the Business and Sports editors. But reporters like Sylvia and Pam had to see her by appointment.

Hale mostly preferred speaking with her reporters via interoffice mail. Sylvia would receive short, cryptic memos from her boss, often with a story attached, which she'd slashed with a red Magic Marker to improve it in this way or that. Sometimes there'd be a Xerox of an article from *Washingtonian* or *New York* or *Savvy* magazine that she'd suggest be duplicated. Lately, it seemed to Sylvia and the other Style reporters that Hale had been asking for more fluff, things like "The Best Cajun Food Inside the Beltway" or "Return of the Manicure."

Where Colette had been territorially threatened by Sylvia's column, surely Hale would be objective and see that Sylvia had delivered precisely what she'd been asking for—a story with heat. Very possibly, Sylvia would bring up the Kokoh King lead with Hale, asking for extra time to pursue the story. Strike while the iron is hot.

The headiness of the last twenty-four hours reminded her of her senior year at UVA, when everything seemed to go her way. She had been dating Max Ridgway, handsome, brilliant, a former football star who'd graduated two years earlier. That golden year, Sylvia had been elected to the literary review. She'd been awarded one of the coveted rooms on Thomas Jefferson's famed quadrangle. And a crew from *Mademoiselle* magazine had come onto campus scouting out college models for their fall issue, and Sylvia had been chosen. Everything she'd touched seemed to turn to gold. And then she graduated.

Hale Gardiner plopped her oversized Coach bag on her desk. Oiled to a high-gloss polish, her walnut desk was the size of a small conference table and was stocked with brass plaques tracing Hale's history of achievements. Awards to the teenage Hale from equestrian clubs throughout the Middle Atlantic states for jumping horses. A plaque this year from the Metro Women's Press Club naming her "Woman of the Year." Dozens of Venetian glass paperweights, varying from the size a plum to that of a boxer's fist, held down stacks of paper and newspaper and served as bookends to columns of letters and memos and restaurant menus. The overall impression of the desk was not one of clutter but of weight—the magnitude of the job.

Saying nothing to Sylvia, Hale purposefully set about unloading papers, books, and magazines from her bag. Hale unclipped a gold earring and set it down on her desk. Punching a button, she lifted the telephone receiver and instructed Luanne to confirm her lunch reservations for one-thirty at 21 Federal. As she spoke, her eyes grazed over Sylvia before moving on, as if her reporter were just another cog in the vast wheel of her interior scenery.

Hale's voice started out slow and quiet, almost tentative. "Maybe Dennis was right," Hale said, tracing the back end of her gold pen meditatively back and forth along the edge of her lips. "Perhaps it wasn't such a good idea for you to try your hand at Colette's beat."

Hale opened the paper to the Style section and seemed to study Sylvia's column for a moment, a furrow forming on her brow. She turned the paper around, spreading it right side up, in front of Sylvia, like a prosecuting attorney.

"Walk with me," Hale began, "if you will, through the process with which you took on—or shall we say put together—this column."

Sylvia looked at her blankly.

"What are we really trying to accomplish here?" Hale asked.

"Accomplish?"

Hale stood up and began to pace the room. At the floor-to-ceiling window, she pushed aside a long curtain and glanced out to the street, before turning back to Sylvia. Hale knew that Sylvia wasn't much younger than she—four or five years maybe—yet she felt as if she were addressing a member of another generation, someone unendowed with her gift for knowing what was appropriate and what was not.

Her doubts about Sylvia's judgment dated all the way back to an incident at UVA, the first time she'd ever met the woman. Sylvia and her cronies, then the leading lights at the *Cavalier Daily*, the student newspaper, had, in their investigative zeal, uncovered a fund-raising scandal involving the Alumni Affairs office. Hale, then a new UVA graduate, the youngest member of the Board of Visitors and herself a former editor of the *Cavalier Daily*, had been called upon to speak to the young journalists to discourage publicizing the scandal.

Her pleas had fallen on deaf ears; Sylvia had refused to suppress the story, despite Hale's argument that the university was handling the matter with dispatch in-house, and that going to press with the material would serve no other purpose than harming the institution.

Hale stitched her lips together soberly. What was it that bothered her so much about Sylvia's column, about her whole approach? A zealousness, combined with a naïveté that refused to acknowledge the reality of the power structure. It was one thing to have some fun in print with the manicurists around town, but it was quite another to do so at the expense of someone like Bob Rossen. In one fell swoop, Sylvia had managed to jeopardize Colette's carefully cultivated contact with the Rossens, as well as needlessly insult a certain senator from Massachusetts who was well known for his personal vanity. The woman needed to wise up. And Hale was not one of those pushover female bosses who swept a problem under the rug. She took it upon herself to confront thorny issues and toughen up staffers, especially the young, good-looking women who otherwise might never learn the rules of the game from the men who overlooked their mistakes. Sylvia Loring fell into this category. It was patently obvious she had Dennis Berman wrapped around her little finger.

"This column is problematic," Hale said definitively. "There are too many elements here." She could see Sylvia bristle at the criticism, but she continued in the same crisp vein. "Hard news, soft news, and fluff all mixed in together does not make for a satisfactory story." And then the final blow: "You might want to set some of this down."

Sylvia looked at Hale incredulously. "I've got it down, thanks," she said with barely concealed sarcasm.

Hale responded with her eyes, which locked into Sylvia's with an unyielding intensity.

Luanne buzzed to announce that the women from the National Women's Political Caucus had arrived.

"Send them in."

As the two women entered her office, Hale leaped up, a confident, gracious smile widening on her face. She extended her hand and immediately took their coffee orders. She was not the kind of boss who made her secretary fetch it. If there was one thing Hale vowed to do with her position, it was to help improve the voice and status of women in the political process. She had immediately accepted the proposition from the NWPC to discuss ways to enhance coverage of elected women in her pages. They would be surprised. She had ideas she wanted to share with them!

Then, almost as an afterthought, Hale dismissed Sylvia with a wave of her hand through the air. "Read through Colette's clips before your Thursday column, will you?"

# CHAPTER
## 5

Colette Daniels scrunched up the airplane pillow and pushed it into her carry-on bag. They never give you enough pillows at hotels, she thought, glancing around furtively at the deplaning passengers. They were all too busy removing their bags from the overhead bins or stretching their legs after the two-hour flight from Washington National to Boston's Logan Airport to notice.

She slid behind the wheel of an ivory-colored Lincoln Continental rental car and headed north on I-95 from Boston. Her pulse quickened as she imagined Ben's reaction when he saw her. Although she'd never witnessed one of his speeches in person, she could picture him up on the podium, immaculately dressed in his presidential dark-blue suit and red rep tie, mesmerizing the crowd with his presence. When he saw her, he would grow wild with excitement, just as he had last night at the Saint-Phalles when he'd led her over to the dark, standing-room-only open bar and positioned her directly ahead of him. "Order me a bourbon, straight up," he'd breathed into the nape of her neck, his voice deep and low. Feeling the magnetic pull of his powerful body behind her, she could hardly contain her excitement.

New England had always held a certain fascination for Colette. It was the land of taboos, of Puritans—a prim place where things happened under the surface, under covers, behind closed doors. Her presence tonight would signal him that she was ready for business, available to do anything and everything he wanted. Here on the road, in the wilderness. Out of Judy Fincastle's reach.

The November landscape outside her window was bleak, trees without leaves, braced for the cold. Colette pressed the open button to let the window down and the cold air stream in. She had learned early in life that you get the most from doing what others don't, from being daring. It wasn't so much that she liked breaking rules as that she never accepted them in the first place. Whoever said that sex should be confined to the marriage bed was speaking against the force of nature. As far as she could see, marriage made people want each other less.

Colette had decided just this morning that she had to have Ben, that she could wait not one more day. She had wanted him last night at the Saint-Phalles, but he had made no effort to lose his dull wife. It occurred to her later, as she lay in bed alone in the wee hours of the morning half expecting her phone to ring, that he'd deliberately aroused her and then slipped away, making her come after him. If that was his game, it was maddeningly effective; she'd always preferred a man she had to figure out to the kind who threw himself at you, who made love to you worshipfully and sent flowers afterward. He knew and she knew that their affair had already begun, even before their first night together.

Once Colette had decided to go to New Hampshire, she'd been in a frenzy, throwing garments from her black lacquer wardrobe out on her bed, trying them on, discarding those she wasn't pleased with.

The press spin on Ben Fincastle was that he was a born leader, a man you couldn't help liking—the Democrats' answer to the humiliation of having lost five of the last six presidential elections. Politically, Ben's credentials were impeccable: He was fiscally conservative, with a moderate, laissez-faire social policy. He had won a purple heart in Vietnam—so solid a military badge of honor that no right-wing Republican could dare question his patriotism—and he had amassed an election record in his home state that was second to none. He was touted as "the most charismatic Democrat to come on the scene since John Fitzgerald Kennedy." But unlike Kennedy, he was not northern or liberal or Harvard. Ben Fincastle was a good old southern boy with a law degree from the University of North Carolina, a man with a down-home storytelling style who could recapture the South—and the presidency—for the Democratic party.

Tonight, Ben's "get acquainted" meeting at the Portsmouth High School gym would give voters and prominent local and state Democrats a chance to rub elbows and eat spaghetti with the candidate. Early polls showed Ben as the front-runner in the state—Missouri's Dan Tison couldn't catch him. And word was that several key politicians were nearing an endorsement.

Colette checked into her room at the Portsmouth Sheraton, pleased to see a scattering of "Fincastle for President" paraphernalia in the lobby and outside the rooms nearby: flyers, thin, one-sheet posters taped to hotel doors, handbills.

Inside her room, Colette removed her silk dress from the garment bag and hung it in the bathroom to inhale the steam from her bath. She once read that William Faulkner sprinkled rose petals on his sheets before he made love, and impulsively, she stripped some of her fading American Beauties (sent by some worshiper) at home for just that purpose. She scattered them on the queen-size bed.

Colette dressed herself slowly, pulling on skimpy, red silk panties and a red-lace bra that barely contained her overflowing breasts. She struck alluring poses in front of the three-way bathroom mirror. Some girls dieted, but she never had, loving all her flesh that could wrap itself around a man. There was more here to feel his every move, his every quiver and sensation. While men might like being seen with reed-thin models, they went wild in bed with a voluptuous body like her own.

The dress was deep green to bring out her eyes, with soft folds at the bodice, a low scoop neck, and a tight waist. The satin-trimmed high heels were open toe, open heel, and added four inches to her stature, bringing her to five-nine in height—as tall as willowy Sylvia Loring.

Inside the Portsmouth High School gym, tables were pressed together in the hallway, supervised by teenagers wearing Fincastle T-shirts and red, white, and blue Styrofoam hats. In the background, Colette could hear the clipped voice of a New Hampshire speaker, introducing Ben Fincastle.

"Want a raffle ticket?" one of the teenagers asked her. "Proceeds go to the Portsmouth Democratic Committee."

Colette pulled out a five-dollar bill and dropped it on the table. The boy tore off five tickets. "Good luck," he said.

The gym floor was packed—two or three thousand people on their feet, clapping loudly as Colette stepped through the entrance, still wearing her fox fur. For a moment it seemed to Colette, startled, that they were applauding her. Then she saw him. Standing tall at the dais at one end of the gym, shaking hands with the man who introduced him, then thrusting both arms triumphantly into the air, was Ben Fincastle, that sly, boyish grin splashed across his face. He was the handsomest man she had ever seen, with his black hair crisply parted on the side and his sensual, full mouth and dark, fiery eyes. In front of the candidate was the inevitable battery of cameras; behind him, on the wall, hung an enormous American flag.

"Thank you!" Ben said, over the applause, in his deep, gravelly voice. "Thank you very much!"

Then it was only the two of them standing—Colette at the entrance, watching—as the crowd hushed with anticipation. "You know," he began, his voice slow and intimate, as if he were about to reveal something confidential to his audience, "coming from North Carolina, naturally I didn't know what to expect from the New Hampshire kitchen. When I got my plate tonight, it was piled so high I didn't think I could finish it all. Not only did I finish, but I scraped my plate."

The crowd loved it—Ben's rugged good looks, his deep-voiced folksiness. As applause echoed once more around the gym, Colette sauntered toward a vacant seat up front, her fox coat draped over her arm. For one long moment, the candidate's attention was drawn to her.

Colette flashed the star a foxy smile.

When Ben looked away, Colette saw Lyons Smith, Fincastle's longtime deputy and now campaign manager, seated to the candidate's left at the table of honor. Colette and Lyons had met for the first time last night, at the Saint-Phalles'. She hadn't anticipated seeing someone who recognized her. Smith's glance lingered on her in cool appraisal. He lit a Pall Mall, exhaled smoke, and frowned pointedly at Ben.

"You know," Ben began with an ironic smile, "the last time I was here in New Hampshire, my wife Judy was with me." He paused dramatically, locking into Colette's eyes, as if to say, "Watch me walk the high wire without a net." "Now, Judy's a wonderful woman—I love her dearly—but you know, being the daughter of an admiral, Judy moved around a lot when she was a kid, and she's got so she hates traveling."

"But you know, I'm wired a little differently. I grew up hemmed up in the Carolina hills, and like Thomas Wolfe, I've always wanted to travel, to see America, to come to a great port city like Portsmouth and breathe in the salt air." As he spoke, Ben's head rotated around the gym like an oscillating fan, pausing briefly to make eye contact at each juncture before moving on. "Sometimes Judy wishes I was spending less time out here and more time back in Washington. But you know, I like it here! I like rolling up my sleeves and getting out on the street and hearing what's on the minds of the American people. Too often, the politicians in Washington lose touch with the real world. And maybe sometimes they feel a little too good for the rest of the world, with all its real problems and real heartaches. Let me make this pledge. Ben Fincastle, as your president, will never be 'too good' for the working men and women of this country."

The crowd sprang to its feet, applauding thunderously. Colette was with them, savoring the delicious irony about his wife that, she knew, Ben had served up for her benefit.

When the applause subsided, Ben continued. "My friends, I have indeed come a long way to be here with you tonight. For Ben Fincastle to be the next president of the United States, yes, of course, there is a little luck involved. But more than luck, there is trust. Trust in the good sense of the American people to choose the candidate who knows the hearts and minds of working people all over this land. Trust between you and me—that I can count on you, and you can count on me—that working together, we can turn this country around after eleven long Republican years of welfare for the rich and corruption in Washington!

"In the great state of New Hampshire," he said, his voice rising to a feverish pitch and his fist thumping the lectern, "we are going to win the Democratic primary this coming February and continue on to the White House next November!"

The man on the dais was larger than life, his voice like rolling thunder, and when he was done, Colette was on her feet beating her hands together till they tingled with sensation. She felt a slow burn all down her body and basked in the warmth of this community of strangers standing around her.

Then, as he was taking his seat, Ben's eyes found hers, triumphant. "Was that worth your trip?" they seemed to ask.

"Oh, yes," her bright hazel eyes beamed back. "But this is only the appetizer."

Ben took his place in a receiving line with the prominent New Hampshire Democrats, and Colette joined the others in a line snaking its way toward the candidate. Her tongue danced wetly along her lips in anticipation. When she glanced up, a short, stocky man with dark curly hair was on the approach. Usually she liked being hit on, if only for the ego strokes of saying no. But not tonight, and especially not from a man with a press badge dangling on his chest.

"You must be Colette Daniels," he said. "I'm Michael Paradyne with the *Washington Post*." Michael's eyes darted around the room as he spoke, the telltale sign of a reporter with an itching palm. Before even enjoying his conquest, he was looking for the next. "So what brings you to New Hampshire? You're up here covering parties?"

Colette never answered questions she didn't want to. "Mike, was it?"

"Michael."

"You're on the national desk, covering the primaries?"

"I'm working exclusively on Ben Fincastle," he said. Just then, Colette noticed that his collar was too tightly buttoned and his tie seemed to strap him down—as if any minute he could burst out of costume. There was something about this man that she didn't like, wanted no part of.

"I'll look for your stuff," Colette said curtly, then turned her back on him and started digging in her purse.

Damn this line, she thought, inching toward her target, who in turn was flanked by the lesser Democratic lights catching, for one night, the reflected glory of their national star. The governor was here, of course—a diminutive man of about half Ben's size, gladhanding his constituents. There were city politicians and state legislators, a long line of toothy smiles and clammy hands for Colette to endure.

Lyons Smith was a portly man in his late fifties with a few lonesome strands of gray hair combed across his glistening dome. He was standing at the outer edge of the receiving line, talking up his man.

"Colette Daniels," Lyons said when she got to him. He laid his meaty hand too firmly on her arm, "I'd like to buy you a drink."

"That would be nice. Sometime."

Lyon's eyes darted to the array of television cameras, photographers, and journalists hovering close to the reception line. "Tonight," he said firmly.

"You're such a southern gentleman, but I'm afraid I have plans."

Lyons fumed as Colette grasped the governor's hand, then caught the eye of the turning Ben Fincastle. "Hello, Senator," she said, deadpan, offering her hand. "That was such a good speech you made."

"Thank you," he replied.

Their hands clasped and, for a lingering moment, held tightly to each other. Then Colette leaned close and whispered into his ear: "Your move, Senator. Room 304. The Sheraton."

# CHAPTER
## 6

Sylvia alighted from the limousine at the large white columns of the White House. After five years as a reporter, she'd thought nothing, nor anyone, could bring on jitters like these. But here they were, as real as B. D.'s arm helping her out of the car. Luckily, he'd spared telling her earlier in the day just how "intimate" this dinner party would be. All day, Sylvia had envisioned a large state dinner where she might be one of a hundred and forty, lucky if she were able just to shake the Great Man's hand.

"Anywhere from twelve to twenty," B. D. was saying, fingering his woven Italian silk tie. "Dinner in the Family Dining Room. Have you figured out what you're going to say in your private audience with the President?"

However playful his question, it failed to loosen her up. B. D. was a celebrity, but at least he was closer to being her equal; he was still in his thirties, and his work as a consultant who analyzed voter trends and social currents bore some parallels to her own. But the President of the United States, the leader of the free world—what did she have to say to him? She wished she could be invisible and just watch.

Sylvia felt B. D. touch the nape of her neck, and shivered. "Stick with me, kid," he whispered in her ear, "and we'll eat here twice a month!"

Before she could respond, a military officer ushered them through the North Portico of the White House, where they were greeted by the President's white-haired wife, resplendent in a yellow, tea-length, silk dress that draped her ample girth.

There'd been calls from the White House in a last-minute security check and to gain her tape-recorded assurance that she was attending as the date of B. D. Cole, not as a working journalist, that anything and everything she might hear that evening would be strictly off the record. Sylvia had phoned her mother at her Silver Spring office, not out of any relish to break the news, but because she was aware of the disappointment her mother would feel if denied advance warning. Not only was there the White House date, but perhaps more importantly, the fact that B. D. Cole had asked her.

Jan Loring was unable to contain her excitement. "I want you to buy a new dress," she'd said. "And shoes and bag and a wrap. Money is no object." Initially, Sylvia had objected, insisting she would bring out her black Louis Feraud, dressing it up with new accessories. But Jan had prevailed, saying that Sylvia must have a new dress for the White House. And this from a mother who'd always been tight with the dollar!

And so Sylvia had found herself in Garfinckle's once again, this time selecting something a bit more daring: a black-and-blue, Empire-style brocade Christian Lacroix dress with passementerie trim. It was a winter dress from last season, thankfully reduced but still over a thousand dollars. The dress drew out her blue eyes, set off her blond hair, and was short enough to complement her long, gorgeous legs. In it, she felt substantial as well as beautiful.

A warm fire crackled and glowed in the Red Room as white-coated waiters moved about taking drink orders. Sylvia ordered a Bloody Mary and positioned herself near the portrait of Dolley Madison. Hearing scraps of polite conversation all around her, Sylvia realized that one reason for her discomfort was that she'd been stripped of the familiar role of reporter. Tonight she was B. D.'s date, not Sylvia K. Loring of the *Washington Tribune*.

She'd felt this way before. Five and a half years ago, spring of her senior year at UVA, she'd attended Ernest Ridgway's annual Cherry Blossom party as Max's date. It had been her first Washington party, and, though she couldn't have known it at the time, it had changed her life.

Sylvia had been The Nephew's Date, and it seemed to her that everyone—but most especially Uncle Ernest, a famous, retired Cabinet member—had been subtly sizing her up. Being on display had challenged her to use the right fork, to say the right thing, and to stand tall. Max had reported that she'd passed with flying colors. It was there that she'd met Judy Fincastle and Digby Reeve. And it was there that it had hit her dead center what Maxwell Ridgway was. He was a member of one of the First Families of Virginia, what people call an FFV. Born a blue blood, he would always be one. And Sylvia—the daughter of a Polish immigrant who had scraped and skimped to put it all together—hadn't wanted to marry someone, she'd wanted to become someone. On her own.

"Bloody Mary," the waiter said, his white-gloved hand delivering her drink from his linen-lined silver tray.

Sylvia downed a third of it in one long draw, wondering for a moment how Colette handled butterflies in her stomach before deciding that she never had any.

B. D. touched the small of her back. "Sylvia," he said. "I want you to meet the smartest political consultant in Washington, Bryce Edgar. And his wife, Katie."

Bryce Edgar, Sylvia knew from reading the papers, was the President's personal consultant, a power in Republican circles.

B. D. launched into a discourse about the Red Room, obviously for Sylvia's benefit. Dolley Madison held her fashionable Wednesday soirees here, he explained, but in her time, the Red Room was actually yellow! B. D. seemed to feel quite at home here.

"He's been reading his Visitors' Guide to Washington," Bryce quipped.

Floundering for something to say, Sylvia realized that although she wasn't working the party, she could still ask questions.

"I've been meaning to ask," she started, eyeing B. D.

"Why does a Republican president ask a Democratic consultant to dinner?" Especially, she thought, a president whose popularity ratings had hit an all-time low.

"Let's put it this way," B. D. said with a confident smile. "He likes my style."

"I could put it another way," said Bryce. "He likes to pick B. D.'s brain."

"And not have to pay for it," added Katie significantly.

The other guests had all arrived now, and Sylvia heard the First Lady telling a famous country-music star—one of the President's most vocal supporters during the last campaign —that the President was running a few minutes late.

The singer was dressed to kill in a shocking-pink satiny number, with flounces and ruffles and bows. Her husband wore a cowboy string tie and rattlesnake boots, polished to a high sheen. There was also an Arkansas couple, contributors to the campaign, "deep pockets," B. D. whispered to Sylvia. A famous Australian media tycoon and his wife were the guests of honor.

All conversation ceased when the tall, square-jawed President entered the room. He wore a wide smile and made a beeline for the tycoon. "So when's the next sailing trip?" he asked, reaching for the hand of his guest of honor and slapping his back. He stepped around the room, extracting kisses from the ladies and making witty conversation where he could. It seemed that he knew something about each one of them.

When the President reached Sylvia, he stopped short theatrically. She was the only woman here whom he'd never met—and also the youngest. "So this is Sylvia Loring, the young lady who brought down Bob Rossen!" he said. He shook his head and tisked his tongue, but his tone signaled that he was more titillated than upset by the Rossen scandal. Then, to his wife, standing nearby, he added, "Honey, you better watch what you say tonight!"

"So you read the *Tribune*?" Sylvia said.

The President's thin lips formed into a smile. "Darn right I do. Every morning. And if I don't get to it, you can be sure that they clip the articles I miss. If I don't read them, they pile up on my desk, and I've got to read them or else they'll think I'm not doing my homework!''

Sylvia couldn't believe it. How could she describe what she was experiencing to her mother or Pam? Here was the President, who appeared so ill at ease at press conferences, just wanting her to like him!

The President paused for a moment, studying her, reaching to extend the exchange. "How's my old pal Digby Reeve getting along?''

Sylvia searched her mind for something, anything of interest she could say about Digby. "You know, he's appointed a young woman as editor.''

"Doesn't surprise me a bit," said the President. "You tell Digby I said hello.''

With that, the President turned and motioned the group into the Family Dining Room. "Let's go get something to eat.''

Beneath a glimmering chandelier, the long table was festively appointed. An enormous vase of carved pumpkin with an autumnal arrangement of orange, yellow, and bronze daisies, mums and pompoms, interspersed with blanched corn husks and rust-colored oak and green galax leaves made the centerpiece. The Lyndon Johnson china, trimmed with delicate wildflowers, was laid out on the table flanked by three glass goblets. Place cards with each guest's name inscribed in elegant calligraphy rested against miniature pumpkins, fronted by brown cloth napkins rolled into logs. Delicate engraved menu cards stood at the head of each plate. It was hard to believe that this setting was considered "informal.''

Sylvia found her seat at the center of the table between Bryce Edgar and the country star's husband.

"Here, let me," said Bryce, pulling out her chair.

Positioned directly across the wide table from Bryce, B. D. tracked him with his eyes. "Now, let's not get too familiar here," he said jokingly, but he didn't look amused.

The Australian media mogul, sitting in the position of honor to the right of the First Lady, launched into a lengthy anecdote about a sailing misadventure with a member of the British royalty.

Waiters appeared with finger bowls of warm water, flower petals floating at the surface.

"Does Ben Fincastle know who's feeding you tonight?" the President asked B. D. as he sipped on the beet soup.

"You bet," B. D. said. "The good thing about my job is I don't have to clear my social schedule with anyone."

"You know," the President said, his eyes twinkling, "we appreciate what a stretch it must have been for you to come here tonight. Having to cross enemy lines and all."

"All for a worthy cause!" B. D. replied. "I can't get crab mousse American in my neighborhood. Not at this price!"

The President sobered. "I understand your man is in New Hampshire now. I'm not sure I like his getting so close to my territory."

"We think he's unstoppable," said B. D. "I'd say he's very close to having the nomination in his hip pocket."

"If he does, and that's a big if," replied Bryce, attacking his mousse, "the real contest will come after the convention. I'll think you'll be surprised at how deep the President's support really is."

"Listen," said B. D., clearing his longish curly hair from his face. "I won't be surprised at anything you boys come up with. Not after the stunts you pulled in '88. But I think we're ready to take you on this time."

The publishing tycoon, who'd been following this dialogue with a poker face, interjected a question. "Why is it in American politics that the Democrats, time and time again, always bungle the election by putting up a candidate too liberal for the electorate?"

"Let me tell you something," B. D. began, shooting a look at the President. "I'm not trying to scare you, Mr. President, but Ben Fincastle is the strongest candidate our party has seen since John F. Kennedy. Stronger, actually. And I'll tell you why. The man is solidly middle-of-the-road. If I had to locate him geographically, I'd place him a little right of center. And he has not only a national constituency, but a charisma that we never had in Mike Dukakis or Walter Mondale. Those men were earnest and awkward. They meant well, and both were good men."

"I know it," the President interjected.

"They meant well," B. D. repeated, "but they were not leaders."

This last seemed to please the President.

The media mogul interjected, "Mr. Cole, your oratorical skills are not lacking. Are you considering running for political office?"

"Never," shot back B. D. "It's not me—I'm more conservative than that. I prefer my role behind the scenes. I let them go to the casino table; I merely stake them."

From Edgar and the President came grudging laughter. Soaking it up, B. D. glanced triumphantly at Sylvia.

She smiled appreciatively. Something in B. D.'s manner —an inner confidence, a take-charge intensity—made him compelling. He was so sure of himself, a man who by his very power could transport her away from herself as he held the entire dinner party. Even the way he looked at her, cocky, possessive, was breaking down doors inside, making her want to get closer, to see the rest of him, to find the rest of herself.

"Oh, come now, B. D.," Bryce was saying. "You're the last person I'd ever call conservative."

"Bryce," B. D. retorted, stealing the next line from Ronald Reagan. "There you go again. Confusing my personal life with my professional life."

Amidst the startled laughter, the President himself sent the next volley. "Your reputation does precede you, doesn't it, B. D.?" And then, grinning, he turned his attention to Sylvia. "If I may be so bold, how did a nice young woman like you get hooked up with this character?"

Sylvia flushed with embarrassment. The President, it seemed, was not her childhood image of God—an imposing grandfather of a man—but as down to earth and gossipy as her friend Pam.

To Sylvia's immense relief, the President's wife intervened. Her eyes smiling, she frowned at the President. "Never ask a woman an embarrassing question!"

"And why not?" the President retorted. "Women reporters ask me embarrassing questions every day. And by the way," he continued to Sylvia, "you tell that publisher at your paper maybe he'd better watch out, too. I'm waiting for the day the press keeps as close an eye on itself as it does on us!'' His glance swung mightily down the table to the Australian. ''Am I right?''

The tycoon shrugged. The question didn't appeal to him.

Sylvia could feel all eyes turn to her, could feel that blinding flash of light when the moment is yours, either for shame or glory. She pushed aside her red currant sorbet.

''Well,'' she began, squaring her shoulders and turning directly to the President. ''Like the President, I suppose, the press isn't perfect. But I think some papers—and some reporters—do have a conscience. We know when we're stretching the truth, or don't have enough sources, or have too much of a bias. Sure, we're not perfect, but we do try to hold ourselves to a high standard of reporting the truth as we see it. I think we have a right to expect that same standard from politicians—even from you, sir.''

The President appeared taken aback, and, for a moment, Sylvia wondered whether she'd said too much, been too brazen. His lips, parted but mute, finally managed, ''I don't know whether to applaud or rebut.''

''I think we've got ourselves a new speechwriter,'' said Bryce, grinning.

''Not on your life,'' B. D. retorted. ''She's ours.''

Sylvia felt a glow the rest of the evening, a golden aura the entire length of her body. It seemed that she was on the brink of change, about to take one of those transcendent leaps from which there is no return. After this command performance, she had never felt more glamorous, more intelligent, more important. She understood for the first time, firsthand, why people claw, scrape, and backbite to insinuate themselves into Washington's inmost circles and, once there, work just as hard to remain. It was for the taste of a wonder drug called power.

Now, as they breezed away from the North Portico in the rented limo, B. D. was at her side, two languid bodies in the velvety depths of the back seat. As B. D.'s space-age chariot eased through the swinging gates and nosed onto Pennsylvania Avenue, passing Lafayette Park and Blair House, it seemed to Sylvia that the city had never been more alive. Wet with rain, the streets were smeared with liquid colors, reds and greens and silvers and golds from a million lights.

B. D. reached for her hand, entwining her fingers with his. "My place?"

With that invitation, the evening offered a dazzling third act. Sylvia hesitated. Something inside her held back. "I don't know," she said. And then, boldly, remembering the awkward moment at the dinner: "Where do B. D.'s women usually go after dinner with the President?"

B. D. stirred in his dark navy suit, whether in protest or in anticipation Sylvia wasn't sure. His body turned slowly toward hers. "You're not just any woman," he said softly.

She was giddy, with the drinks and now his words, so giddy she didn't recognize herself, what she said, her tone of voice. "Flattery," she said, "will get you everywhere."

"Look," he said, suddenly curt. "I never flatter. You have something. You should be an actress. I'm going to put you in touch with people you should know. Directors in Hollywood."

He was so close, so intense—and the idea was so absurd—that Sylvia had to laugh.

"I'm not joking," he said. "You're too beautiful for print journalism. And you have something I rarely see in this godforsaken town—especially among journalists. You have soul."

"Thank you," Sylvia said, at a loss for a reply.

"Don't thank me," he snorted. "This town reeks with hypocrites, but I'm not one of them. If I tell you something, I mean it."

Sylvia shifted in her seat. Something in the air had changed, making her a little uncomfortable. She hadn't meant to make him defensive. Instinctively, she sought to recapture the mood by shifting the focus from her to him, by drawing him out. "I really don't know much about you," she said, "only what I read in the papers."

"Don't believe everything you read in the papers. Especially your own."

Sylvia laughed. B. D. smiled, seeming to savor his little

witticism. He leaned forward toward the driver and said something in a low voice.

"How about we drive around a bit," B. D. asked her, "and get acquainted?"

Sylvia made no protest. The limo cruised down Constitution Avenue, past the phallic thrust of the Washington monument, and up and around Capitol Hill, the dome a milky white against the overcast sky.

B. D.'s journey from a lower-middle-class home in Denver to political fame in Washington was riveting. He told Sylvia about his mother, who worked at the Coors plant in Golden, and his truck-driver father, who died of a heart attack when he was only nine. He told her of making 1590 on the SATs, of his magna cum laude degree at Northwestern University, and his meteoric rise as political soothsayer in Washington, where ambitious politicians latched on to his readings of developing trends. There was much to admire in this man who'd single-handedly hoisted himself up by the bootstraps without connections or advantages.

"Getting where you want to go is actually quite easy," B. D. said. "It's a matter of having the courage to follow your convictions."

Sylvia didn't share B. D.'s enormous success or celebrity, but she identified with him. Whatever she'd achieved had been of her own making. And simply being in his presence challenged her to push beyond.

They came down off the Hill and threaded their way into the cobblestone streets of Georgetown, B. D.'s home. The limo stopped outside of a tall, brick town house. "How 'bout a nightcap?"

Their excursion had bought her time to prepare for this moment, and Sylvia had convinced herself she wanted more from the evening. But not on his turf.

"My place," she said crisply.

B. D. hesitated, then nodded. Without another word, except for giving Sylvia's address to the driver, they arrived in Adams-Morgan, passing the Red Sea with its late-night diners. Sylvia's apartment was just a few blocks away, down a dark, quiet street.

Sylvia turned on the light. B. D.'s eyes darted over the tiny apartment, past the TV, the couch, the nook of a kitchen, and the closed door to the bathroom. The bedroom door was half open.

"Cute," he said, breaking a silence that to Sylvia seemed deafening.

Sylvia's heels clattered toward the kitchen. "What would you like?" she asked, laying her coat on a chair.

"Scotch. On the rocks," he replied.

"I have wine, beer, and vodka," she said. When she returned with B. D.'s beer, he'd shed his jacket and loosened his tie.

She turned out the light and lit a candle, kicking off her heels as she sat down beside him with the drinks. B. D. drank. Sylvia drank. Sylvia hesitated. This was harder than she had thought. Back in the limousine, in the last ripe moments of silence, she had pictured everything: two drinks, a candle, making out on the couch, then gliding into another world. She hadn't counted on feeling so uncomfortable. But she was determined to get it right. She just needed time. She needed to get a little high. She drank some more, but her throat stayed dry.

B. D. pulled her toward him and kissed her hard. "I want you," he whispered.

She kissed him back, and he threw himself on her. She could feel him on her thigh.

Then she couldn't go through with it. It was too fast.

"B. D.," she said, pulling away. "I can't. Not yet." She looked at his face and could see disappointment and a hint of an emotion she couldn't yet read. Anger? Passion?

"What are you waiting for?" he asked evenly.

She wanted to say love, that she had to be certain she loved a man before giving herself to him. The reason was simple: it hadn't worked for her when she didn't. But she couldn't bring herself to utter that word, love. Not around a man as worldly as B. D, a man who probably thought love was an outmoded concept.

"I don't know," she stammered. "It just doesn't feel right."

His fingers cupped her chin. "You're a little green." He lowered his face toward hers and kissed her lips. "Let me take care of that." His free hand slid down her back and worked its way around toward her hip and over to her thigh.

"I am not green." Sylvia shot upright. Of course, he was right. But she didn't know him well enough to admit it.

As she closed the door after him, Sylvia sighed in relief, wishing she could just will that last part of the evening away. She flushed with the sudden image of how she must have looked to B. D.—like a child, afraid and inexperienced.

Next time, she told herself, she would be ready.

# CHAPTER
## 7

"Senator," Lyons Smith was saying, steering the candidate through the crowd toward their waiting Mercedes, "we're doing that *Boston Globe* interview tonight in your room."

"We are?"

"That's the schedule. Nine-thirty P.M. on the nose."

"Christ, Lyons. How about a night's sleep for a change?"

"Not tonight. You damn well don't mess around with the *Boston Globe*."

The two old friends, men who had known each other since Ben's first term in Raleigh as a state senator, climbed in. Joining a short procession led by a Portsmouth police car and flanked by two on motorcycle patrol, the car glided past gawking faces and waving hands into the empty night streets of Portsmouth.

"Hell," Lyons said, feeling the sting of Ben's silence but sensing the urgency of this moment. "The whole damn hotel is crawling with press. You can damn well bet they'd all love to hang your head on their trophy rack."

Ben turned to Lyons, glowering. "What the hell is that supposed to mean?"

"I think you know, Ben," Lyons said carefully.

Ben was silent. Lyons studied him through another one of his smoke rings as the Mercedes made its way toward the Portsmouth Sheraton.

Still dressed—her fantasy was that he would undress her —her legs crossed seductively on the bed, Colette looked at her watch. It was quarter to twelve, and the table was all set except for the main dish. Half a dozen times she'd been back to the mirror for minor alterations. The sheets were turned up, with their sprinkling of rose petals. The curtains were drawn, the light was rosy and low. But where was Ben? Had he gotten cold feet? Could something or someone have detained him? That killjoy Lyons Smith?

The telephone exploded from its receiver. Colette started, then, smiling in anticipation, answered it. This would be him.

Ben's voice came on the line. "You know," he began, grasping for words, a different man altogether from the polished orator on stage, a man now torn and uncertain. "This can't be. You and me. We can't . . . not now, not with media people all around."

Colette wasn't used to being turned down, especially by a man who wanted her, a man whom she knew from an ace source to have roamed outside his marriage bed. She'd gotten some men who'd never cheated on their wives, but had never not gotten one who had. There had to be a way. Her heart skipped, her body began trembling as she rallied the necessary powers of concentration on this moment. She could feel it from him over the line; he was teetering and needed only a little shove to push him over the edge.

"Ben," she purred, camouflaging her own desperate urgency. A man she'd once dated had told her that of all her sexual charms, her voice was the sexiest. "Ben," Colette continued. "I've got something for you. Something very important for your campaign. I've come all this way to deliver it. I have to see you right away." She would have gone on, dangling this carrot, even making up more stories if she had to, but he didn't need any more persuasion. He said he'd meet her in half an hour in the wharf district, where no one stirred at night.

She jumped into her car, dashed to the destination, and waited. Thirty minutes passed, and she began cursing him for keeping her. Being late had always been her prerogative. But still she waited.

Then a golden Mercedes nosed around the corner, moving onto the street. It was Ben. He pulled his car alongside hers, one car facing north, the other south. The cars almost touched at the drivers' windows.

He rolled down his window, then she hers. They sat for what seemed like forever just looking at each other from their separate metal cages, not saying a word, until it was just too ridiculous.

"Get in," he said.

She climbed inside, her fox coat falling open into a gaping V over her dress. As she settled in, she hiked her hem so that more of her legs would show. Her shimmery Midnight Mist stockings were held in place by a black garter belt. A garter belt was a woman's best weapon, she had learned, the item that never failed to drive a man crazy.

He had thought they would talk and tease and commiserate about what might have been. That they would part friends with the vague promise of later, sometime after the election. It occurred to him more than once that Colette might be his booby prize if he lost. If he lost, then he could have her—nothing to lose, no campaign to damage. He could wait, and he would. He had planned to explain how crucial it was that he stay clean just now, take no chances, just as Lyons Smith had told him time and again. He expected that Colette would understand, would defer to the higher calling of his career. He knew also that it got him going, knowing that she was hot for him, that his presence alone could ignite someone as young and desirable as she.

As soon as she climbed into his car and settled in on the butter-soft leather upholstery, as soon as he felt her force, her pulsing energy, he wondered if he would follow through with his plan, if he would say what he had intended.

The temptation to take her right then and there was great. He needed to move, to get away from there. He stepped on the gas and moved them through the streets, out the north end of Portsmouth onto the bridge that crossed the river into Maine. The speedometer climbed higher and higher, close to ninety on the straightaway.

Moonlight from the sky outside drew his gaze to the swell of her breasts, then to the hair that formed a silky halo around her face. It was someone else, some force beyond him, that reached for her and drew her body next to his, her thigh pressing deliciously against his own.

This was supposed to be their talk, but neither of them said a word.

Colette studied a face that was now completely in her command. Without taking her eyes from him, she slid out of her coat and draped it casually across her lap, spreading it onto his.

"Hi," she said, feeling suddenly shy, her voice sounding a little funny to herself. She reached for his tie and gave it a suggestive tug.

Ben said nothing. One hand still on the wheel, his other reached for her breast, lightly stroking. Colette held her breath as his hand rode the wave of her breast and sailed down the silk of her gleaming green dress to the smooth satin of her inner thigh. Her eyes closed, and she felt the hand, smooth and commanding, spread ripples across her thigh and wash up, slow and undulating, toward the soft, wet center of her. She sensed the car change direction, going somewhere off to the right, then felt the hand, as delicate as a feather, graze the gossamer skin of her panties and touch, pressing gently, where she wanted to be touched. Colette moaned, and the hand, only a finger now, slid up and over her panties, as light as rain, and down under them, grazing flesh until it found her again.

"Ben," she whispered.

Somewhere in the widening circle, the growing storm of sensation, she knew that the car was slowing down and that all around was darkness and the sound of surf.

"What are you doing?" she said, suddenly realizing that the car had stopped, the engine was running, and Ben was hoisting her onto her fur coat. He crouched over her, stroking, magically stroking.

He laughed softly in answer. She knew what he was doing; she was begging for it. Colette moaned, feeling her insides spinning like a whirlwind.

It was afterward—after Colette gasped his name, shaking and screaming and digging her fingernails into him, after Ben had pumped all of himself into her with one sustained, savage cry—that she saw the headlights, bursting like a flare on their windshield.

"Ben!" Colette screamed.

He rolled off of her and, together, they saw the police car cruising toward them across the beach.

His voice was eerily calm. "Quickly," he commanded. "Get yourself together."

"Ben," she said, panicking, "what if they see me here with you?"

He looked at her and said, "Quiet."

Ben clambered into his pants, his hands smoothing his tousled hair. He had spoken with such confidence that she could muster no reply. Where she felt fear, felt like running, he rose up above himself and her, too, ready to do battle. Colette drew her coat around her just as two policemen stepped to the car window.

The patrol car behind them sent a probe light into the Mercedes, and the beam played accusingly across Ben's face.

"Good evening, gentlemen," Ben said, rolling down his window.

Two young, mustachioed officers peered in at Ben and Colette, wearing the shield of the Kittery, Maine, police department.

"Driver's license," the first one said tersely.

Ben handed it over. When he read it, the officer's expression changed. He showed the license to his partner.

"You aren't Senator Ben Fincastle?"

"Yes," said Ben. He nodded toward Colette. "My wife, Judy."

The two officers glanced at Colette, then looked at each other, overtaken by the significance of the moment.

"Senator," said the first, "we apologize for the inconvenience. We only wanted to let you know that there is no overnight parking on Kittery Point Beach."

"I appreciate it, gentlemen," Ben said. "Keep up the good work. And I hope you'll vote for me when the time comes."

"Yes, sir!" one said.

As the officers reached their patrol car, the second one turned and called, "Senator, good luck with your campaign."

When they were gone, Colette breathed in relief. "Ben, I can't believe you said I was Judy."

A devilish smile played on his face. He seemed to inhale her now as if she emitted a drug.

He reached for her, again.

They unhitched slowly all that had just been so hurriedly hitched. And more slowly this time, they played with each other, brought each other out again.

The night had grown colder, and on the windshield a few fine flakes of snow fell, like eiderdown.

Ben turned on the engine for its heater, and they lay in each other's arms dozing off together. When they finally awoke, he shifted into action, steering back to Portsmouth to where they'd left her car.

She started up her car, and from her rearview mirror, she could see him following behind her most of the way to the Sheraton.

# CHAPTER
## 8

Sylvia did not sleep. Still wearing her million-dollar dress, she stared out the window into the pouring rain. The pale light from the streetlamps illuminated the spare furnishings and the lithograph on the wall of Jefferson's quad at UVA.

Her mind would not rest. Over and over she replayed the last scene in the night's drama.

Sylvia's body twisted on the bed, tormented by her thoughts. B. D. was right. She *was* green. He barely knew her, but he'd sized her up in an instant.

Sylvia had turned off a man who was challenging, extraordinary, sought after, one who'd put himself right out there for her, making no attempt to conceal his agenda. She could have handled him differently, she thought. She could have talked to him, bent him toward her way of thinking.

Slipping out of her dress, sitting on the side of the bed in her underwear, Sylvia knew that the real problem was fear. Aimlessly, she strolled back into the living room, grasped her unfinished drink, and sat down on the couch. The digital clock on the VCR read 5:15. What was she so afraid of? All her life, since junior high school, the other sex with its hair-trigger lust had been hitting on her, wanting the fruits of her blond bounty. Disgusting at times, sure, but nothing to fear; that was just men, just testosterone. Sylvia sipped her drink. It wasn't men's bodies she was afraid of either, was it? Sex itself, the physical stuff, didn't scare her. It was the mind stuff, something inside herself. Sylvia set down her drink, and the sudden thought rang out like a shot: she was afraid of herself.

That had been the case with Max. She had been afraid of what would happen inside her. Max Ridgway—the only man she'd ever known who was a soul mate, who loved not only her face and body but her very being. What would be left of Sylvia Loring if she lost herself in a man like Max? Letting go with a man she truly cared for meant losing her own life. Miserable as it could be sometimes, at least this life was hers and hers alone. Loving a man meant becoming another woman, a woman she was afraid of.

Sylvia downed the last of her drink. No, that's not right, she thought, a little drunk now. Fear had nothing to do with it; thank you very much, Max Ridgway, but she did not want to be another kind of woman. Who she was was just fine, thank you.

Besides, Max was gone, forever.

Sylvia stepped into the bathroom, in the mirror glancing over the body that men wanted so miserably. She stepped into the shower. It had been a long night, but this was progress: now she knew what Sylvia Loring wanted. Sure, she wanted a man, but not one who would march in and take over. Maybe B. D. was just right, a man who could show her a whole new world, but would not engulf her in it.

Sylvia dressed. She toasted a bagel and downed a cup of coffee. She was ready for another day at work.

As Sylvia reached her desk, her eyes searched the newsroom for Dennis Berman's rumpled presence. The boss was generally here by now, quaffing his first cup of coffee, scanning the wires on his computer screen. Sylvia couldn't deny the disappointment she felt over his absence. Dennis was a kind of father figure. She counted on him, as he did her. Their adoration was mutual, although unvoiced.

As soon as he came in, Sylvia parked herself in front of his desk.

"What are you doing here?" he asked, his eyes grazing over her fondly. "Society reporters never check in at this hour."

Sylvia was in no mood for repartee. "I need to talk."

Her tone commanded attention, and before another reporter or editor arrived in their section, they were well into a strategy session beside his desk. Sylvia got his go-ahead to explore the Kokoh King lead. Dennis suggested caution in her dealings with the woman, and questioned whether Sylvia could find enough to run with a story of this magnitude. But, as always, he lauded her enterprise.

"Take her to lunch," he said. "Then see me."

"Fine, but what do I do if she sticks to her story? She'd be my only source."

"I told you it wasn't going to be easy."

Sylvia plunked down in Dennis's chair. With a sigh, she rested her chin in her palm, thinking. "All right," she said abruptly. "Somebody has to get up on the Hill. Don't they?"

"Easier said than done," Dennis replied. "Obviously, our man Rossen is El Stonewall-o."

Sylvia's mind moved ahead to another obstacle, this one closer at hand. "Dennis, you know my little love fest with Hale yesterday didn't exactly turn out that way."

"Oh?" said Dennis, surprised.

Sylvia described her strange session in Hale's office. The editor's reaction was doubly perplexing given that Sylvia's scoop column had run all over the country in late editions yesterday. "Her parting words were that I should study up on Colette's clip file," Sylvia said.

"You've got to be kidding."

"Would Hale ever get behind a sex-scandal story?" Sylvia wondered.

"Let's get the story first," said Dennis. Then, with a dismissive flick of his wrist, he added, "Out of here! I've got work to do."

As Hale Gardiner studied the cafeteria selections, she wondered why she bothered: the sandwiches were tasteless, the bread stale, and the soups insipid. All the *Tribune* cafeteria had going for it was bottled sodas, but her personal office refrigerator was already well-stocked. She kicked herself for having made the fatal admission to her publisher this morning that she had no lunch plans today.

Right behind her in line was fifty-two-year-old Digby Reeve, a well-meaning, recently widowed man. To a self-starter like Hale Gardiner, he was the perfect boss; he let her alone to do most everything she wanted and stuck his nose in only inconsequential matters.

One of his most galling peccadilloes was his insistence on patronizing the employee cafeteria, which he'd built in 1965 and where he assumed the convivial air of a restaurateur. Occasionally, Hale suspected him of an added motive: coming here as a way of trimming the expense budget.

Digby set a heaping bowl of clam chowder next to the roast beef sandwich on his tray, running his finger along the side of the green plastic bowl where the chowder had slopped over the side. Digby licked his finger unceremoniously—a detail that did not escape Hale's sharp eye. The ladies behind the counter always made sure to fill his bowl to the brim, and Digby teased them appreciatively, always calling them by name.

"You're going to have to buy me a new belt, the next size up, Marian," he joked.

They unloaded their lunches at a side table, with Digby disparaging Hale's selection of a house salad and soda. "You've got to build your strength for the big speech," he said. As he sat down, his portly frame jostled the rickety table, spilling his chowder onto the table. Merrily, he sopped up the spillage with a napkin.

"As you know, hospice is Mother's pet charity," he continued.

"Yes, Digby, I'm aware of that," Hale said, warily eyeing the stream of reporters drifting into the lunchroom. She'd try to make this as short as possible. It made her uncomfortable being exposed like this. Some impertinent reporter or editor could just walk right up and put her on the spot. There was no Luanne in her outer office to screen her visitors, no paperwork to focus on when someone tried to waste her time.

"So you agree to make the speech?" he said.

Hale had no choice in the matter. She could put Digby off, but not Phyllis Reeve. Still, Hale let his query hang in the balance for a moment. Then she drew in her breath. "I'll clear my calendar," she said.

Hale knew that Phyllis Reeve had been skeptical ten months ago when the *Trib*'s longtime editor stepped down and Digby decided to appoint Hale. A woman, and a young one at that. Even though Phyllis was controlling shareholder of the Washington Tribune Company, she treated her only son as the real powerbroker, and Digby himself had let it slip that he'd stuck his neck out for Hale, overruling Phyllis's objections about her. He had argued that she was dynamic, in touch with the young people that their paper needed to attract to once again turn a healthy profit.

From the day Hale first came to the *Tribune*, she could tell that Digby had admired her style. And as editor, she hadn't disappointed him. Her first act on the job was to call the staff together and announce her intention of putting the *Trib* back on the map. "I want a Pulitzer Prize in the next three years," she'd said. And she'd sent a ripple of anxiety through the room with her announcement. "Dead weight is no longer welcome here." Digby later confided that her performance had been so commanding that Digby wondered for an instant whether she might let him go!

Hale glanced at her crystal-faced, titanium watch. "I really must be going, Digby." Her untouched salad lay under a dollop of garish French dressing in its humble barklike bowl.

"Miss Gardiner," he said, mockingly pulling rank on her. "Your leader hasn't called closure on this meeting yet."

"Oh, Reeve," said Hale reprovingly, while resigning herself to extending their little chat another five minutes.

What was one to do with this man? He had been much more forward ever since naming her editor.

Hale watched as a long line of employees streamed through the cafeteria line: security guards, printers, reporters. She watched as Sylvia Loring and Pam Tursi stepped to the cash register. Noting that Pam was showing more leg than a reporter ought to, Hale lamented yet again the lack of a dress code.

A telephone rang noisily and was answered with a sigh by the cashier.

"Mr. Reeve," she called out, practically screaming his name over the clatter of the lunchroom. "Urgent call!"

Digby stepped up to the phone and cradled the receiver. "Yes, yes," he sputtered. In great agitation, he turned to Hale to see if she was watching. She was.

"Hello Mr. President," he said, sending a hush over the cafeteria. "Actually, sir, you caught me in the cafeteria! Our ladies serve up a mean clam chowder."

For a few moments, Digby listened, beaming and fiddling with his tie. The cafeteria line was frozen in place. The servers stopped ladling chowder and slicing sandwich meat. Not a fork moved.

"Yes, Mr. President," he said finally. "We think so too, sir. We're awfully proud of the job she does for us."

Hale stirred in her chair. A spate of articles about her—the first female editor of a Washington paper—had recently appeared in the *Washington Journalism Review*, the *Wash-*

*ington Post, Washingtonian* magazine. It was apparent that the President had noticed and was finally giving her her due. Smoothing back her cowlick, Hale swallowed in anticipation of Digby calling her to the phone. Perhaps the President would ask to have a word with her.

"I'll certainly tell her, Mr. President," Digby effused. "I'm sure Sylvia will be very pleased to hear it!"

After a few remarks about the upcoming campaign, Digby returned the receiver to its wall-mounted roost. He turned to Sylvia Loring, still standing with tray in hand. "No one ever told me we had a celebrity in our midst! Dinner at the White House?"

"Well, lunch here sure is easier on the nerves," Sylvia countered, embarrassed.

Digby made his way back to Hale and took his seat with an air of great importance. "Seems the President thinks we're doing a fine job."

Hale drew herself up in her chair. "Oh? He must have noticed the changes over the past few months."

"He sure admires our Sylvia Loring!"

Hale said not a word in response. She glanced over at Sylvia and Pam, who were surrounded at their table by colleagues. Her lips clamped together, Hale rose from the table and, with a nod to Digby, made her exit.

The main item of news the reporters carried up from the cafeteria that Tuesday before Thanksgiving was not so much that Sylvia Loring had been to the White House the night before, but that she'd managed to come and go without attracting any newsroom notice. Sylvia realized that in a town where the invitation to the right dinner party was a major coup, often netting professional rewards, she'd unwittingly pulled off the biggest coup of all: dinner at the White House. But after the way the evening had ended, she was convinced it was a dead-end experience, albeit a glorious one. At least the Rossen story might go somewhere—and she would be at the wheel, doing the steering.

Sylvia headed straight for Frank Glover's desk. Highly

respected, Frank was the *Trib*'s senior reporter on Capitol Hill. Frank's twice-weekly syndicated column, "On The Hill," was second only to Colette Daniels's in popularity. A Washington native and graduate of Howard University, Frank knew the city's precincts like the back of his hand.

Frank looked up from his desk at Sylvia with a sly grin. "Now, what I can't figure out is how you send a perfectly decent, down-to-earth reporter over to cover baubles and beads, which as far as I'm concerned has no place in a newspaper in the first place, and suddenly she goes uptown on you."

"Cut the crap Glover," boomed out Andy Ferraro, without so much as turning his head or interrupting the movement of his fingers on the keyboard. "What you wouldn't give for a White House invite!"

"More of that lip out of you Ferraro," Frank retorted cheerfully, "and you're back to obits."

Sylvia loved hanging out with the hard-news reporters, who always seemed to be in the thick of battle. Every Style reporter—and Sylvia was no exception—lay in secret awe of the Cityside reporters' one-hour deadlines, and the combat zone into which they were so often sent. She liked this crusty, old-boy stuff—it made her think of old Hollywood movies and how she'd first gotten the journalism bug.

"Are you on deadline?" Sylvia asked Frank.

He was in fact on deadline, but gave her five minutes anyway. Frank told her that her column was still the talk of the Hill and that he personally had never been a great fan of Bob Rossen, his understated way of praising her work.

When Sylvia revealed that there might be more—perhaps a major sex scandal in the offing—Frank listened with interest. His mind seemed to be clicking, making his own connections, developing his own theories.

"If I come up with anything, would I be stepping on your turf?" Sylvia asked.

"Yes," he said bluntly. "But frankly, this isn't the kind of story I want to handle, period. If you want to do it, fine. But," he said, lowering his voice, "if you get what you're after, don't expect a welcome mat on the Hill anytime soon. You're going to royally piss off a lot of people, and I'm not talking only about Bob Rossen.''

Frank's overstocked Rolodex was the only thing he ever bothered to lock up at night. He rotated the 360-degree wheel to ''S'' and pulled out a name, someone inside Rossen's office. ''Don't use my name when you call her. Debra Sugahara is gunning for Rossen's ass, and she might be ready to spill.''

# CHAPTER
## 9

Kokoh arrived at Ola's House of Yogurt off DuPont Circle twenty minutes late. Sylvia was waiting, already on her second coffee refill when Kokoh made her entrance, decked out like a movie star in disguise in dark broad sunglasses, her long, black hair pulled into a tight ponytail. Sylvia felt only relief to see her show up at all, given Kokoh's wavering on the telephone.

The place was Kokoh's choice. Sylvia soon learned why. Kokoh's ''early dinner'' was a jumbo yogurt split, heaped with banana, vanilla, and chocolate yogurt mounds topped with chopped walnuts, chocolate chips, crushed Oreo cookies, and shredded coconut. Talking like a convert, at a rapid-fire pace, Kokoh extolled the virtues of yogurt for a future model. ''It's good for your complexion and your health, and you don't gain weight.''

Sylvia pulled out her notebook. ''So, Kokoh, did you see the paper yesterday?''

Kokoh nodded her head vigorously, while theatrically sucking yogurt from her spoon like a grade-school birthday girl.

"Were you pleased with how the picture turned out?" Sylvia continued.

"Listen, I'm really not sure we should be talking about any of this," Kokoh said.

"Why not?" Sylvia asked quietly.

"I don't know," Kokoh blustered. "Maybe this isn't cool."

"I thought you said you'd tell me anything I needed to know."

"I never promised you anything, did I?" Kokoh said.

With a sinking feeling, Sylvia began to suspect that this scattered beauty had cooked the whole thing up—probably high on cocaine at the French ambassador's party—just to get attention. If that was true, Rossen's indignant AA might even have cause for complaint.

"Look," Sylvia interjected. "Don't waste my time. If you're just making all this business up, let's leave it at that. No hard feelings."

Sylvia's skepticism seemed to provoke something inside Kokoh, and she gathered herself in indignation.

"You don't believe me?" Kokoh snapped.

"Why should I?"

Kokoh stood up, grabbing her sunglasses and bag. "Okay, I'll tell you. But not here."

They strode out together into the darkening evening, marching past the handful of homosexuals braving the cold at DuPont Circle and into a neighborhood of seedy old Victorian row houses. Kokoh lived in one of Washington's many changing neighborhoods; it was a mixture of poor and lower middle classes, with a scattering of the gentrifying yuppie element.

Sylvia followed Kokoh up a dark flight of steps into an apartment that was a far cry from what Sylvia had imagined. She smiled at her own preconception, which had pictured velvet couches and plush carpet and the smell of sensual oils. Instead, Kokoh's apartment was barren, with a shabby couch and dingy hardwood floors. Not a single picture or poster hung on the walls. The only suggestion of extravagance lay in the form of a sleek Italian telephone with built-in answering machine that sat ingloriously on a window-sill.

Kokoh bolted the door behind them.

"You don't entertain men here?" Sylvia blurted out.

Kokoh laughed out loud. "Where have you been?" She explained that the girls always went out on call—to hotels, private parties, even offices on Capitol Hill. "We're supposed to put on this big act like we're all little rich girls," Kokoh said. "Like we have our nails done in the morning and facials every afternoon."

"So with Bob Rossen, do you generally go to his office?" Sylvia asked.

Kokoh paused for a long moment, thinking. "I really shouldn't be doing this," she said finally. "Not that I don't want to lay it to Rossen where it hurts, but I'm already in deep shit for this." Kokoh produced a slip of paper from a kitchen cabinet drawer and handed it to Sylvia.

It was a charge slip, with Bob Rossen's signature for $195 for Temp-Time Help. It was dated two days ago, the day of the party.

"This is for your sexual favors?" Sylvia asked, feeling sheepish about putting it so bluntly. But everything had to be made perfectly clear.

"I made it out myself!" Kokoh said.

"May I have this?" Sylvia asked.

"No way! I gotta turn that in to get my money. I should have done it two days ago." Then, with a laugh, she added, "But it's okay for hookers to be ditzy."

Sylvia convinced a reluctant Kokoh to go back outside and get it photocopied. As they walked, Sylvia quizzed Kokoh further about the operation.

"Don't you think I've said enough already?" said Kokoh testily.

They made the Xerox and returned to the apartment. "Look, I've gotta go to work," Kokoh said.

"What about the other clients you mentioned. Who are they?"

Kokoh said, "I can't tell you that right now."

"Why not?" Sylvia asked.

Kokoh looked at her. Sylvia could only guess that the "deep shit" she'd alluded to meant that Kokoh's boss, whoever it was, had put the squeeze on her after seeing the photo in the *Tribune*.

They heard a key turning in the lock. "Oh, shit!" Kokoh screeched. "The shit hits the fan every damn time!"

In walked a tall, busty blonde wrapped in a smart, tailored wool coat. The woman eyeballed Sylvia. "Who are you?"

Before Sylvia could reply, Kokoh said, "This is that reporter I told you about. Shana, this is Sylvia."

"You are one dumb . . . ," Shana hissed to Kokoh, then turned her gaze to Sylvia. They studied each other; Shana looked every inch a college girl, rosy-cheeked and wholesome with an expensive, blunt haircut and a preppy pearl choker. "What did she tell you?" Shana demanded, throwing a nod to Kokoh.

"So you work with Kokoh?" Sylvia replied.

"I'm staying out of this," said Shana haughtily, then eyed Kokoh. "And if you knew what was good for you, you would too."

# CHAPTER
## 10

Breezing through the revolving-door entrance of the Willard Hotel, Hale spotted her cousin Eleanor Gardiner seated in the Willard Room at the far end of the long, elegant hallway. Impeccably tended palmettos in giant Grecian urns rose from the lush mosaic carpet alongside three-foot-wide ashtrays with the hotel's seal imprinted in white sand. Blessedly, Hale never ran into anyone she knew here. Certainly not newspaper people. The Willard was patronized mostly by out-of-towners of wealth and position, along with the occasional Washington VIP.

Dining at the Willard Room every other Wednesday was the Gardiner cousins' unbreakable ritual. Hale's secretary had called the first of the year and made reservations for twenty-six lunches. As girls, Hale and Eleanor had been inseparable companions, spending summers together and most holidays. They rode horses and shot skeet; they dressed up together in their mothers' finery and went trick-or-treating.

"Miss Gardiner," intoned the maître d' as he guided her to her accustomed corner table, overlooking the hotel foyer.

Black, fluted columns and red velvet draperies divided the spacious Willard Room into private enclaves where intimacies could be easily exchanged. There were no economy measures here: the traditional white linen tablecloths were changed after every patron. Cut flowers were fresh every day.

Eleanor was already sipping her usual Bloody Mary, handsome and statuesque in a white wool designer dress. She possessed the proud, patrician bend in her nose that would send lesser women to the plastic surgeon, but not a Gardiner. A year Hale's senior, thirty-three, Eleanor owned and operated a small portrait photography studio in Georgetown that, to Hale's knowledge, barely earned her a decent living.

"Dotty!" Eleanor said, using the moniker for Hale's christened name, Dorothy. Long ago, Hale had trained her mother and father to call her Hale, her mother succumbing more quickly and approvingly than her father, flattered by her only daughter's election of her own maiden name. "I'm so glad to see you today," Eleanor continued. "I was afraid you wouldn't make it."

Hale never stopped wondering when Eleanor would find the right man. God knows, it wasn't easy. Her own marriage at twenty-three to an Oxford-educated, English aristocrat had fallen apart in seventeen months. They'd married too quickly—after less than three months of meeting—and the man had changed almost overnight. Once married, he'd expected her to wait on him hand and foot: cook his meals, clean his London flat, and warm his bed. On occasion, she'd wondered if she'd bailed out too quickly. Next time, she was determined to make it work.

Eleanor was a curious case. Status and wealth in a man didn't seem to matter to her, although she'd once had that infamous crush on the dashing Maxwell Ridgway. How Hale had wanted him for her Eleanor!

Eleanor was certainly attractive enough to land a catch despite the distinct liability of her career in the arts. She'd never displayed the slightest aptitude for business and just seemed to flounder along, a job here and a commission there.

Partly from guilt, partly from loyalty, Hale had always been only too anxious to help. She had snared for Eleanor a fat commission to shoot a series of portraits for the paper: oversized, black-and-white photo-portraits of Digby Reeve, Phyllis Reeve, and herself that hung in the Tribune Building lobby. She also threw Eleanor the occasional plum photo assignment for the *Trib*, sending her out as a free-lancer to occasions where she might meet clients and eligible bachelors. And Hale would brook no criticism of her cousin; when word reached her desk that some of the photographers were grumbling about Eleanor's receiving special treatment, Hale called in the photo chief. "Eleanor is doing me a personal favor by working for us at free-lance rates," she'd said, setting him straight. "I'd like the department to show her some appreciation the next time she comes in."

The waiter came around with another Bloody Mary for Eleanor and a glass of Cabernet Sauvignon for Hale. "I don't know," Eleanor mused. "I've been feeling rather on edge this week. Perhaps it's just the holidays coming on."

"I've felt the same way," Hale chimed in, and proceeded to rattle off a litany of woes, starting with this speech that Digby had enlisted her for.

"As a boss, I must set an example," Hale said. "And I must be careful never to let my hair down. I can't understand why I get so tense about giving these speeches. I think I'm in control, but must not be if I feel this unnerved."

"Oh, don't give it another thought. You'll knock 'em dead. You're the best speaker I know."

This cheered Hale momentarily, but a dark frown crossed her face when she thought of Sylvia Loring, and the Bob Rossen affair.

"Plus," Hale added, "we've been having staffing problems at work. With Colette Daniels gone, I've got a substitute who just isn't up to par. Did you see Sylvia Loring's column yesterday? What did you think?"

"That photo of the congressman being doused," said Eleanor, delicately cutting into her duck, "didn't seem like the sort of thing you usually run."

"Absolutely not, but some of our reporters come from nowhere," said Hale, conveniently forgetting that she'd personally tapped Sylvia to fill in for Colette. "They've been bred by *Dynasty* and *Falcon Crest* and these godawful public schools. They don't know the difference between society and unrefined gossip."

Hale broke open a crusty roll and spread butter. "And the most galling part of it is somehow these people always manage to push ahead."

"Well," Eleanor said, recoiling from the turn in the conversation. "Not everyone has had the advantage of money and a good family."

Hale fell silent, ruffled by Eleanor's interjection. She knew that Eleanor also referred to herself, convinced that her father had been condemned by the Gardiner family and, by extension, so had she.

One day in their teens while they were out riding, Eleanor confessed to Hale her darkest secret—that she had caught her father "doing it" with another man. This had bonded them together with the invisible glue of conspiracy. Only later did Hale realize that therein lay the reason for the discreet distance her family had put between itself and Uncle Dwight Gardiner, why after the death of Eleanor's mother he had never shown the slightest interest in another woman.

That Dwight's large inheritance had been significantly reduced was the one thorn that pricked relations between the two cousins. Even to this date, Eleanor always seemed to expect things from Hale: the occasional interest-free loan; making long-distance phone calls from Hale's house; borrowing expensive outfits or jewelry that Hale alway had to remind her to return.

"So," Hale said, "the holiday is upon us. We must cheer up!"

"Cheers," said Eleanor, lifting her drink.

Together the cousins drank, the tense moment having passed. Despite her troubles, Eleanor possessed an irrepressible spirit, though lately, observing these second and sometimes third Bloody Marys, Hale wondered whether her cousin had been drinking too much. What Hale felt most of all for this dear woman across the table was a keen feeling of protectiveness; they were family, after all, and family must take care of each other.

"Listen, my dear," Hale said, "why don't you make an exception this year and join us for Thanksgiving dinner. Papa and Mother will be there, of course, and Charles and Aunt Win and Uncle Taylor and God knows who—the usual lot of foreign dignitaries away from home, just like old times! How can you refuse?"

Hale painted a rosy picture with her words, of the Gardiner estate in the rolling Virginia hills west of Middleburg, a fire roaring in the huge flagstone fireplace, the long table groaning with the weight of the feast. Afterward, they would don riding breeches and go dashing into the woods, horse to panting horse on the leafy path as they had done as girls.

For a moment, Eleanor paused, a frosting of pleasure on her lips. Then, as if jarred by a sudden recollection, she said abruptly, "No, Dotty, I can't."

Hale couldn't believe it. Eleanor wasn't still wasting her time with that crude Rich Kurtz! The subject was off limits now, had been ever since Hale had asked Eleanor point-blank what Rich did for a living. Eleanor had replied that Hale could never see Rich for what he was, and the discussion had ended.

"Why can't you come?" Hale demanded.

"I do have to work," Eleanor said.

"Oh, nonsense!" erupted Hale. "How is it that you always 'do have to work' on holidays? A day away from your work would do you wonders."

Eleanor smiled lamely.

Hale downed a fortifying sip of wine. "Who's kidding whom? It's not your work."

Eleanor sighed. "Let's get the check, shall we?"

When Hale got back to her office, she thought of another person to invite. She dialed Colette's number on the telephone, reaching only her blasted machine.

"Colette, dear," Hale spoke into the answering machine. "If you're in town, do come out to the country for Thanksgiving dinner tomorrow. Call any time day or night. We can drive out together. I'll be at the office till six today."

# CHAPTER
## 11

Back in the shadowy rear booth, Debra Sugahara could barely be seen as Sylvia shut the door on the chilly night wind and walked the narrow length of the Tune Inn, past mounted trophies of bear and elk and horny men ogling her from the booths. Debra had suggested it as a place where Bob Rossen was sure not to spot them—a dark, grungy bar down the street from the Hawk 'n' Dove and Duddington's and the other trendy Hill hangouts.

"Robert Redford's favorite hangout when he comes on the Hill to lobby," Debra said after the introductions. She spoke in a soft, ironic voice with bell-like clarity. "Must feel like he's back in Utah."

Above their booth perched a stuffed hawk, a yellow hard-hat, and a mounted swordfish, and over the rest rooms across the aisle were the mounted rear ends of two deer that Debra pointed out to Sylvia with a glance. "Witty, huh?"

"Very." Sylvia settled back against the hard wood seat and examined her own prospective trophy more carefully. Raven-haired with a smart, short haircut framing her pale face, Debra sat straight but low in the booth. She was lovely in that china-doll way, her eyes burning black out of the shadow like a wild animal cornered in the night.

In the notebook of her mind, Sylvia was already scribbling rapid-fire notes, taking in all the details, even the Bob Seger song, "Night Moves," which someone had punched up on the jukebox. She had already decided to capture this scene here in the article. They ordered drinks from a muscular, hard-boiled waitress, and Debra went on about Redford, about how he came breezing in to lobby Bob Rossen on his pet environmental issues, leaving behind a whiff of glamour for all the staffers to inhale.

"Like Bob, Redford's very short," Debra added dryly. "Unlike Bob, he's very sexy."

Sylvia reached for her notebook. "Is that my cue?"

Debra's face tightened. She drew a breath and said in a shaky voice, "I can't believe I'm really doing this."

Sylvia said nothing. The woman was nervous, and her instincts told her not to push—not unless she had no other choice. On the phone, Debra had said yes; she'd seen Sylvia's column and was willing to talk. But how far she would go was very much in doubt.

"You can't use my name," Debra commanded. She took a long sip from her gin and tonic. "If I tell you what I know about Bob Rossen, and he finds out it's me . . ." With her finger, she made the sign of a knife slashing her delicate throat.

Despite herself, Sylvia shuddered. Whether Debra meant that she'd lose her job—or something worse—wasn't clear; what was clear was how much trust Debra Sugahara was putting in a perfect stranger. It was frightening sometimes, Sylvia realized, how much impact she could have on someone else's life. "I won't use your name," Sylvia told her solemnly.

Debra's glance darted anxiously toward the two men with

their pitcher of beer in the next booth and pressed her head back against her seat, biting her lip and avoiding eye contact with Sylvia.

A panic attack, Sylvia thought. She leaned confidentially across the table. "Debra," she said gently, "where are you from?"

"You're not going to use this?"

"No."

Sylvia drew her out skillfully. Debra Sugahara was from Sacramento, the youngest daughter of Japanese-Americans who had been farmers in the Central Valley before World War II. After Pearl Harbor, the family land had been expropriated and the parents interned. "At Manzanar," Debra said, her voice expressionless. "On the other side of the mountains. With ten thousand other Japanese-Americans." After their release, unable to reclaim their land, Debra's parents had moved to Sacramento and her father had gotten into the real-estate business and done "very well for himself." Debra laughed. "If Bob finds out who spilled the beans, I can always go back to the family business."

Sylvia was encouraged. Debra was loosening up—even ordering a second gin and tonic before Sylvia had half finished her screwdriver. "How did you get started with Bob Rossen?"

Debra drank, then looked at Sylvia thoughtfully. "Dad's a pretty brave guy, but he's also no dummy. He told me the way to avoid any more Manzanars was for Japanese-Americans to get active in politics. Besides," she said, flashing a cynical smile, "we all know Bob has a thing about Japanese women."

Sylvia took a swallow of her screwdriver, remembering Kokoh's raunchy comment at the French Embassy party. "So it seems."

"Oh, yes," Debra said, dragging out the "yes" suggestively and taking another shot of gin. She leaned toward Sylvia across the booth, lowering her voice to a stage whisper. "If it has two breasts and a Japanese face, Bob just can't resist. How do you think I got hired? I only had a B-minus average at San Francisco State. Of course," she added wryly,

"I thought at the time it was my energy and enthusiasm that got me the job."

The whole story involving none other than the powerful chairman of the House Judiciary Committee was so sordid that a part of Sylvia's brain kept telling her this just couldn't be true. Yet here it all was, told flatly and convincingly by this levelheaded assistant, his top liaison to the business community back in his Sacramento district. It was the clincher to the long-standing Washington precept that Democrats get caught with their pants down and Republicans with their hand in the cookie jar.

Bob Rossen, Debra said, had been a pilot in the Pacific in World War II and—here she confirmed what Kokoh had said—after the war had been stationed in Japan. "He was married at the time," Debra said. "A nice Jewish girl, the woman he was supposed to marry. We've all heard him brag about it. Let's just say that over in Japan Bob acquired a certain yen"—Debra giggled at her pun—"for Japanese females."

Sylvia smiled, ordering a second screwdriver. She had to be careful with the booze, but here at the critical moment, she didn't want Debra to think she was drinking alone and clam up.

"So," Debra said. "Bob keeps the old Japanese fires burning here in town. But what's amazing is, the more power he's gotten on the Hill, the more brazen he's become."

Sylvia let her pen do the grunt work of the job as her mind stretched to process the incredible. On numerous occasions, Debra had seen Bob Rossen escort Kokoh into his inner office and lock the door. "He can't get enough of that girl," Debra said. "I've seen Kokoh go in there at all times of day. Once he tried to pretend that he was trying to help her father with something—she's an Air Force brat and her dad's in the service—but it's like, wink, wink. All the staffers know what's going down."

"What else do you know about Kokoh?" Sylvia asked.

"All I know is I think she works for something called Temp-Time Help. I saw a copy of a charge slip one time on Bob's desk."

"Kokoh said she has a lot of clients from Capitol Hill," Sylvia said. "Know anything about that?"

"No. All I know is Bob Rossen. Bob takes all these junkets to Japan—look it up, okay. What's he doing in Japan—conferring with Toyota? I'll give you two guesses. No, old Bob's giving new meaning to the term 'geisha girl.' "

"How do you know that?" Sylvia said.

"Everybody on his staff who's been over there with him knows that. Me, for example. When I first started working for him, innocent little me, Bob took me on his little Japanese junket."

It wasn't until later that Debra asked to go off the record. Not until she'd told how Bob had put the moves on her in Kyoto and she'd resisted; how Bob, in a fit of rage, had brought a Japanese woman into Debra's bedroom and right before Debra's eyes made love to the woman on Debra's mat.

"And that's not all," Debra said. And then, realizing: "Oh, no. You can't put all of this in there."

Sylvia hesitated. For the moment, she decided to skirt the issue of what to do with that last material. "Go off the record," she said, "if you want to tell me more."

Debra told her more. She told her how one weekend, at Bob's house in the northwestern section of the city, he had put the moves on her again after a party for the staff. His wife Sally had been there, a seemingly impassive witness to the whole thing. He was just going to take Debra upstairs and do it.

"What happened then?" Sylvia asked.

"He was drunk. He hit me with his fist. His wife jumped in and tried to stop him, and then he hit me again."

Sylvia went stone cold. "Were you hurt?"

"I ran out to my car. I had cuts on my face, but nothing requiring stitches."

Debra's matter-of-fact tone sent another chill down Sylvia's spine. "You didn't press charges?"

"I was afraid to. Even now, Bob keeps threatening to fire me if I don't sleep with him. Of course, he never does it— I guess he figures that would ruin any chance he's got. So, what he does, just to torture me I'm sure, is every time Kokoh comes in he gives me this look before he closes his door. I can't describe it. It's like, 'Fuck you, Sugahara.' "

"Why are you telling me all this?" Sylvia said.

"I called my dad today after I talked to you. He's known about all this. He said if I didn't speak out about Rossen, he was going to do it himself."

Every time Sylvia had to sit and watch Dennis Berman read one of her stories, it set her on edge. From Sylvia's desk, she had a clear shot of Dennis at his desk. The Rossen story was the first thing he looked at when he came in that Friday morning. He read it from start to finish at least twice, a furrow on his brow, his lips grimly pushed together in a look that would spell disapproval to anyone who didn't know him. His pencil slashed and stabbed at parts of the story. She tried to distract herself from trying to read his verdict from the nuances on his face and turned purposefully to the bottomless-pit pile of magazines, papers, and press releases that accumulated on her desk, but she just couldn't concentrate. She'd written the story the day before—Thanksgiving Day. She couldn't wait to pour out the story while it was still fresh in her mind. Debra had called her back after the interview. She'd decided not to stay on in Rossen's office under the circumstances.

"Even if Bob didn't know for sure I was the one who'd talked, he'd suspect it, and that would be just as bad. I've decided to resign," Debra had said, her courage gaining magnitude with her new decision.

"And if it'll help make your story, go ahead and use my name," she'd continued. "Just not the part about his making it with other women in my hotel room. But you can say that he beat me up."

Apparently, Sylvia had won Debra's trust. Debra even gave her the one thing her story still needed: another source inside Rossen's office, someone willing to confirm her observations off the record. "He's looking for another job right now on the Hill, so his name cannot be used," she'd stressed. But he had been at home then, willing to talk. It had taken her all day to write the story, but she had managed to get to her mother's house for a late Thanksgiving dinner.

Dennis signaled her from across the room, and they walked into a conference room where they could talk. He asked her if all her sources were sound, and she said they were. He asked if she would share them with him, and she said she would. He told her that if the story got by Hale—and he stressed the *if*—she would of course have to call Rossen and get his comment on these charges. She said she understood that, though she hadn't actually thought of it till just that moment.

Dennis removed his glasses, setting them atop the printout of the story that he'd carried with him into the room. "This story is hot as hell. Let me congratulate you right now." No characteristic zinger followed, no note of levity. She had never seen Dennis so serious.

He walked her back to her desk. "When did you write this?" Dennis asked.

"Yesterday," she said.

"It could have waited one day," he said reprovingly, but she could tell he was impressed. Not another of his reporters cared this much.

Dennis seemed as anxious as Sylvia about the story, cruising up toward Hale's office every fifteen, twenty minutes to see if she'd come in, apparently eager to get the dialogue with her started before half the afternoon was gone.

The sound of riding boots thumping the linoleum floor announced Hale's arrival at twenty of twelve. Wearing her prized burgundy boots was a rare indulgence, in keeping with her jaunty holiday spirit.

Dennis Berman was waiting in her office, dismantling a paper clip.

"This is urgent; it can't wait," he said, thrusting Sylvia's story into her hands. Without asking for her consent, Dennis lifted Hale's phone and summoned Sylvia to her office.

When Sylvia arrived, Hale correctly invited her to sit.

"You should be congratulated for your enterprise," Hale started.

Sylvia flushed with pleasure.

"But," Hale continued, "I believe sexuality is a private matter and should not be subject to the probing eye of the press."

"I'm not sure that prostitution should even be against the law," Sylvia said. "But as long as it is, we need to cover it."

Hale was unconvinced by this argument. She pulled the printout of Sylvia's story off her desk, lifting it up like a loose accordian; she glanced at the first page, then the second. She began to shake her head, slowly at first. The one thing she didn't want attached to her editorial hand by the big boys, the powers that be in the journalism establishment, was the sleaze factor, the accusation that she parlayed sleaze to sell papers. "I'm just not sure of the relevance of these allegations, even if they're true," she said.

Dennis could no longer restrain himself. "While none of us thinks that prostitution is up there in the pantheon of sins against society," he began, throwing Hale a probing glance, "and all of us have been caught with our hands in some cookie jar at one time or another, stories like this one don't come around every day. If we sit on this one, you can damn well count on it showing up in the *Post*. I don't know when, but it'll be there."

Hale's head shot up, as if momentarily stunned. She was obsessed with the competition, with being respected by them, with beating them to the punch. She reminded herself of something her father frequently repeated: Your competition respects you more if you knock them out than if you stand idly by.

But she needed time to think it through. "Why do you say that?" she asked.

"You know as well as I do, Hale," said Dennis. "Sylvia's sources have spoken to her because they want to go public. Two women are putting themselves on the line here. Her main source, who's resigning effective Monday, wants to get into print. If we don't print, she'll go to the *Post*. And by the way, Monday is the day this story should run. Banner headline, page one."

Hale knew that being decisive was one of the most important qualities a leader could have—even if she didn't feel that way, as she didn't just now. "Okay, we'll run with it, but not page one," she said.

Dennis argued the point, insisted that's exactly where it should go. But Hale wouldn't back down. "Top right-hand corner, page three."

# CHAPTER
## 12

It was strange, Sylvia thought as she and B. D. sped toward RFK Stadium in B. D.'s gold Jaguar the following Sunday. A man could make the moves and be rebuffed, call her green and then not phone for three days—and then? And then he could call and invite her to a Redskins game as if nothing had happened. Very strange, but oddly intoxicating to be courted by this powerful man who was inviting Sylvia to join him in his powerful clique.

Without so much as a mention of their late-night encounter, B. D. began to talk football. He seemed to take for granted that Sylvia understood the nuances of the National Football League until he realized that she did not even know the city represented by today's rivals, the Giants.

"You've got to be kidding!" he said, flashing around a curve to reveal the huge stadium on the skyline ahead.

Sylvia sighed. Sports talk always opened up an abyss between herself and men—any man, even Max, whose football heroics, glorious though they apparently were, had been lost on her. Perhaps that was one reason Max had adored her so much—she was never one of his hero-worshiping fans.

"New York!" B. D. bellowed. "The New York Giants!

Let me tell you something. You know what the great binding cord of this town is?'' He paused as if revealing an official secret, one known by only a select few. ''You think it's politics? No way. It's the Redskins.''

B. D. gave his name to a stadium cop and was waved on through to a VIP lot, where his Jaguar took its place beside a white Rolls Royce. In his car trunk, he opened for Sylvia's inspection a wicker picnic basket, containing a bottle of Dom Perignon with two crystal champagne glasses, crackers, and an assortment of cheeses.

Sylvia had to laugh at this display. What she really liked about the man was that he wasn't afraid to be himself; he said what he thought and got away with it. And upscale German cheeses and wicker baskets didn't jibe with B. D. Cole.

''You should have told me and I would have made some peanut-butter sandwiches to go with,'' Sylvia teased.

B. D. let out a hearty laugh, having some fun at his own expense. He steered her inside the stadium, his hand light on her back as they emerged from a tunnel into the sun-drenched arena, awash with the vivid colors of the crowd, pennants snapping around the upper rim in a stiff breeze. Sylvia shivered inside her long camel's-hair coat, half from delight at the spectacle, half from the chill.

In a section below, a mob of beer-guzzling, bare-chested men, wearing war paint and Indian feathers, was doing some kind of circular war dance and singing the Redskins' fight song, ''Hail to the Redskins.''

''These fans go berserk when the Giants are here,'' B. D. explained. ''During the week,'' he added with a knowing smile, ''they're all bureaucrats at the Federal Reserve.''

They boarded an elevator, going up.

''My God,'' B. D. said, staring at a heavyset man in full Indian headdress whose face was painted in red and gold, the Redskin colors. ''Marv, is that you?''

''B. D.! How are ya?'' said the man, clasping B. D.'s hand.

''You're looking good, Marv. Never better.''

The elevator doors opened, and Marv staggered out, as if under the weight of the headdress. "Let's have lunch," he said.

"Call me," responded B. D. as the doors closed. The elevator continued up. "That was Marv Stein," B. D. explained with a chuckle. "Washington bureau chief, *New York Times*. Hell," he added. "I should have introduced you."

"Forget it." Sylvia shrugged.

"Don't you want to work at the *Times*?"

"It's never exactly been my dream."

"Oh, you'd prefer the *Post*."

"Actually," Sylvia started, "I'm really quite happy where I am. I think a smaller paper in a major market, where you have freedom and flexibility, is the best of all possible worlds." And then, thinking the picture sounded a touch too rosy, Sylvia added, "The only downside is salary."

Just then it occurred to Sylvia that unless Hale reneged at the last minute, they'd all know her name tomorrow: Marv Stein, the heavies at the *Post*, everyone. Even as they were speaking, her Rossen story was being set into print.

The doors opened, and they were at the top of the stadium, looking down as if from the sky on the lush green turf, and on the crowd, ringing the field like a giant pointillist painting, dots of color everywhere.

"This way," B. D. directed.

They arrived dead-center above the middle of the field in a row of private boxes, each a warm enclosure against the wind, with plush seats and bars and glass panels. Inside the booths, groups of people were clustered, eating and drinking and wielding binoculars.

B. D. ushered Sylvia through the door and introduced her all around to members of Washington's power elite, at least half of whom were household names. The two of them took their seats in the front of the booth, only to rise again for the national anthem.

"Glad to see this veritable excrescence of patriotism in you, B. D.," observed one well-known columnist, dressed in a seersucker suit and bow tie.

"If it isn't the prince of polysyllabic palaver." B. D. grinned, shaking hands with his friend.

Sylvia laughed. She loved the way B. D. could put a celebrity in his place. He had been this way with the President, with the Australian publishing tycoon. She had always been intimidated by the wealthy and powerful, painfully apparent in the way she behaved around them. B. D. was so confident, never deferential, and he had them eating out of his hands.

"A line worthy of Spiro Agnew!" the columnist retorted.

It was going to be that kind of afternoon, thought Sylvia, full of dry political thrusts and bon mots, while on the earth below grown men crashed headlong into each other with no apparent purpose other than self-destruction and moving a leather ball from one spot to another.

Then, as the anthem ended and the crowd roared, Sylvia felt her heart stop in her chest, and her body, angled against the glass panel, go eerily weightless, as if her soul at this very moment were leaving it behind. Climbing directly toward her, a tall man making his way through the crowd, was Max Ridgway.

It was Max, unmistakably. Sylvia could not yet make out his face, but no one else in the world walked like that, with his gliding, effortless gait. No one else in the world carried himself that way, erect yet relaxed, a body of broad shoulders and angular lines, an athlete's body. And, before the face came clear, she recognized that hair from the streets of Charlottesville, a thick brown shock streaked with dark reds and golds, now whipped into threads by the stadium wind.

He was not alone. In the lead was his uncle Ernest, his handsome face creased with age, followed by a voluptuous brunette who could be hardly older than nineteen. Who was that, Sylvia wondered? Surely she did not belong to Max.

And Max. God help her, had it really been five years? The face had something of its old self: a broad, expressive face, keen-eyed and sharply intelligent. It was Max—but older, much older. Gone were the apple cheeks of the man-child and with them the old collegiate air of nonchalance, the boyish innocence. In their place was something intangible but no less striking. The five years had burned into him something Sylvia could just as easily have registered in herself: an air of weary irony, a harder edge that showed in his rugged, weatherbeaten good looks, the look of a soldier home from combat.

"Someone you know?" B. D. asked, following Sylvia's gaze.

Max was coming straight at her, as if from a far corner of her life into its very center. In confusion, Sylvia abruptly sat down and turned her face to one side.

Then, feeling his gaze through the glass as if there were a spotlight on her cheek, Sylvia turned and looked into the cool blue depths of Max Ridgway's eyes.

A smile, ironic, strangely triumphant, tugged at the corners of his mouth. Sylvia rose and went to the door, ushering them inside the warm box.

"Hello, Sylvia."

"Hello, Max."

There was an awkward silence. Then, suddenly aware of where they were, Max turned to his left.

"You remember my uncle Ernest."

"Yes. Of course." She shook Ernest Ridgway's hand.

"And this," said Max, gesturing to the woman, "is Nicole."

The voice was high-pitched and vulgar. "Hi, Sylvia."

Astonished, Sylvia stared at this girl, a decade younger than Max if she was a day, unable to believe the obvious, that she and Max were together.

B. D. came forward and extended his hand to Max. "B. D. Cole."

"Oh, yes," came Max's retort, as if he knew the name but refused to let that recognition register visibly. He introduced himself.

"Of course!" B. D. exclaimed upon meeting Ernest Ridgway. "A great pleasure, sir. Will you join us?"

"Actually," replied Ernest, "thank you, but our hosts await us over in the next booth."

"Well, then," B. D. said. "Maybe at halftime, then."

"Fine," Ernest said, with a smile.

They moved on, Max throwing a final glance, neither distant nor friendly, at Sylvia.

The game had started. Sylvia stared absently down at the field as if the uniformed men were tiny figures in a board game she didn't know how to play.

"So," B. D. rumbled in her ear. "Who is this Max?"

"Someone I used to know." Sylvia turned to look at B. D. It was all so bizarre. Max Ridgway was different, as she should have known he would be by now. And so was she, here in the company of this man, his eyes clouding with incipient jealousy, silently demanding some explanation. "We knew each other at UVA."

His eyes still following the game, B. D. sucked in his lip. "I take it you're pleading the fifth."

"If you don't mind," Sylvia said, "I think I'd like some of that champagne."

B. D. opened the Dom Perignon, pouring a glass for Sylvia and offering it around the booth. Their companions declined; they all had drinks and, for the moment, at least, were happily intent on the game.

"To the future," B. D. said, his crystal glass ringing against Sylvia's. He smiled pointedly and touched her glass once more. "Certainly not the past."

As the game wore on, Sylvia listened politely to B. D.'s explanations, but her thoughts kept returning to Max, who, hidden by a wall, could hardly be more than ten feet away. Why was he so much changed? Why had he left so quickly? What had he meant by that parting glance? Why had he made no effort to arrange to see her again?

And that woman—was it possible that Max Ridgway, Renaissance man, admirer of Thomas Jefferson, had settled down with something like that?

There were no answers. There was only their past.

They had met her sophomore year at a Saturday-night fraternity party. That in itself was ironic: Max despised fraternities, refused membership. Challenged by her best friend,

Ann-Marie Walters, to "get your butt out of your books for a change," Sylvia had come to the party reluctantly, planning to stay only briefly.

It was a post–football game party. The Virginia Cavaliers had beaten someone out at the stadium for the first time in twenty years, and a lot of the guys at the party were football players. That was why Max was there.

Sylvia remembered how it happened. Ann-Marie, who was something of a Kentucky blue blood herself, having been raised in the horse country outside Lexington, had let out a piercing shriek that could be heard above the Rolling Stones.

"What's wrong with you?" Sylvia said through clenched teeth, meeting a fusillade of stares in the crowded room.

"Don't look now," Ann-Marie whispered, "but see that gorgeous man over there in the corner? Do you know who that is?"

Sipping beer from a plastic cup, Sylvia spotted the man in question, his lean body poured like steel into close-fitting jeans and a red flannel shirt. Except maybe in the movies, she had never seen a body that looked as strong—not muscle-bound, just incredibly solid and perfectly filled out, from his wide shoulders to his beat-up old tan cowboy boots. His head bobbing excitedly, he was talking with a little preppy shrimp of a guy with tortoiseshell glasses.

"That's Max Ridgway."

"Who?"

"You don't know who that is?" said Ann-Marie in astonishment. "That's the star of the football team. He scored three touchdowns today. Let's go talk to him."

"Wait!" Sylvia said, grabbing Ann-Marie's arm. "We don't know him."

"You're not intimidated, are you?" Ann-Marie said, her tone so mocking that Sylvia's pride could be salvaged only by going with her.

As they approached, elbowing their way through the bodies, some of them dancing, Sylvia could pick up snatches of the conversation between Max Ridgway and the preppy. She could hardly believe her ears. The subject, with great animation on both ends, was the poetry of Walt Whitman.

"I prefer the Civil War poems to his nature poetry," the preppy was saying as they arrived.

"Hi," Ann-Marie interrupted, taking a gulp of beer and turning to Max. "I'm Ann-Marie Walters. Who are you?"

"Max Ridgway," he said in a low, startled voice.

It had been terribly embarrassing. Ann-Marie went on and on, congratulating Max on his performance that day and exhausting her knowledge of football, while Max squirmed in the corner, plainly uncomfortable and wanting to talk about someone else.

"Who are you?" he blurted suddenly to Sylvia.

When she told him, Max's face lit up and he said, "Right! I read your stories in the paper all the time. You're a really good writer."

Sylvia blushed. "Thanks. I have to work at it."

"No," Max objected, his voice rising with great intensity. "That's what I like about it—you have this effortless style, it's not forced like some of those writers at the Cavalier, it just seems to flow!"

Sylvia's cheeks were on fire. No one had ever praised her with such enthusiasm.

His voice was a little shaky. "Would you like to dance?"

Sylvia looked up. No, he wasn't talking to Ann-Marie. He was looking right at her. "Sure," she said in a small voice. "Great!"

It was vintage Stones stuff. Heads turned as they started dancing and, at first, Sylvia felt terribly self-conscious. It seemed everyone was watching. Here she was with a gorgeous football hero in the middle of a mob scene, when all she'd meant to do was stay twenty minutes, then crack the books. It was simply impossible not to feel on the spot. And to make matters worse, they were the tallest twosome on the floor, seeming to tower over the other dancers.

Max was magic on that floor. For such a big man, he was smooth. There wasn't any wasted motion or show-off stuff in the way he danced, just an easy, fluid rippling from his lean hips to those mountainous shoulders. And it was catching—she was loosening up, letting her long body undulate to the pounding music, forgetting herself.

Then "Satisfaction" came on. All around her, like some preliminary chant to a gang bang, Sylvia could hear frat boys singing in unison: "I can't get no satisfaction/But I tried/and I tried . . ." "Satisfaction" had always put sex front and center stage, and made her virginity, at age nineteen, seem like some unmentionable disease, a secret so dark she would rather die than admit it. Even Ann-Marie didn't know about it; she had always assumed—and Sylvia hadn't disabused her—that Sylvia had been deflowered by a boy back in Silver Spring.

"Dumb song," Max said, as if reading her mind.

"What?"

"Dumb song!" Max shouted above the blaring music. "You listen to the lyrics, the guy wants to jump into bed with her, the girl won't let him, so the guy makes the girl feel like she's to blame for all the pain!" Max grinned. "Good beat. Bad lyrics."

Sylvia could hardly believe it. Since when did a football jock, just maybe trying to hustle her into the sack with a soft sell, adopt the point of view of a woman?

Then a slow song was playing. Max said nothing, only moved into her with an innocent, no-holds-barred shine in those blue eyes that made her heart leap into her mouth.

He clasped her right hand with his left and planted his right hand in the small of her back and drew her close against his powerful chest.

It was all she could do to suppress a sigh of pleasure. In high school in Silver Spring, her boyfriend had been editor of the student paper. Andrew Lewis—a tall, gaunt kid who trampled her feet every time they danced—was smart as a whip, a good guy, but just not attractive. And their bodies had never been in synch; Andrew was a verbal genius but all thumbs with his hands.

Her breasts pressing lightly against Max's chest, Sylvia had never touched such a rock-solid body. Her left hand lay on Max's shoulder and, as they swayed together, she nuzzled her cheek against his chest. She could feel the weight of him against her, his body relaxed; he smelled of lightly scented soap and the clean, sensual smell of his own body. She followed his steps, feeling the soft flannel of his shirt against her cheek.

Then the music stopped. "Thanks for the dance," Max said.

Sylvia smiled. She was aware of other women, watching her with more than a touch of envy. "It was great," she said.

The place was growing loud again with drunken shouts and conversation. Max suggested they get some air.

As they pushed through the crowd to the door, Sylvia's eyes caught her friend's across the room. Ann-Marie glared at her, apparently furious at this turn of events. Then Sylvia lost sight of her and was out beside Max on the fraternity steps.

"Pretty night," Max said, scanning a luminous October sky where a full moon rode high over University Avenue. "Feel like walking?"

"Like where?"

"Oh, I don't know. Down to the Corner, maybe."

"Going to be a mob," Sylvia said.

"I know a place," Max said mysteriously.

Sylvia hesitated. He was standing on the steps, with the moon over his shoulder and a dark, serious intensity in the shadowy depths of his eyes. There was something larger than life about him, something that was pulling her like gravity.

"Okay," she said. "But I can't stay long. I've got a paper due on Monday."

In silence they swung onto University and strode past Jefferson's domed Rotunda, glistening white in the moonlight, toward the Corner, a beehive of shops and student hangouts. On a Saturday night after a home game, the Corner was a street scene, teeming with guys and girls in orange-and-blue YOO-VEE-AY sweatshirts, with tweedy alumni and good-timing out-of-towners, with wolfish frat boys in rugby shirts on the prowl for stray coeds.

"What's your paper?" Max said.

"It's on Melville."

"American Lit Survey?"

"Yes, as a matter of fact."

*"Moby Dick?"* Max asked, his voice rising with excitement.

"How'd you know?"

" 'And I only am escaped alone to tell thee,' " Max said in a passably good Yankee whaler's voice. He grinned. "Just call me Ishmael."

Sylvia laughed. "Not bad, Ishmael. Actually, that's Melville, quoting Job."

Max halted, staring at her. "No. That's Ishmael speaking. At the end of the book."

"Look it up."

They had reached the edge of the Corner, pedestrians swerving around them under the bright street lamps. "All right," Max said, unconcerned about blocking traffic. "How much do you want to bet?"

Sylvia thought it over. "A dollar."

"You hungry?"

"A little bit. Why?"

"I'll bet you one Gusburger."

Before Sylvia could reply, Max was beckoning at her from inside a bookstore. "Do you have *Moby Dick?"* he asked a teenage clerk at the register with a punk haircut.

"Moby who?" asked the boy.

Grinning at Sylvia, Max found a copy and tore into it, pinning back a rear page. Sylvia peered expectantly over his shoulder.

"Here it is!" he announced triumphantly, his forefinger zeroing in on the quote. Then he sobered. "Well, I'll be damned." He turned to Sylvia. "Job?" he said, cocking his head at her with just the shadow of a grin. "Job never said a thing like that. Must be a typo."

Sylvia laughed, poking her finger into the steel of his arm. "One Gusburger. Pay up!"

A Gusburger, Sylvia discovered, was a burger cooked by Gus Vallianos at the little White Knight Restaurant, well past all the hot spots, the Virginian and the College Inn restaurant and Macado's, way down University in a dimly lit area not too far from University Theater, the art flick house. There was a counter and a few booths, a jukebox and a small black-and-white TV—and no students. Two cops were drinking coffee in the pale light, and a couple of guys with grease and calluses on their hands manned a booth.

"Nice game, Max," said Gus, a short, rotund man with warm brown eyes, from behind the counter. "Watched the whole thing on the tube." Grinning, he faked left, then swung his body right, imitating the way Max had dodged would-be tacklers. "You sure had some nice moves on that last touchdown."

Max introduced Sylvia to Gus, who received her warmly.

They took a booth and ordered coffee and two Gusburgers. The place was cozy, and Sylvia's burger was the best she'd ever had, cooked Greek-style with feta cheese.

The talk began as soon as the burgers ran out. It started slowly, punctuated by long sips of coffee, then began to ignite as Gus brought more brew, a second cup, a third. "This will keep me up all night," Sylvia protested, stirring in some milk.

"That's the way I want it," Max said, smiling.

When the place closed at two A.M., they were still immersed in conversation. All night they walked, then sat on the steps of Levering Hall and talked in low, intimate voices, watching the moon set with a fiery glow. When the sun rose and they had reached Sylvia's dorm, it seemed they'd just begun. By this time, Max knew all about Sylvia's parents' divorce, and she'd learned that he believed he could communicate better with horses than with people. The chord they touched in each other was that of kindred spirits—loners, idealists. From that day on, Max and Sylvia had been inseparable.

A marching band stepping onto the field brought her back.

"Halftime show," B. D. announced, getting up to stretch.

Sylvia felt a knot in her stomach. Max would be here any minute. It was incomprehensible that he wouldn't want to hear about her last five years as much as she did about his. There was so much to fill him in on. The *Tribune*: did he even know she worked there?

They hadn't been one of these modern couples who'd kept up the friendship after the breakup. She knew of some former boyfriend-girlfriends who were attendants at the other's weddings, made friends with the new mate. Since she'd broken off their romance, she figured it was in his court to make a move in the direction of friendship. He had surprised her by never doing so.

If only Max hadn't pressed for a commitment. If only he'd given her more rope, more time to evolve on her own terms, things might have worked out differently.

Ten minutes passed, and still he didn't appear. Sylvia tried to conceive an artful approach into Max's booth, tried screwing up her courage to go. God, she wished sometimes she had half the moxie of Colette Daniels. She made small talk with guests in the booth without paying attention.

Twenty minutes passed, and Sylvia realized that Max wasn't coming and that it was up to her. If she tried to stop by casually, as if they were dear old college pals, he might throw it back at her with one of his looks, asking why she had never so much as approached him after all these years. For the first time, it occurred to her that he might have expected her to make a move. Then came another, more devastating thought: perhaps after all these years she meant no more to Max than Andrew Lewis, her high-school boyfriend, did to her now.

Sylvia slipped out of her booth and walked the short distance to his. Through the glass wall from behind, she could see Ernest Ridgway gesturing energetically as he talked. She opened the door and heard him saying, "I don't trust Ben Fincastle. I'd have to reluctantly go with Dan Tison."

"Careful, Uncle Ernest," Max interjected, his eyes lighting on Sylvia at the door. "B. D. Cole's antenna has arrived."

There was an edge in Max's tone that Sylvia did not recognize. Didn't he know how hard it was for her to approach him, and that he only made it more difficult by placing her in an enemy camp?

Sylvia would have to do it; apparently, there was no other way. "Can we talk for a minute, Max?" she asked.

Max glanced at his watch. "The game's just about to start

up. What's on your mind?'' He motioned to the chair in front of his.

Sylvia wished that she could just swat Nicole away like a fly from the booth; the girl seemed to be leaning even closer to Max since Sylvia moved inside. This was not how she had imagined a second meeting with him.

Max reached into a full cooler of beverages packed in ice and extracted a frosty bottle of imported beer. He unscrewed the cap, tossed it behind him in the air, and took a sip. "Something to drink? Beer? Wine?" he asked.

"No, thanks," she laughed, trying to strike a light note. "I've had more than I should already."

He made no reply.

Finally, she said, "How's the horse business?"

Max's eyes met hers, and there was something knowing in his gaze. "I better go easy here," he joked. "This could wind up on the *Washington Tribune* Society page."

So he did know where she worked! And unless he were guessing, he even knew her beat this past week. What did he think of the column on Rossen? she wondered. She wracked her brain for some acceptable way to suggest he pick up tomorrow's paper, but could find none.

It was clear that Max was not going to let himself fall into the familiar male trap of being interviewed. He never had. That had been one of his many charms; he always threw questions back her way, and seemed more interested in her response than in hearing himself talk. Often, they used to wrestle verbally over who would ask the questions.

"So this friendship with B. D. Cole," he started off. She could see in his flashing eyes and tell by the ironic way he pronounced B. D.'s name that he was not impressed by him. "Is this, ah, a strictly professional alliance?"

Damn it, she thought, it was the same old Max, cutting right to the heart of the matter, knowing her mind somehow better than she did.

For an instant, Sylvia was at a loss for words. She couldn't admit what was true, that she was seeing B. D. because she was intrigued and flattered. And, yes, curious about the world in which he moved so nimbly and how he did it. Still, she didn't want Max to get the impression that she was in love with B. D.

He seemed to read a response in her hesitation, and his face turned suddenly serious, as if he were moving through some private experiences of his own. For the first time, she noticed the vertical lines that had set like fence posts in the cheeks flanking his wide mouth. "In response to *your* question, I've had it with horses," he said succinctly. "I'm getting out."

Sylvia was stunned. It was difficult to imagine Ridgway Horse Farm closing its gates. Surely, he didn't mean it. Back at college, Max had said Colin Ridgway was getting to the point where he just couldn't go it alone, but that it would just about kill him if he had to retire. "You mean you're getting out but your father will carry on?"

"You're putting words in my mouth, Sylvia," he said, suddenly and uncharacteristically impatient. It was a verbal warning shot that she was treading on sensitive terrain. "I'm getting out, and I think that Dad is unable to 'carry on' without me. It's really not a very pretty business."

Sylvia couldn't believe what she was hearing, or maybe she didn't want to. Ridgway Breeding Farm was one of the oldest in the business; it had produced two Kentucky Derby winners and one Triple Crown winner. But besides its success, there was Max's pure, unadulterated love of horses. Did they mean nothing to him anymore? Was it possible for a person to change so completely in just a few years?

"What will you do?" she said, trying to subdue the alarm in her voice.

Max took a long sip on his beer, and smiled. It was a kind of proud, cocky smile, as if daring her to disbelieve him.

"I'm looking into options right now," he said. "Moving inside the Beltway before too long."

Nicole murmured something appreciatively and squeezed his thigh near his knee. This was, evidently, a move she applauded.

"You know," he continued, "something practical like the CIA. I'll have to pull a few strings."

As Sylvia stood to leave, she felt her knees go wobbly as

if they might give out on her at any moment. Amazed at how shaken she felt, she suddenly realized how important it had been, deep in the recesses of her mind, for Max to have stayed Max. Whenever she thought of him—which was often—she always pictured him out on the farm, walking, trotting, and galloping the horses, cleaning the stalls and brushing down horses, as she had seen him do so many times. She had never seriously entertained the thought of his having really changed.

"The CIA?" Sylvia repeated. "Max!"

A smile tugged at the corners of his mouth. This outraged reaction was exactly what he seemed to want or expect of her, she wasn't sure which.

"I guess I'd better get back to my booth," she said.

He made no effort to stop her, or to invite her to join them for the game. She wanted to tell him how glad she was to see him again, or just touch him, but it didn't seem appropriate now. She wanted to say she'd see him around.

"So when do you think you'll be moving to Washington?" she said, still standing. It was the best she could do. She was aware that anyone in the booth who was listening in would assume she was one of many women chasing Max.

"Monday after Thanksgiving," he said.

Only after she left did she realize that that was the next day.

# CHAPTER
## 13

B. D. took Sylvia to a small Italian restaurant in Georgetown near his home where the owner seemed to know him. "A favorite haunt," he told her. There were no menus here, only dishes scrawled in chalk on blackboards. B. D. ordered two plates of Milanese-style pasta that came served on warmed china dishes with an abundant blanketing of fresh-grated Parmesan and hot, fresh-out-of-the-oven garlic bread.

Sylvia didn't let on that her mind hadn't left RFK Stadium. Despite her vocal enthusiasm over the meal, she was turning over in her mind the encounter with Max, unable to make sense of it. Could he be happy with Nicole No-last-name? Could he possibly be serious about leaving the horse business and joining the CIA?

"Is it hard to get into the CIA?" she asked suddenly.

B. D. looked surprised. "These days it is, unless you have something special going for you: aptitude in languages, connections. What, are you thinking of joining?"

"No, just curious." She laughed.

"But why?" he said. That was one of the things B. D. was famous for, pushing until he got his answer.

"Some man I met at the Saint-Phalle party said something about his son wanting to join the CIA," she lied. Sylvia had never been comfortable lying, but she couldn't bring up Max's name—especially after defecting to his booth during halftime, something that had plainly irritated her date. She felt guilty for accepting B. D.'s ticket, drinking his champagne, and now eating dinner at his hangout without giving him her undivided attention. She turned the subject back toward him, asking whether he'd been surprised that the Redskins had pulled it out in the fourth quarter.

"Surprised, no; astonished, yes," B. D. said with a smile, apparently pleased that he had piqued her interest in sports. After giving his version of why they'd won, B. D. added, "Sports isn't the only thing I'm going to teach you about."

Sylvia made no reply.

When the check came, B. D. grabbed for it. But Sylvia was there first. "This one's on me," she declared.

"Don't be absurd," B. D. said. "I invite you to dinner, I pay."

"You got the tickets to the game. I'd like to buy you dinner."

"Sylvia," he said firmly, plucking a pink, powdery mint

from the silver check tray and popping it into his mouth. "This is my treat."

As they stepped outside into a breathtaking sunset, B. D. took her hand. "Ben's on TV in fifteen minutes. *Washington Watch*. I live four minutes from here. Wanna come over and catch it with me?"

Sylvia hesitated.

"Or I'll put you in a cab."

On impulse, she said yes. As they departed together, she thought again about Max. Leaving him, she assumed he was the injured party, but maybe she'd been hanging on to him all these years. A sudden determination took hold of her: she had to get on with her life, had to break out of whatever old shell she'd been in and leave the shadow of Max Ridgway behind.

B. D. lived in a renovated old carriage house overlooking Rock Creek Park on Dumbarton Avenue. As they entered, B. D. explained with no uncertain pride that when he'd bought the place it was on its last legs. "Drunks used to sleep here, and its windows made target practice for vandals." He'd had the interior gutted and, working with just the building's shell, had transformed the place.

The living room was long and sparsely furnished with a low, leather, sand-colored sectional couch that wrapped around the corner. Framed political posters dating back to Harry Truman's 1948 campaign stood out against the otherwise severe, white expanse of wall. An enormous widescreen television—on which B. D. was already busy adjusting color, contrast, and sound—sat imposingly in front of the couch. He inserted a videotape into the VCR to record the program as they watched.

From the built-in bar at one end of the wide room, he called out to her: "Wine, beer, something harder?"

She requested white wine, and he poured himself some Stolichnaya on the rocks.

B. D. sat quite literally on the edge of his cushy seat as Ben's image blinked onto the screen. "Wrong line," he called out when Ben started in about losing the 1972 congressional election to a victor whom he'd booted out of office two years later and who had never been heard from since. "Goddammit, Ben, how many times do I have to tell you not to bring that one up?" He spoke at the screen as if Ben Fincastle were sitting right there in person.

After the show was over and drinks and refills had been downed, B. D. took her hand. "Would you like to see the rest of the place?"

Her glass of ice cubes in hand, Sylvia let him lead her upstairs to the loft, where the tour started and stopped, where she knew she would let him make love to her. He kissed her first on the forehead and then the lips, and together they eased down into his king-size bed.

B. D. turned off the lights, and she heard him hurriedly strip.

Still, she felt shy and left on her long-tailed shirt. Suddenly, his bearish body was in bed beside her, his voice murmuring how he'd known from the moment he saw her that she was right for him. He gently slipped off her shirt, and his hands were all over her body, heating her up as he waited for the moment to make his final move. "I want to bring you with me," he whispered.

An electronic ring sounded at the phone by his bedside.

"Damn," he said in frustration. Then, remembering a previous commitment, and evidently a higher priority, "That's Ben. I've got to get it."

His naked back to her in the semidarkness, he was suddenly all business, making crisp analytic remarks about Ben's performance on the show. "That 'seventy-two campaign. Clean it up Ben. You're letting them set the agenda on that loss. Counterpunch. From now on, I want to hear nothing but positives."

Sylvia stared out the loft window toward the lights across Rock Creek Park, hugging her knees to her chest. Through the wintry trees of the park, she saw headlights flickering along Massachusetts Avenue as it headed south toward Dupont Circle. Where was Max right now, she wondered? Somewhere in the city, maybe at Uncle Ernest's stately house up the Potomac. She pictured him in his big red Chevy pickup, the one he'd had at UVA, the one they'd taken so many drives in together. She remembered the feeling of being high above the road in that spacious cab, that intimate feeling at night when it was just the headlights and the two of them talking in the darkness, their bodies pressed together.

B. D.'s voice cut through the reverie. "Sorry," he said, climbing under the sheets beside her.

"That's okay."

They lay in silence for a moment, B. D. peering into her eyes that did not meet his directly. "You are the most beautiful woman I have ever seen."

Sylvia closed her eyes, savoring the compliment, wanting this to work. His lips touched hers, soft and lingering, then smothered her breasts with kisses as he knelt over her. Her hand reached and, for the first time in what seemed ages, felt a man's hardness.

"Oh, Christ," B. D. groaned.

He pulled back a moment, breathing hard, then entered her and began to stroke, slowly, finding her and spreading a sweet ripple of sensation throughout her body. Sylvia moaned softly. The feeling deepened, became more intense, streaking up the alleys of her body, floating her out on a lazy blue lake, sending shivers of tension through her at the same endless moment. Time was a boat on the lake, going nowhere, drifting in circles.

Suddenly, his weight settled on top of her, an ungodly weight, and Sylvia felt him slip away from her as he rocked back and forth in his pleasure.

Something was wrong with her. Something had always been wrong with her. She had been afraid to sleep with Max, had never let him, not even in the heat of passion making out in that old truck, not even when they spent the night together in her room at UVA.

And that broker in New York—the same old thing that was happening now, getting excited, going out to the edge of a cliff, then pulling back, afraid to let go, to jump off. Something was wrong with her.

B.D. was looking down at her. "What's wrong?"

"Nothing," she murmured.

His finger worked to urge her on. Nothing. Sylvia closed
her eyes and tried to focus. She had not meant to think of
Max. But he had broken his way through the front wall of
her brain, with his handsome face and lean body.

"Am I doing something wrong?" B. D. demanded. "This
isn't happening. What are you thinking about?"

Sylvia sat up against the head of the bed. All he needed
was reassurance. All she needed was time. "B. D., it was
wonderful. It's been a long time for me, after all."

This seemed to appease him.

"Next time it will be better," he said. "Next time we'll
go away somewhere where no one can find us."

# CHAPTER
## 14

As she walked into the Style section that Monday morning,
Sylvia spotted an enormous, freestanding ice bucket filled
with a couple of magnums of champagne, and Pam Tursi
assembling screw-on plastic champagne glasses. An enormous banner, hastily drawn in black and red Magic Marker
on the back of a long computer printout, was taped to the
wall above her desk. It read: "Congratulations, Sylvia Loring!"

Patricia thrust a sheaf of messages, all of which had come
in this morning, into Sylvia's hand. "This is the *Trib*'s biggest
story since Hale was named editor," she exclaimed. "*Washington Watch* called twice. They want you on the show next
Sunday, and they're trying to get Rossen, too!"

As Pam moved Sylvia forward to uncork the champagne,
Dennis Berman, toting his ubiquitous coffee-stained mug,
and almost all of the Style staff crowded around to toast her

triumph. The Rossen story was the lead news item of the morning, running on all the wires and dispatched on radio news programs nationally. When word reached Cityside that liquor was flowing over in Style, Frank Glover, Andy Ferraro, and others put in appearances.

"My hat's off to you!" Frank told Sylvia. "I hear that Rossen's calling a press conference tonight at five-thirty."

"Wanda gave you some flak about it, didn't she?" needled Andy Ferraro, referring to the phone call he'd just overheard.

In mock self-deprecation, Frank admitted it was true. His wife had called him and asked why he hadn't gotten the Rossen scoop. "I told Wanda that Sylvia Loring is like Leroy Brown: you don't mess around with her."

Sylvia smiled. The spirit of camaraderie, the triumph shared by her fellow reporters gave her a glow. But she could not help but wonder again, as she had since she first saw this morning's paper, if Max had read the story.

Never one to hang back from a scene, Colette smoothed her red suede suit and sauntered over to Sylvia's desk. She walked right up to Sylvia, who was leaning against her desk, sipping on the bubbly.

"Congratulations for pulling down Bob Rossen's pants," Colette said sarcastically.

"Thanks for your support."

"No, really, your investigative skills are quite beyond me," Colette continued in the same sniping tone.

"You called that one," came a response from one of the Cityside boys. "She goes to work every day and works!"

Such thinly veiled barbs never failed to get to Colette. She didn't mind a good cat fight with Sylvia, but to have all these Cityside reporters admiring their virgin queen—and by implication putting her down—was more than she could stomach. How could they be so entranced by Sylvia? Even B. D. had fallen under her spell, grilling Colette for details. Sylvia's beauty appeared so effortless, as if she never worked at it, never tried new colors, didn't spend endless hours at stores and boutiques searching out the right outfit to give the right effect, never thought about how many calories something had before she ate it. In fact, Sylvia seemed to view her beauty as if it were almost irrelevant. It was enough to make Colette sick. She stared down the offender, then put in a last word to Sylvia.

"I hope this article brings you pleasure. Pleasure seems to be in short supply in your life." Colette headed for her desk.

When Hale Gardiner learned that Colette had just arrived, she strode through the Cityside section and into Style, holding her head high, her eyes fixed forward with the air of concentrated intensity. This was her usual carriage, adopted to avoid unnecessary eye contact with her subordinates. It seemed to Hale that everyone wanted a nudge, a nod, some encouraging words, and she was not about to compromise herself by issuing compliments lightly or dispensing valuable time as if there were a bottomless supply. One of the American University interns had recently stopped her in the hall and invited her to lunch. Hale had been so flabbergasted at the girl's nerve that she'd told her to check back with Luanne next week. Of course, the lunch would never come to pass —there'd always be some handy excuse—but it made her uneasy just knowing that people were gunning for her.

Tucked under her upper arm was a manila folder filled with ideas and clips for Colette she'd collected during the past week. Of course, there were the parties to cover, of which there naturally would be quite a flurry during the upcoming holiday season, but she wanted to help Colette stretch beyond herself, go for something bigger. Perhaps a series on D.C.'s burgeoning art world. Maybe some important profiles. Colette was, after all, one of the very few *Tribune* writers for whom the word "serviceable" would not be a compliment as applied to her prose.

When Hale arrived at Style, all her troops, it seemed, had gathered around Sylvia Loring's desk, laughing and joking and making a fuss over the Bob Rossen story. In one swift glance, Hale took in the banner and the nearly empty champagne bottles and Sylvia riding high on adulation. Who had orchestrated all of this? Why had she not been consulted? They should have obtained her consent first. She made a mental note to speak to Dennis Berman about it. No one except herself ever seemed to consider the cost to a paper in lost time: twenty people taking off twenty minutes each amounted to almost seven hours of unproductive paid time.

Then she spotted Colette leaving the party.

"Colette," she said. "Welcome back."

"Bob Rossen must be peeing in his pants right now," Colette muttered.

"I can't help but wonder if we haven't done something of a hatchet job," Hale concurred.

"Hale!" bellowed Dennis. "How about some champagne?"

When Hale declined, Dennis meted out the remaining liquid into the competing plastic glasses of a large number of claimants.

"I've got it," said Dennis, a creative gleam crossing his face. He hoisted the mug from which he was drinking champagne. "Here's to Hookergate!" At that, the crowd—all wordsmiths themselves—roared in approval. Sylvia's editor and mentor had just coined a new phrase.

Hale clapped her hands together. Everyone turned as if expecting some kind of toast or tribute.

"Back to work!" she called out. Then, turning to Colette, "Do you have a minute?" Together, the two women walked to Colette's desk, where Hale set down her file folder.

"So," Hale said, "did you have a nice Thanksgiving?"

"Oh, yes," Colette exclaimed.

"Splendid," Hale replied, struck by the sudden flood of pleasure on the woman's face. Colette had no family in town. Though, granted, her invitation had come at the last minute, Hale still wondered what other gathering could have been preferable to the Gardiners'. "I really was disappointed that you couldn't join us for Thanksgiving dinner in the country."

"I got your message," Colette said. "I was really dying to come. I'm so upset I had to miss it."

"You must have had a prior commitment."

Colette returned Hale's gaze, her lips curling up into the slightest satisfied smile. "Actually, I was in Banff, skiing," she said. "Nothing quite like it to make your blood race!"

Hale nodded, impressed. That was one of Colette's many magnetic qualities, and one she liked to believe they shared: she was adventurous, always off on some new escapade. So capable in so many different areas, though she'd never pictured Colette as a skier! Another similarity between them was that there was money in Colette's family. There had to be. There was simply no other way she could dress the way she did and do the traveling on her salary—even though it was half again as much as her fellow reporters made.

"Skiing the whole week?"

Colette nodded brightly.

Hale turned the subject to the business at hand: Colette's work. "Good as you are," Hale started, "we must now begin to think of you not only as a society writer, but as a reporter in the broadest sense, someone who examines the culture of this city in all its depth, all its richness. I'd like to see you win some prizes for the *Trib*. I'd like to shepherd you along."

As Hale went on, talking of new "vistas" for Colette, of series on this and profiles on that, Colette assumed a more comfortable position in her seat. She glanced over at Sylvia, now tossing a champagne-doused newspaper into the trash, clearing up the debris from her little party. While Colette's peers might view her as a second-class reporter, her boss did not. Hale recognized her special capabilities. She knew there was nothing in journalism of which Colette was not capable. Someday, she would show the sniping reporters that she was every bit as good a journalist as Sylvia Loring.

"I would like very much to broaden my horizons," Colette said.

Following Colette's glance toward Sylvia, Hale bade Colette good-bye and approached Sylvia at her desk. This was the moment, Hale decided, to make clear that Sylvia's anointment was a bit premature.

"Sylvia," she said brusquely. "I want your notes for this story on my desk. ASAP."

Sylvia stiffened. "What for?"

"As anyone can see," she said pointedly, implying that Sylvia perhaps might not, "this is a controversial story, refuted by Congressman Rossen and, perhaps, even your sources. I want to be certain you are accurate.''

Hale watched the effect of her words as Sylvia paled slowly. It was important for her reporters to know, Hale thought while making for her office, that she was monitoring the accuracy and integrity of their work.

Sylvia's phone rang continuously at Sylvia's desk as it had throughout this most extraordinary day in her career. Everyone, it seemed, had called. Her mom wanted to know how the Redskins game with B. D. had gone. For once, Sylvia felt so triumphant and magnanimous that she didn't stop to point out to Jan Loring the glaring omission in their conversation—nor did she even let it bother her. Digby Reeve rang her up from his office, praising her work extravagantly, telling her that paper sales had "gone through the roof" that day. "I'm looking forward to reading your follow-up stories," he'd said with fatherly encouragement. Even B. D. Cole had checked in, lightheartedly admonishing her for keeping the lid on the Rossen scoop yesterday.

Sylvia hadn't complied with Hale's request to submit her notes. Nor did she have any intention of doing so. Sylvia felt a kind of uplifting surge of power from this newfound show of independence, a move she never would have made in the past, a move designed to retaliate for Hale's incredible, stink-pot attitude about the Rossen story from start to finish.

Sylvia was growing exhausted, and she wanted to husband her resources to get a good night's sleep for a change and be able to come in fresh the next day to figure out her follow-up story. She looked forward to her long-delayed evening out with Pam; they were going out for Chinese food tonight, a week after she'd canceled to have dinner at the White House. There was so much to catch up on.

The phone sounded. That was Pam, Sylvia thought. She lifted the receiver, speaking before spoken to: "Pam?" she asked.

"No way, this is Kokoh," came the voice on the other end, edgy and rapid-fire.

"Kokoh!" Sylvia responded, happy to hear from her informant, but suddenly anxious about Kokoh's safety. She lowered her voice. "What's going on?"

"I can't talk long, I'm going to work. Hey," she said. "I've been thinking about what we talked about. More names. Remember what I told you? Rossen's just the beginning."

"You said that, yes."

"Maybe I want to name more names. Maybe I want you to use my name this time."

"Kokoh, I'm worried about you. This story is bigger than anyone expected. Everyone in town knows about it. I'm afraid you might be in some danger. I don't think you should go in to work today. Maybe not ever again."

"I'm not scared," Kokoh said, dismissing that topic and moving on to what was on her mind.

"I've decided I want to go for it: fame, money, the whole bit. Why mess around with this crap when I could be on the cover of *Playboy*! Right? They'd love it—ex-hooker becomes famous fashion model. Will you write another story and use my name?"

"I don't know, Kokoh. We'd have to see if there were enough to run with."

"Oh, I could give you enough to run with, all right! More than you could imagine."

"Okay, Kokoh, when can we meet?" asked Sylvia. This was getting out of hand. Now her source was willing to give more, dropping what could be a major follow-up story into her lap. It seemed to Sylvia that fate was leading her down a path the end of which she had no way of seeing. "Tomorrow?"

"Yeah, sure, same yogurt place. You remember."

"Sure, Ola's House of Yogurt." As they talked, Sylvia flipped to her notes from last week and read back the address to Kokoh. "How about I take you out to breakfast?"

"Breakfast!" Kokoh exclaimed, outraged. Apparently, even for fame getting up for breakfast was too big a price. "Breakfast at three o'clock."

Just as she hung up, the phone rang again. In a prescient

flash, Sylvia saw that this one was no ordinary call. It would be Max.

Wrong again. It was Jan Loring, who, for the first time Sylvia could recall, sounded close to hysterical. She said she'd been trying Sylvia for twenty minutes and was about to place an emergency interrupt.

"Uncle Marek just called," she said. "It's Nana, she's had a massive stroke, and the doctors think she may not last the night."

"Mom," said Sylvia. "No."

"I've booked two tickets for us on the ten-twenty flight to Cleveland. I'm paying, of course. Can you make it?"

"Of course, Mom," said Sylvia before the follow-up for the Rossen story flashed into her mind. "It's just that there's this big story I'm working on . . ."

A steely silence sounded through the line. Jan Loring was not about to understand. Sylvia wished now that she had told her mother before about the Rossen story. She'd have to tell her now.

"Mom, have you heard the news today?"

In a small voice, her mother murmured no.

"Well, I've just published the biggest story of my career, about Congressman Bob Rossen, chairman of the House Judiciary Committee, who may have to step down because he's been linked to sexual harassment and using prostitutes."

"I'm sorry to hear that," said Jan soberly.

"Well, it's bad news for Bob, but it's a huge scoop for me and my career."

Sylvia could hear her mother sigh on the phone, and she knew that her mother's mind was on one track, understandably, and that track held no room for Bob Rossen or any piece of journalism.

"Sylvia, can you come with me or not?" said Jan, her voice rallying strength as she spoke. "I can't hang on this phone any longer."

If she didn't go, her mother would never forgive her. Her mother didn't appreciate her career, but she did love her—maybe too much. Sylvia remembered her appeal for the new dress, the pride in her eyes at Thanksgiving. How could Sylvia even think of herself when her mother's own mother was about to die? Sylvia thought of Nana, precious Nana, the gentlest woman she'd ever known, so loving and good. Yet she was strong, too, strong enough to make it through the war in Poland with two small children to support, strong enough to somehow make her way to the United States with no close family to help, only the flimsiest and most distant of connections with some neighbors who'd settled here. Once, during the worst period of the war, Nana had bartered her gold wedding band for a bag of potatoes.

"Where do I meet you?" Sylvia said.

After making the arrangements, Sylvia hung up, leaned back in her chair, and stared at the ceiling. Everything was happening all at once. She felt a pang of guilt, thinking of herself first like that, of the story, when Nana was lying in a hospital room at the end of her life. For once, her mother could take credit for not letting her off the hook.

"Meditating on the meaning of success?" came a familiar voice. It was Dennis Berman, mug in hand, puzzled and concerned about the troubled expression on Sylvia's face. She said nothing, but looked as if she were about to burst into tears. "Success isn't all it's cracked up to be," he said.

"I just got a call. My grandmother's dying. They don't think she'll make it through the night."

Dennis pulled up a vacant chair, straddled the seat, and leaned his chest into the chair back. "I'm sorry," he said. When Sylvia told him where she lived, he asked if she was going.

Sylvia nodded. Dennis was so sympathetic that she felt she could tell him anything. "I've been meaning to spend more time with her, wanting to tape-record the story of her life, and now it won't be possible. Here I spend hours listening to manicurists and restaurant owners and hookers, and I never took the time to put down my grandmother's story, how she got out of Poland . . ."

"Don't guilt-trip yourself," Dennis interjected. "Leave the Jewish guilt to me, okay?"

"She had an incredible life. Her husband died at Auschwitz, and somehow she made it through the war with my mother and my uncle."

Dennis arched an eyebrow. "I never knew you were Jewish."

Sylvia was thrown for a moment. "I'm not."

"You said your grandfather died at Auschwitz."

"He did," Sylvia said. "My grandfather was in the Polish Resistance. When they caught him, the Germans shipped him to Auschwitz, then lined him up against a wall and shot him in a mass execution."

Dennis stroked his chin thoughtfully and nodded. There was something in his gaze that seemed to be taking a second look at this young woman, adding a new calculation to the equation.

"So," he said gently. "Where does this leave your story?"

Sylvia told him about the call from Kokoh King. "I'll try her right now," she said. Kokoh's answering machine was on. As Dennis sat beside her, Sylvia left a message, saying she had to cancel the three-o'clock meeting and would call her as soon as she got back from Cleveland, which would probably be Wednesday. Thinking it might incriminate Kokoh in case her employers somehow heard the message, Sylvia did not leave her name.

"Don't be long," Dennis warned as they both rose. "You know Hookergate won't wait," he said, a twinkle in his kind eye. "Your lady might go to the *Post*."

Sylvia froze. "Am I doing the right thing?"

Dennis gave her shoulder a quick squeeze and flashed an encouraging smile. "What do you think, my friend?"

# CHAPTER
## 15

Naked, Ben Fincastle lay on his back atop Colette's low-slung, jet-black, Italian lacquer bed—the hub of her bedroom universe. "The den of iniquity," Ben teasingly called it, composed as it was of a slick and oily dresser and bed thrust against the outrageously steamy, mauve walls that were like some tropical, wraparound sunset. Ben had never slept, never made love in such a place. With Colette, lovemaking was full-blooded, unashamed, unreal.

If only Judy knew how to turn a man loose. But, of course, Judy—with her proper upbringing, her proper military family, her proper tone of voice, her proper do-gooder causes, and her proper, boring body—had no knowledge of the kind of seduction on which Colette Daniels had a patent. Colette, voluptuous Colette. Even her name had the hiss and the steam of sex. There she was, her body fairly smoking with heat as she closed in on him, descending upon him in her scanty pink bra like some busty opera singer, all breasts and raspy, bourbon voice, speaking the words of seduction.

"You don't know me." Colette laughed. Ben loved that laugh: rich, suggestive, a harbinger of sensual pleasure. Ever since that near-tragic night on the beach in Maine, they'd stolen as much time together as they could, whenever they could. Her arm swung slowly from behind her back. "You don't know Colette Daniels." Dangling from her hand was a black, velvet blindfold.

"My God," he said. That was the thing about this woman: every time he came over, always in his sunglasses, always instructing B. D. to cover with Judy if need be, Colette had some new trick up her sleeve. He loved the way she took command, plundered his body exactly the way she desired.

Colette strapped the blindfold around his head.

Ben's world went dark. He felt her fingers claim his prize, now hers.

"Do you trust me?" she asked, with provocation in her voice.

"Shouldn't I?"

"I wouldn't trust me if I were you," she said. "You don't know anything about me. I'm a perfect stranger."

Ben heard a soft hiss, then felt her hand slather something cool and damp on him. Cool Whip. Another hiss and he felt the cool, wet mass mounding higher, patted in place by her delicious fingertips.

Then he felt something else. Something that sent shock waves through his body: the unmistakable nip of a razor, cutting its way slowly through his pubic hair. His hand jumped up toward the blindfold, but she pinned it back.

"Colette," he called out. "What the hell are you doing?"

She nibbled at his ear, then huskily commanded, "Give it up."

He felt the gliding razor again, God help him, an instrument of pleasure on his skin. No words in response, but the surrender on his face betrayed his answer.

"You like," she said, stating the fact. "So did my grandpa."

Ben lay perfectly still, her words not registering. So Colette had shaved her grandfather. So what? Surely not there.

Colette had not anticipated this kind of power. With all her sexual experience, all her tricks, her knowledge of men's most primitive desires, she had not expected to bring the next president to his knees. Why was she, of all the seductive women in America, chosen to be here, privy to the most intimate secrets of the land? No one but she would ever know Ben Fincastle's sexual yearnings, his hunger for release in her knowing body.

By blindfolding him and slathering on shaving cream, by removing his hair, Colette had taken another big chance, as she'd done by following him to New Hampshire. But she didn't weigh odds and calculate. Not when it came to passion. She seized upon an idea and followed her instincts, which were turning out to be damn good.

Then, calm as a glass of water, she added, "My grandfather was my first."

His body froze, and Colette wondered for a moment if she should have bared her soul.

Ben quivered with excitement at the thought of incest. More than once, he'd fantasized about his own daughter and her friend Kelly, their nubile, young bodies, so innocent, with no knowledge of men. Of course, he would never touch them. He'd once heard an expert testify that incest dealt a girl a crueler emotional blow than did rape. "Oh, Colette," he murmured.

"Don't feel bad. I loved it."

God, this woman aroused him in a way he hadn't been since his youth, trying to lose his virginity with girls in the back seat of his '56 Chevy. Colette found barriers inside him and pushed him through. "No," he said, shrouding his excitement in mock disapproval.

"Yes, many times. Holidays. During the summer when I was out of school."

Then there was the razor again, its smooth, rhythmic stroke making his heart pound. He could feel the matted hair cutting free of its roots. This was a game, he thought. She was making this up to excite him. And she was succeeding. "How old were you?"

"It started when I was nine."

Ben reached for her breast, kneading it gently. "What did he do?"

Colette slowed her words to a crawl. "At first, he was just fondling me. Slipping his hand between my legs and rubbing."

Ben's hand wandered up her thigh.

"Later, when I got older, he started rubbing his thing against me. Then," she said, "he asked me if I wanted to go all the way."

"And?" he asked, breathless.

"I said yes."

"It was wonderful," she continued, still shaving him. "My grandfather was an incredible lover—it made me want to do anything with men."

Ben savored that one a moment. Then, his fingers drifting into port, he made Colette gasp, then docked, making slow, easy waves with his touch. Colette moaned more deeply. "And your parents?" Ben said.

"They never knew," she whispered, as if they could be eavesdropping at this moment. "We'd find all kinds of ways to do it without their knowing."

"How long did this go on?"

"Until I left for college. I told him there were younger men I wanted."

"How did he take that?"

"It was heaven," she said dreamily. "He wanted to do it one more time, for old times' sake. So we checked into this hotel in St. Louis—my grandfather was very successful— we checked into two rooms. Then, that night, he came strutting into mine." Colette moaned, her breath coming more rapidly. "He was a large man, still strong and virile at seventy-one. He took off my clothes and lay me down on my bed. He kissed me all over, up and down my thighs, and his tongue darted in where he knew I liked it. I was dying. . . ."

Ben groaned. "*I'm* dying!"

Colette sank her body tantalizingly onto his, her wetness grazing over him. "Then he turned me over on top of him; I'd never done that before. One last lesson from the old guy. Something to remember him by."

The memory got her once again, and then him. Shuddering together, they lay entwined.

"Incredible," Ben said afterward. "You're very convincing. The playacting."

"Ben," she said, removing his blindfold. "I wasn't playing."

Ben sat up on his elbow, staring at this tigress in the half-light. This woman was either a hell of a liar or very honest, honest in a way that people weren't. He couldn't tell which, but it was precisely this mystery about her that had made him unable to forget her this past week, even while the horror of being discovered preyed on him constantly.

"I never would have turned him in," Colette continued. "I was having too much fun."

Ben smiled lustily. "And picking up a few tricks, I see." He studied her with admiration; lies or truth, either way he was hooked. "You amaze me, Colette."

Colette poured a glass of brandy from her bedside decanter. One glass for them both to share. Colette talked about herself all the time, but rarely opened these doors. Now that she had exposed her darkest secret, she felt a strange urging to tell on, to unfurl the entire fabric of her past for his inspection.

Colette had grown up in slow, sleepy Herrin, Illinois, where the biggest thing that ever happened was when a gangster named Charlie Birger was hanged in the 1920s. Her mother's father, the infamous grandfather, and most of her mother's family were wealthy. Like her father, G. "Dan" Daniels, a failed businessman, Colette had always been in awe of the Refner relatives, had always felt different, had always wanted to impress them. The Refners had fine homes in St. Louis and lived in style. On holidays, they spent a small fortune on food, drink, and gifts.

Colette's mother, Helen Refner Daniels, a tall, sedate beauty, had been drawn to the charismatic young Dan Daniels, a hyperactive bundle of charm and energy whom she'd met at a dance. From the standpoint of money, Dan Daniels was no catch—he had none. But the young man had undeniable sex appeal and a fast-talking optimism that Helen had admired.

The marriage, of course, was a fiasco, though they'd stuck it out. Colette had never met two people less suited for each other. To make matters worse, Dan Daniels had turned out to be the world's worst businessman. Starting out as a car salesman, he'd eventually purchased the Chrysler dealership in Herrin and run it into the ground, going bankrupt with overambitious schemes, bad cars, deceptive sales techniques, and sloppy management. As many of his disgruntled customers as there were kicking around Herrin, it was a wonder he hadn't been strung up like Charlie Birger.

Colette entered her teens on the edge of poverty, enduring the disdain of the town's rich kids as her father drank and repossessed cars for a former competitor, and her mother, who'd never worked a day in her life, took a job as a secretary. Having defied the Refners to marry Dan Daniels, Helen had remained too proud to accept money from her family—or admit that her marriage had failed.

This much of Colette's story was true, and she was pleased to see its aphrodisiacal effect on Ben. Stroking her hair, he was obviously lost in her past. Taking the last sip of brandy and pouring another glass, Colette decided to impress him more.

And so she lied. After graduating valedictorian in her high-school class (in fact, she'd had no upper ranking), Colette had accepted a scholarship to Northwestern. (In fact, she'd gone to Western Illinois University, her tuition paid by her randy grandfather.) At Northwestern, Colette went on, she'd been in the famous drama program. She had intended, she told Ben, to be an actress on the Broadway stage, and would have been had she not developed an interest in journalism as a senior editor on the school paper. It was an agonizing choice, she concluded. "But I've never looked back."

You weren't supposed to rattle off such things, Colette knew, but she viewed these little fictions as a form of creativity, true in spirit if not in fact. After all, everyone created a personal myth, remade the past. Especially Ben, who was shaping himself into the presidential mold, and who, after all, had introduced her as Judy to those cops in Kittery.

"And you never will," Ben said, running his finger down her cheek, where it was caught by Colette's lips as she sucked the finger in.

# CHAPTER
## 16

Hale wanted those bloody notes. She had made her request; here it was a day later, and the woman was openly thumbing her nose at her. Now Sylvia Loring was not answering her phone, Luanne reported, even though it was almost noon. Rather than coming in and earning her pay, Sylvia was at home or somewhere in the city celebrating the dubious triumph of bringing down Bob Rossen.

Of course, it had become obvious to Hale by now that the Rossen story—with its this-is-just-the-tip-of-the-iceberg innuendo—had made waves. Yesterday's *Trib* sales had been the highest in two years, and even her father had called to congratulate her on the scoop. Hale was being deluged with interview requests from various sources, including a famous Harvard political scientist who was studying the issue of sex in political journalism. Hale had indeed opened a Pandora's box in running the Rossen story, but once open, she was committed to continuing the exploration. And now, the purveyor of the story was holding her up.

"Get me Dennis Berman," she instructed Luanne.

"Dennis," she demanded when he came on the line, "where is Sylvia Loring?"

"Cleveland," he said matter-of-factly.

When he had explained the situation, Hale said, "This was not authorized."

Dennis bit his lip. "In my book, a death in the family is reason enough."

"May I remind you," Hale retorted, "the grandmother isn't dead. And," she added significantly, "as you are fond of pointing out, Dennis, we have the *Post* to worry about, don't we?''

"In what respect?"

"In the respect," Hale said, enunciating each syllable with acid precision, "that our reporter seems to be missing in action. And we have a follow-up story to write. Heaven knows what the *Post* is up to, even as we speak. She's certainly left us with a pretty mess, hasn't she, Dennis?"

After she hung up, Hale suddenly burst out, startling Luanne in her outer office. "Ring up Colette! Tell her I want to see her immediately."

"She won't be in yet," Luanne said.

Hale rose from her desk, pacing. "This won't wait. Call her at home."

"Colette," Hale said when the connection was made. "I want you to meet me at Herb's in half an hour." Colette protested, saying she wasn't dressed, but Hale was adamant. "Forty-five minutes, then. And don't be late—this simply won't keep."

Herb's was a cozy little café at 17th and Rhode Island, below street level, with intimate booths done up handsomely in pink and turquoise stripes. Near the entrance, its walls lined with signed celebrity photographs, the owner had set up a huge, round oak table reserved in evenings for writers —"Algonquin South," it was called. Though the prices were modest and one could find there just anyone off the street, even students, Herb's was an easy walk from the *Trib*, and Hale was fond of the owner, an affable man who often threw benefits here for the arts. Besides, she liked the literary associations of the place, the fact that one could happen upon Washington's most eminent writers, not to mention the occasional *Post* editor with whom it was always good business to have a pleasant little chat.

It was no surprise that Hale arrived first, escorted personally by the owner past the outer booths, where light flooded in from the street above, past the horseshoe bar with its tall sculpture of an American eagle to a dimly lit rear booth he knew Hale preferred.

Hale ordered a glass of white wine, listened to a bluesy piano piece, and watched the candle flicker, sending shimmers of light down her wineglass. Then she saw Colette.

"You amaze me," Hale exclaimed. "How you throw yourself together at the drop of the proverbial hat. That sweater," she said, admiring the luscious apricot cashmere that in the candlelight set off Colette's creamy skin and dark beauty. "I simply must have one like it. Where on earth did you find it?"

The sweater was actually a gift of only yesterday from Ben, who showed a surprising talent for dressing her. Rare was the gift from a man that she kept. "Oh, I've had it for a while," Colette said blithely. "Believe it or not, I got it in London my last trip there."

"Oh?" Hale said. Despite the ordeal of her short marriage, she had remained an Anglophile; this was something else she and Colette shared. "I must know where in London you got it."

Colette, of course, had never set foot in England, had never been anywhere in Europe, but she remained unfazed by this latest test of her quick-witted imagination. "I can't imagine where," she purred. "It was a gift from a man. A very lovely man."

This was such fun, Colette thought, registering the effect of this last remark. Hale's face was serious, intelligent, aristocratic, but apparently she would believe almost anything. Of course, there was a grain of truth here; a very lovely man *had* given her the sweater.

"Colette," Hale said. "You recall our talk yesterday. Well, I think I've found just the thing for you."

The waiter arrived, dapper in khaki pants, a pink shirt, and black bow tie. Hale ordered her usual, an appetizer of golden American caviar on potato pancakes, followed by an entree of Cilantrano fruit salad with grilled chicken. Colette, at Hale's recommendation, ordered the same, along with a cappuccino.

"Bring me a cappuccino as well," Hale instructed the

waiter. She turned to Colette. "Now, then. I assume you've been following the Bob Rossen story." When Colette nodded, Hale went on, "This story is much too important to let flounder. Sylvia Loring has let us down. Not only has she failed to submit her notes, but at this critical moment she's taken an unauthorized trip to—can you imagine?—Cleveland."

The waiter brought their cappuccinos. Both women sipped. Hale allowed the ensuing silence to swell the suspense.

"I've made a decision," she began finally. "It's a decision, I think, that neither of us will regret. In the Rossen story, you'll remember there are allegations that could be substantiated, making the story much bigger—that there may be a prostitution ring operating on the Hill. This is the kind of story that could make a journalist's career."

Hale could see the effect of this last remark on Colette. Her eyes lit up, as if anticipating what was coming.

"Sylvia was covering your beat when she happened upon the Rossen story. The story, by rights, belongs to you. Therefore," Hale said, pausing for one last sip of cappuccino, "as of this moment, I'm officially passing the baton to Colette Daniels."

As she drove to the *Trib*, Colette pictured Sylvia's reaction when she got the news that the prostitution story now belonged to her. Boy, would Sylvia be furious. And the next celebration would be on a much larger scale—and in her honor!

She stepped up to the Style editor's desk, determined to show Dennis she was to be taken seriously, that she meant business. Dennis turned from his computer terminal. "Say that again."

"I said, Dennis," Colette repeated firmly, "that Hale's put me on that Rossen story. She suggested you pull Sylvia's contacts for me."

Dennis stared right through her. Though she had mustered the right tone, the fact was that Colette had always been intimidated by this man. Dennis was a hopeless throwback to the old school, a reporter with a capital *R*. He made no bones about the fact that he doubted her abilities.

Dennis rose. His face had reddened. Without another word to Colette, he marched toward the sanctum sanctorum.

Luanne greeted him in the outer office. Dennis stormed right past her as if she were a potted plant.

"Excuse me . . . Dennis?" Luanne said, rising in alarm. But he was already at Hale's desk.

The chief continued scribbling on a pad, letting him wait until she was ready.

But Dennis didn't wait. "What the hell's going on? Since when does a good reporter get bumped from a story on which she's doing a bang-up job?"

At first, Hale appeared startled by his anger, then she looked up at him sharply. "This is not a matter for discussion, Dennis."

"I think it is."

"I think," she said, pressing the point of her pen into her notepad, "that you are here without invitation."

Dennis burned from ear to ear. "The least you could do, Hale—the very least—would be to call her up in Cleveland and give her the chance to get back here on the next plane."

"It isn't just a matter of her presence," Hale responded. "It's a matter of what's good for the *Tribune*. A matter of excellence."

"Excellence!" Dennis erupted. "You call that puffball 'excellence'?"

It took a few moments, but Hale finally seemed able to get a grip on herself. "If you are referring to Colette Daniels," she said in a chillingly formal tone, "may I suggest that you reconsider your opinion when you see her work on this story."

Then, as Dennis was turning to leave, Hale added, "Do you know how many Phi Beta Kappas we have on the editorial staff?"

Dennis stared dumbly.

"No, I didn't think so. There are three. And Sylvia Loring is not one of them. Colette Daniels is."

"Eleanor, you just can't imagine," Hale was telling her cousin on the phone, "what it's like here at times." It was almost six o'clock, time for Hale to leave the office, but after what she'd endured this afternoon—first Dennis's, later Digby's objections to reassigning the prostitution story to Colette, all of which she managed to stubbornly override—she needed a sympathetic ear. "This sort of thing would never happen if I were a man. But because the editor of the *Washington Tribune* happens to be a woman, they have the gall to question my judgment at every turn."

"It's awful, isn't it?" Eleanor sympathized. "Now, tell me, what sort of tack do you think Colette will take on the story?"

Hale's mind had already jumped ahead. Why hadn't she thought of it before? She would arrange to have Eleanor and Colette meet.

"Eleanor, you must meet Colette. You will get along famously. She's a delightful person."

Eleanor seemed reluctant, that old hood of insecurity creeping up again. Hale would fix that. While it was true that Colette was extraordinary, it was also true that she was approachable.

"I have it!" Hale said. "Let's have Colette do a Society Sketch on you."

Hale pointed out how good it would be for Eleanor, how it would enhance her reputation around town.

"Dottie," Eleanor protested, "won't this look a little nepotistic?"

"Don't confuse nepotism with loyalty." Hale's eyes misted as she imagined how much difference this kind of spread could make to Eleanor. At the same time, it was impossible not to feel the absence in her own life of someone who looked out for her interests and offered uncritical support. No question about it, the cliché was true. It was lonely at the top. "Sweetie, the fact is you're struggling, and I'm in a position to help. You would do the same for me if our roles were reversed."

# CHAPTER
## 17

Sylvia sat in the first pew of Our Lady of the Sacred Heart Church in Cleveland on Thursday morning, between her mother and her uncle Marek, as the priest read Nana's funeral service in Polish. It bothered Sylvia that she couldn't understand Polish, though she could pick out a few words here and there from her earlier exposure. The language—with its hard-to-pronounce combinations of $c$'s, $r$'s, and $z$'s—was entwined in her mind with her amazing grandmother. Nana had always called Sylvia by the diminutive of her middle name, "Kasia," short for Katarzyna. Sylvia Katarzyna Loring. Was that all that was left of her Polish heritage? The initial $K$? Nana had died late Tuesday, much to the relief of Marek and Jan and Sylvia. There had been no chance of her revival, and so they had all wished that her suffering would be as short as possible. And it was.

The past drifted into Sylvia's mind. When Sylvia was eleven and spent the summer with Nana and Uncle Marek, a whole new world opened up to her. Nana would plait her long blond hair every day and teach Sylvia the things her own mother never had time for: cooking, embroidery, tending a garden. Instead of being bored, Sylvia was fascinated. While her grandmother spent only minimally on clothing, furniture, utilities and transportation, she spent extravagantly on food, buying the best cuts of meat, the finest fruits, vegetables, and Colombian coffee. Special rye bread from the Polish bakery, imported Hungarian paprika would grace their table. "I wish your grandfather could come back to eat with us for just one week," she said one evening. She'd adored the hand-

120

some Grzegorz Starzynski, a physician before he joined the Resistance. Although they had only a few years together, during which time Jan and Marek were born, she mourned his loss for the rest of her life as if he had died only yesterday.

That summer they cooked enormous batches of *bigos* (the Polish hunters' stew), *barszcz* (red beet soup), and *golabki* (meat-filled cabbage rolls). Sylvia perfected the *tort cytrynowy* (lemon tort), *paluszki* (pastry fingers), and *konserwowane wisnie* (brandied cherries). Every Friday, they would load food into large baskets and travel all around Cleveland on the city bus making deliveries to the aged and shut-ins. Despite all her grandmother's tragedies, she radiated a sense of joy in living and had a drive to help anyone in need. "During the war, when we barely had enough food to survive, there were many who were kind to us," she once told Sylvia. "I vowed then to help feed anyone who was hungry when I could."

While kneeling to pray, something Nana had said that summer flashed into Sylvia's mind. "When you get married, I will prepare for you a magnificent feast!" A sharp pang overtook Sylvia as she realized now that Nana's wish would never come to pass.

Sylvia felt as never before the gray chill of being alone. Life was short, and at its end was the bleak prospect of lying trapped on a bleak institutional bed, hooked up to life-support machines by a maze of wires and tubes. You had to make the most of your youth, your beauty, your talent, while you still had it. Life was bigger than the narrow confines of the newspaper, and somehow, Sylvia knew, she had lost her way. Time was passing quickly—every year it went faster—and she was burning up her best years at work. Work she was proud of, but that was all she had to show.

Five years ago, at UVA, it had all been so simple. God, had it really been five years already? The whole world had been ahead of her, glistening with possibilities, and Max Ridgway was at her side.

She thought of Nana, gone now, but at least having had, in the memory of old age, the satisfaction of having married and lived a few years with the man she loved.

Times had changed, Sylvia thought. No doubt her grandfather wasn't perfect; no doubt he had faced the machine guns at Auschwitz with mortal terror. But men like that, brave men, real men, were hard to come by these days. This was the age of paper heroes, of media stars with feet of clay, of talk-show glibness and public relations. A real man was hard to find.

She had had him, of course—hers for the taking, strong, gutsy, larger than life. Now, she wondered idly as she stood for the final blessing, could she ever have a man like that again?

Boarding a flight out of Cleveland that Thursday afternoon, Sylvia was snapped back to her life in Washington by the cold fluorescence of the airport. She suddenly thought of the newspaper, of Kokoh King, and fought off a strong feeling that the young woman was in danger, the sense that she'd left her in the lurch.

Sylvia reassured herself that since Nana had just died, she was overly susceptible to morbid thoughts. Nothing of importance could have transpired since she'd left D.C.—especially since Dennis and Pam had her uncle's Cleveland number and that of the hospital with instructions to call anytime.

On impulse, at the departure gate, Sylvia dialed Pam Tursi's direct line at the *Tribune*. After briefly relating news of her grandmother's death and funeral, Sylvia asked what was happening at work.

Her question was met with a pause, and then, "Hale put Colette on the prostitution story."

Sylvia went numb. "No way. Tell Hale I'll be back in the office this afternoon. I can work tonight."

"I hate to be the one to break it to you," Pam said, "but you ain't getting this one back. Berman's already busted his gut fighting Hale on this thing. What can I say? The word around the office is that Colette is perfect for Hookergate. I mean, how much research does she have to do?"

Sylvia fell silent. Pam's intentions were good, but the joke about Colette wasn't funny. Not right now. "I'll see you tomorrow,'' Sylvia said abruptly, and hung up without saying good-bye.

Sylvia stood motionless at the phone, feeling as if the breath had been knocked out of her. Although at times during her five years at the paper she'd gone along with things she wasn't proud of, never before had she been robbed. The prostitution story was no routine assignment: it was her baby; it could put her name on the map. Sylvia stared at the passengers starting to board at her gate, her eyes stinging with tears. As soon as Sylvia had turned her back, Hale had handed Colette a knife and together they'd stuck it in.

The thought of boarding that plane with total strangers, unable to vent her fury, suddenly terrified her. Perhaps the plane would crash and she would die, too. She dialed Uncle Marek's number, where her mother—who was staying on through the weekend—answered.

"Mom, Hale Gardiner's given my story to another reporter."

"Hale Gardiner?" her mother said blankly, evidently not recognizing the name. "Story? Sylvia—where are you?"

"Mom, you don't know who Hale Gardiner is?" Sylvia accused, blinking back fresh tears.

Jan thought for a moment. "Oh, yes. The editor. Sylvia, aren't you on your plane yet? You're going to miss your flight."

"Will you listen, please? I've come all the way to Cleveland, and you're not listening." The line went quiet. Sylvia heard herself say, "Mom, I think I'm going to resign."

"Sylvia," her mother said sternly, "I don't want to hear you so upset. Now, calm down. This is a situation where the best thing is just to turn the other cheek."

"Mom," Sylvia roared into the phone. "Are you hearing me?"

"Calm down," her mother commanded. Her voice plummeted to a stage whisper. "Now, don't forget about B. D. Cole. You'll lose him if you quit."

Sylvia's voice was a shout. "This is not about B. D., this is not about catching a husband, this is about my work!" She slammed down the phone.

Boarding passengers were staring at her. Even the ticket agents were looking up from their stations. Sylvia strode in the opposite direction from the gate, so furious she was almost ready to spring into the air. Here she was, wanting somebody—anybody—to say, "How awful," and all her mother could think of was B. D. Cole. And there was something accusatory in her tone, the way she said his name, as if to say, "Here's another opportunity you're passing up, you fool."

Well, Sylvia thought, coming to a halt at a down escalator, it figured. After all the tension in Cleveland, now that Nana was dead and buried it was time for a real *blow*out. Thank God she didn't have to live with the woman—they'd explode in each other's faces every forty-eight hours.

Her flight number sounded in her brain. No, it wasn't her brain, it was the public-address system, announcing the last call for the flight to Washington. Why bother, Sylvia thought? What's to go back to? Then, having no good answer, she walked toward the gate.

# CHAPTER
## 18

Christmas is the cruelest season when you're depressed and mourning. So Sylvia thought as she stepped off the Metro train at the Friendship Heights stop that Saturday afternoon and walked the short distance to the Dolls' House & Toy Museum. It was almost more than she could take—seeing Pam and her precocious son Jesse along with the other bug-eyed children prancing through the world-famous Victorian Christmas exhibit. But there'd been no way to beg off; she'd put the date on her calendar before her grandmother had died. And last night, when she had been thinking up excuses for

Pam, little Jesse had come on the phone line. "Aunt Sivvy," he'd said. "I bought you a red-and-green candy cane." She suspected Pam of putting him up to it, but even still, how could she refuse?

And after the longest day she'd ever lived—watching the morning talk shows, trying and failing to read first a serious South African author and then a popular proselyte of love and traditional values, finally climbing the walls—this kind of distraction was probably good for her. She knew it. Pam knew it. Anything to get out of the black hole she was in.

"You're late," announced Jesse, one mittened hand safely ensconced in the suede glove of his mom as they waited on the front steps of the museum. The other dangled the promised candy cane.

"No matter," said Pam, waving Sylvia's already-paid-for ticket. "You must be dead to the world."

"Fighting it," said Sylvia, kissing Pam and her son.

"What's dead to the world?" chimed in Jesse.

"Don't ask," said his mother. "You'll find out soon enough."

"What's dead to the world?" he said, refusing to be brushed aside.

"It's when you don't feel like moving," Sylvia said. "But you do anyway. I jogged four miles this morning."

"I wish I could be that purposeful."

"Don't make me laugh," said Sylvia. "Want me to define the word for you? 'Purposeful': See also Pam Tursi. The act of mothering a four-year-old while working at the *Trib*."

Sylvia was feeling better already as they made their way through the rooms teeming with true-to-period dollhouses filled with incredibly intricate carved and upholstered furniture, miniature chandeliers, petit point, even details like doll-size cutlery. They paused at a quintet of Baltimore row houses that were dressed for the season with pine-cone wreaths and bonzailike Christmas trees, decorated with Lilliputian holiday trim.

"How would you ever wrap a gift like that?" Pam said, pointing to a wrapped and ribboned hatbox, the circumference of a silver dollar. Pam launched into her favorite fantasy, which was taking all the knowledge she'd learned in her five years at the *Trib* and starting her own business. What type of business was the variable in the constant equation of her dream. The other variable was start-up capital—where she'd ever find it. Not surprisingly, her fantasy of the hour was a shop specializing in quality, stimulating, nonviolent toys.

"Jesse is already asking me for an assault rifle for Christmas," she said. "Somebody's got to put some sex appeal into alternative toys."

Sylvia smiled. Pam could make you forget yourself.

The woman had moxie. And it wasn't easy to raise a day-care child, live in an expensive city, and make your living at a place like the *Trib*, where reporters were underpaid and overworked. Still, Pam prevailed. The bumper sticker on her Ford Escort defined her spirit: "It's never too late to have a happy childhood."

The museum was crowded, elbow to elbow with Washington kids, as anticipated on this the first Saturday after the Christmas exhibit went up. As luck would have it, they bumped into neighbors from Pam's apartment complex with their preschool son, who invited Jesse to join them in inspecting the miniature trolleys, trains, Model T Fords, and an exhibit of Teddy Roosevelt on safari.

"Can I, can I, Mommy?" asked the voluble little boy, like it was the most important matter in the world. Permission granted, he scampered along.

Sylvia wished that she could enter into the Christmas spirit. And though she tried to look cheerful, her heart wasn't in it.

Seeing Sylvia's mind was elsewhere, Pam suggested they grab one of the few benches for tired parents near the faux Christmas tree of pointsettias arranged on a platform of steps. "Okay, pal," Pam declared. "We're going to Plan B here. Time to talk turkey."

The truth was, though Sylvia had lost her grandmother, had a bloody fight with her mother, and watched a career-making story go down the tubes, what was gnawing at Sylvia most was Max. And Max was the one subject, proud as she was, that she did not want to discuss with another woman.

"You're trying pretty hard," Sylvia observed coolly.

"Every way I know."

Sylvia dodged the real subject while answering Pam's inquiries about Nana, the funeral, the relatives, her mother. She dodged her by admitting bitterness over losing the story to Colette. She then let it slip, quite casually, that the strangest thing had happened at the Redskins game: she'd run into Max Ridgway.

Jesse bounded into Pam's lap with his treasure: a gold-painted twig that had broken loose from a nearby reindeer display.

"You're still in love with the guy," Pam said, more as a statement than a question. Pam had of course heard about Sylvia's collegiate romance and had seen pictures. But Sylvia had never couched it as a going concern. Here Pam had stated it present tense. No holds barred.

"I was then, I think. But I didn't know what it meant."

"No more?"

Sylvia glanced from Pam, her face earnest now under its mantle of dark curls, to the little face of her son, looking up at Sylvia inquisitively, as if he, too, wanted to know. She pictured herself talking about Max while this little tyke listened in, and it made her suddenly want to laugh. Then she felt tears welling up, which she squeezed back. This was tough.

"Hey, listen," Pam said. "Whatever we talk about, it's strictly off the record. My lips are sealed. Just between you and me."

"And me!" Jesse exclaimed.

The two friends guffawed, laughing until they almost fell over. Then Sylvia talked. She talked about how Max had been on her mind constantly lately, about the peculiar sensation of seeing him at the game. "I must sound very confused about him," Sylvia admitted. She failed to mention—because she had not yet accepted it—that he was in the company of another woman.

Pam nodded her head sagely. "One thing to do, and one thing only," she said. "You have to find out if there's anything left for either of you. And *you* have to do it. Don't wait for him."

Sylvia stewed a few moments. "Assuming that's what I want to do, how would I go about it?"

"Got it! You ready? Hale has got to be feeling guilty about giving you the shaft."

Sylvia's face spelled out skepticism.

"Okay, maybe a little guilty, anyway," she continued, "enough to make this work. You said Max was getting out of the horse business. The Ridgways breed racehorses, right?"

"They also race them," Sylvia said.

"There's something rotten in the manure here somewhere. You don't just walk away from a multimillion-dollar business unless there's deep dung in the barn. You know anything about the horse business?"

"Just what I read in your piece."

Pam had written a story on the Virginia horse business that Sylvia had read with enough interest to retain some details: how owners can lose their shirts when they buy bad horses, or when a million-dollar filly suddenly dies of a rare disease. Something interesting, surmised the business reporter—always working a story, even on her day off—had happened or was still happening to Ridgway Breeding Farm. Whatever it was, it would make a good story for the *Trib*.

"But one more thing," Pam went on. "When I did my story, the older Ridgway wouldn't talk to me. Not exactly a publicity hound, that one. At the time, I didn't know you knew Max, or I would have done some heavy name-dropping."

"Okay, so what are you suggesting here?"

"I'm suggesting that you walk into Hale's office Monday morning and ask her to send you out to horse country a couple days."

"But Max isn't out there," Sylvia objected.

"Find out where he is. He'll have to be interviewed for an in-depth story, right? Call the old man. I'm sure Mr. Ridgway the elder is still kindly disposed toward the beautiful young ex."

Sylvia was silent for what seemed forever, her body motionless while her mind and memories raged, a war zone of conflicting emotions. Something inside her objected to using the *Tribune* as a cover to explore her feelings for Max. "Colin Ridgway probably doesn't remember me."

"Aw, come on, of course he does," Pam said a tad impatiently. "You're not the type of person people forget. What do you have to lose?"

On the first Wednesday in December, Sylvia drove in her sparkling white Chevy Nova (which she'd run through an automatic car wash before leaving Washington), down Route 50 into Loudoun County and on to the Ridgway Breeding Farm. It had proven surprisingly easy to get Hale's permission to do the story. Now, dressed in her finest professional winter outfit, a turquoise gabardine suit and ecru silk blouse with lace insets, her long blond hair knotted to the side, Sylvia tried to mentally prepare herself for the coming encounter.

Colin Ridgway had always intimidated her. Max's father was tall, aristocratic, and aloof. He was even more handsome than his famous younger brother, Ernest, whom he'd viewed as somewhat forward. When Ernest Ridgway had been named attorney general, Max had remembered his father telling him it was "no big surprise." Unlike Max's mother, Betsy, who had been so kind and attentive during Sylvia's many visits with Max to the farm, Colin had always seemed to be too preoccupied with the business of breeding and racing to take much interest. She still used the canvas carryall bag, her name stenciled on in red and green block letters, that Betsy Ridgway had given her that last Christmas she and Max were a couple.

Sylvia usually thought most interviews through in advance, jotting down questions, maybe doing some reading, depending on how familiar she was with a subject. She was generally confident enough to think on her feet, to follow her instincts during the interview and formulate follow-up questions as they went along. For this story, however, she'd read for two days straight, everything she could get her hands on about horses and the business and where Ridgway Farm fit into the picture. She'd learned that Colin Ridgway was past president of the Virginia Thoroughbred Breeders Association, but aside from references to him in that capacity, there had been almost no press. She jotted down enough questions so that if her mind went blank, the interview could continue.

She'd taken directions, but they were unnecessary, because she still remembered the way. It was just noon when she pulled into the farm, nestled in the foothills of the Blue Ridge Mountains. She recognized its familiar hanging sign: RIDG-WAY BREEDING FARM, EST. 1762, and the black, creosote-soaked fences that delineated the gently rolling pastures. It was all coming back, every detail. Sylvia steered her car up the long gravel driveway, lined with gracefully ancient oak trees and sugar maples. About two hundred yards from the public road began the low, gray fieldstone walls that dated back to Colonial times. The Ridgways, of course, had been slaveowners, and their slaves had built these walls without mortar or cement—so exactingly, Max had told her, that to this day you still couldn't stick a razor blade between some of the stones.

Sylvia hadn't forgotten the imposing brick facade of the two-story, four-chimney, pre–Revolutionary War home, where Max and his sister Laura had grown up. Max had once explained that from his father's point of view the antebellum mansions built nearly a century later were "nouveau."

Wearing a gray houndstooth jacket, Colin Ridgway stood at the door of his house to greet her.

"You're lovelier than I remembered," he said, taking her hand and shaking it. "I can see why my son did not quickly forget you."

Sylvia didn't know how to respond to such courtly talk. "I haven't forgotten you either," she smiled. His handclasp lingered on hers for just a minute longer than necessary, and then he ushered her into the den, where a fire blazed in the stone hearth.

Colin Ridgway looked a good bit older than when she'd last seen him. According to Sylvia's calculations, he was now sixty-six. His hair had grown lighter, and the bald patch had extended its scalp-top territory.

"I wish I could offer you lunch," he said, "but my help comes in only on Tuesday and Friday."

"That's all right," Sylvia answered, wondering where Betsy Ridgway was. She surveyed the room, sensing that something was different about the den. Piles of *Racing Form* and *Thoroughbred Record* stood in disorderly stacks on shelves and tables and his ancient, leather-covered writing table.

"Can I get you a drink?" he offered. "Scotch?"

She said yes, because she knew that he wanted to drink and wouldn't if she refused. "That would be nice."

He handed her a low crystal glass with a napkin that cupped up around it and took a seat in an oversized wing chair opposite her.

"Mr. Ridgway," she began, turning on her tape recorder, "you have always been publicity shy. I feel it's a great honor that you granted me an interview, but I'm puzzled as to why."

He seemed a bit disconcerted by the question. "Maybe I'm a smarter man than I was three years ago," he began. He scratched his scalp, and it seemed that he was just as nervous as she. "You know this business isn't what it used to be. When my father came into the business, thoroughbred breeding and racing consisted of a handful of grand old families who were in it for pleasure and sport. The money was good, but it wasn't the reason you went into it. Today, big business has come in with all of its apparatus—syndicates, promoters, agents, even public relations."

She thought of Max, wondering why he had left. It was too early to ask, but she would have to before she left.

"What are the three most important changes Ridgway Farm has undergone in the last five to ten years?" There. That was broad enough that he could steer the conversation where he wanted to and loosen up a bit.

Colin Ridgway leaned back into his chair, fiddling with his drink. "Changes over the last five to ten years are not so important as what's happening right now. Ridgway Farm is going to be syndicated. It's the way to stay in business, of course."

Sylvia was stunned. Clearly, Ridgway Farm had run into serious financial trouble. And, from her research on the horse business, she knew what syndication meant. "Are you saying," she said, trying to mask her disbelief, "that your family will no longer own Ridgway Farm?"

Colin Ridgway cleared his throat, choosing his words carefully. "We will own a certain percentage of Ridgway Farm. Under the new arrangement, there will, of course, be other owners as well."

"What percentage do you expect to retain?"

Colin stiffened visibly in his chair. "I'd rather not comment on that."

So Pam was right. There was deep manure in the barn. Not only was the Ridgway family losing sole ownership of the farm, but by the way he'd ducked her last question, Sylvia suspected that Max's father—and Max, if he were somehow still involved—would no longer be even controlling owner.

Sylvia took a sip of scotch. More quickly than she had anticipated, the interview had become sensitive. Though widely ignored in Washington, it was always a good rule to interview people you knew as seldom as possible. Already, she was torn between wanting to respect Colin Ridgway's privacy and wanting to get the real story.

How had this happened, she wondered? She decided to ask a couple of questions to warm him up. "Ridgway Farm has been in the family for how many generations?"

"I'm the tenth generation."

"And how do you feel about this change?"

"Oh," he said in a clipped tone, "I accept it as inevitable. As you know, the expenses of a horse farm, particularly a farm on the scale of Ridgway, are virtually prohibitive in our day. There's certainly every reason to disperse the costs among a number of owners."

She'd made a mistake, Sylvia realized. Obviously he wouldn't admit his real feelings, certainly not to a reporter. Rather than being a gateway to what had happened, his feelings weren't even going to be accessible.

There was a sudden restlessness in his tone. "What else can I do for your story?"

A warning light flashed in Sylvia's brain, signaling that the interview could abruptly burn out, like an engine with no oil. "Did the business suffer financial reversals?" she blurted out.

Colin Ridgway stared at her—Max had his piercing eyes, she thought—then forced a laugh. "That's a very pointed question from such a beautiful young lady. I don't recall your asking questions of that sort when you were out here with Max."

"Mr. Ridgway," she said after a moment, "I'm a reporter now."

"Yes, I see that," he said pointedly, the clear implication of disapproval in his tone. "To answer your question, yes, there were several 'reversals.' Quite frankly, I don't intend to get into them." He took a long swallow of Scotch. "Can I freshen your drink?"

Sylvia shook her head as Colin poured himself more scotch.

"When do you expect the syndication to go into effect?" she asked.

"Quite soon," he said. "Perhaps as early as the first of the year. We're in the process of reviewing prospective investors and so forth. Making good progress, I should add. Ridgway is an enormously attractive investment, one that every serious investor should make himself aware of. We're one of the oldest continuously running horse farms in the United States. We have an extraordinary record of achievement in thoroughbred breeding and racing."

As Colin went on, rattling off the names of winning horses and races they'd won, the names of buyers, the impressive prices Ridgway horses had sold for at auction and so forth, it occurred to Sylvia why he had agreed to do the story. It was so obvious that she hadn't seen it: the story might help him in putting the syndication together, for while the *Trib* was not the *Post*, a number of his "prospective investors" were bound to see the story.

Sylvia did not prolong the interview. Though Colin had relaxed somewhat, she knew now that he would never reveal anything about the farm, past or present, that could be construed as negative by an investor. "By the way," she said casually as she was readying to leave, "I ran into Max at a football game. He said he was moving into the City."

"Yes," Colin answered, stiffening again.

"I was surprised to hear he was leaving the farm."

"Yes, well, Maxwell was not happy here."

From his tight-lipped expression, Sylvia deduced that she would get no more information about Max from him. "I don't believe he mentioned Mrs. Ridgway," she went on. "Is she all right?"

"Oh, yes. Quite all right."

"Is she here, by any chance? I'd love to say hello before I go."

"I'm afraid not." He took a bracing sip of scotch. "Betsy and I are divorced, you see."

"I'm so sorry to hear that," Sylvia said quickly, totally unprepared for this turn of events. She could hardly imagine the scenario that might have brought it about. "Is she . . ."

"Living elsewhere, yes."

Sylvia nodded. "I see." Hastily, she packed her tape recorder in her bag and rose. "One more thing," she said, getting this out as if it were an afterthought, when in fact she had wondered how best to raise it ever since she had left Washington. "Do you happen to have Max's new address and phone number? We forgot to exchange them at the game."

# CHAPTER
## 19

Mabel Stoneman was a feminist therapist who wore expensive, vibrant clothing and turquoise-and-silver Navajo jewelry. Rings adorned every finger of her left hand except her thumb. Mabel listened attentively as Colette—stretched out on a soft velour couch—spilled out the secrets in her heart.

Therapy was Colette's favorite form of escape, second only

to sex. To no one else could you talk about nothing but yourself and be guaranteed a sympathetic ear. You could tell about shoplifting, about trysts with married men. You could let off steam about your boss or reveal jealousies and ambivalence of emotion. Of course, long ago—in their first session—Mabel had heard about Colette's incestuous relationship with her grandfather, how she liked it. At the time, Mabel had said sagely that Colette was naturally attuned to "alternative sexuality" by virtue of her initiation.

Colette was telling about her latest encounter with Ben, whom she called Ken in therapy; she knew that despite the cloak of therapeutic confidentiality, in Washington, political gossip fell into another category. Political gossip was a hot potato that no one could hold. She'd taken control of Ken by shaving him clean, she was saying, and he seemed to like it. But what was most on her mind today was a strange feeling that was overtaking her: how for the first time in her thirty years, Ken was making her crave something more than just fun and games. She had found herself wanting commitment. Even, heaven help her, marriage.

"These are very normal feelings," Mabel responded, "to find someone who's right for you and want to be with that person."

Mabel never referred to a lover by gender, always couching her responses in neutral words like "lover," "mate," "person," "significant other." Though they'd never talked about it, Colette assumed that Mabel was lesbian. Mabel had a teenage daughter whose photograph was prominently displayed in a rich, burled-wood frame on her desk, and Colette believed that Mabel—who when young must have been a lovely woman—had been with men and in the course of her spiritual and therapeutic evolution, discovered that she loved women more. Colette liked her all the better because of what she took to be her sexual seasoning.

Mabel gave her blessing to the relationship. "Since Ken is in an unhappy marriage, you might want to encourage him to resolve it," she said.

"He hasn't made love to his wife in a year," Colette said. "He'll have to get out soon, right?"

Mabel paused. "You'll have to give it time, my dear. Sometimes a man stays with a woman for reasons even he doesn't understand."

This last did not please Colette. "But he doesn't want her; he doesn't even love her."

"Men are different from us," said Mabel. "Some of them can separate love and sex into different drawers, different compartments of their lives."

Colette smiled devilishly. "Some of us can do that, too!"

Fifteen minutes remained in Colette's allotted fifty-minute session. Mabel asked about her work.

Colette said she had a big assignment at work—"a chance to stretch beyond Society, but I can't seem to get anywhere on the story."

"How do you feel about the story, Colette?" Mabel asked.

Colette had so focused on the results of the Hookergate story—gaining respect around the office, making a bigger name for herself outside the *Tribune*—that she hadn't taken stock of her feelings about the story itself. "You know, the whole idea of prostitution being illegal seems absurd to me. If someone wants to pay someone for a little pleasure, it doesn't bother me. I can think of worse ways to get off." Colette shrugged her shoulders.

"Maybe you don't want to expose this ring," Mabel suggested.

"Oh, yes, I do. I really want to get this story," Colette insisted. "Hale expects so much of me. And Sylvia, I have to show Sylvia."

"It's what you expect of yourself that's important, Colette."

Sylvia was sitting at her desk on Friday morning staring at Max Ridgway's phone number and trying to think of what she'd say when she called, when Colette presented herself at the periphery of her view. "I'm sorry about your grandmother." She spoke tentatively, as if to convey remorse.

After all of Colette's cutting remarks and shabby treatment, it was hard for Sylvia to believe anything she said.

"Thanks," said Sylvia coldly.

Colette would not be dismissed. ''I guess you're thinking I'm a real schmuck for taking your story and all.''

For the first time, it occurred to Sylvia that maybe she'd blamed Hale unfairly; perhaps Colette had lobbied for the story. It made sense. Colette always wanted other people's things—other women's husbands, now Sylvia's story. What better way to make a national name for herself than to hijack a story that had already proven its publicity value? Sylvia certainly did not intend to reassure Colette that all was fine and dandy between them. ''So how's it going?''

Colette launched into an explanation about the round of lunches she was scheduling with people who might give her leads. As she talked, her painted fingernails shredded a Styrofoam cup, cutting into it as if with a knife. It was obvious, despite her report, that Colette had been unable to turn up anything of significance. Perhaps she was cozying up to Sylvia for help.

''What about Kokoh King?'' Sylvia interrupted.

''Who?''

Why did Colette have to play games? She knew perfectly well who Sylvia was talking about. ''Kokoh King,'' she repeated impatiently. ''Didn't you get her name when I was gone?''

''Oh,'' Colette said, ''the call girl. I can't seem to reach her. I must have left half a dozen messages on her machine.''

''That's odd.'' Sylvia stiffened, suddenly concerned about Kokoh's well-being. Then she relaxed. Perhaps Kokoh simply did not want to deal with another reporter.

''I'll call her,'' Sylvia said. ''Maybe I can get through.'' She saw Colette's dark glance. ''On your behalf, of course.''

Colette brightened. ''Thank you.'' Smiling, her wide eyes beckoned Sylvia's. ''Friends?'' she said.

Sylvia couldn't believe it. One small favor, and she wants the whole bag. The woman was incredible. She thought all could be forgiven overnight, that friendship was obtained as easily as a new outfit. ''Colleagues,'' Sylvia corrected with no warmth in her voice. God, this was hard. It would be easier to feign friendship with Colette, issue smiles, kiss and make up, but Sylvia had resolved one thing over the weekend, in the wake of Nana's death: she would fight for what she believed in, apply the standards of honesty and truthfulness to all aspects of her life.

"Come on, Sylvia," Colette appealed. An edge of whininess laced her voice, like a child who hasn't gotten her way on the verge of a tantrum. "What have I ever done to you? I got the Society job for you where you met B. D. Up in New Hampshire, Ben told me B. D. was wild about you. . . ."

Sylvia's heart skipped a beat. This was unreal. It had just slipped out: Colette had been with Ben up in New Hampshire last week. What other Ben than Ben Fincastle? From the obvious sincerity of the moment, it had to be true. Like everyone else, Sylvia had been hearing the rumors for weeks. But, Jesus Christ, Colette had just admitted she was having an affair with the probable next president of the United States.

"Wait, I didn't say that," Colette said. Tears came to her eyes. "Sylvia, you won't tell anyone. Promise you won't."

Sylvia Loring spotted her lunch date, Judy Fincastle, as she got out of a cab in front of the National Press Club at 14th and F streets. Judy was a petite, slender woman in her mid-forties. With her air of faded beauty, she didn't look like the typical well-tended political wife. She'd once told Sylvia it went against the grain for her to spend much on herself when so many went hungry.

Sylvia had always loved the Press Club's atmosphere, and she seized any excuse to eat here or introduce someone else to the place. So when Judy had called right after Colette's strange confession, suggesting they have lunch, Sylvia chose the Press Club.

Sylvia and Judy had first met at Ernest Ridgway's Cherry Blossom party years ago, and ever since, had been twice-a-year friends. They met for lunch, did each other the occasional favor, and checked in with a phone call every now and again. In Washington, you could be luncheon friends with a woman with whom you didn't socialize in the evening, whom you liked personally but who didn't further your husband's interests. Sylvia understood that this was the category into which she fell.

"Congratulations on the Bob Rossen story," Judy said after they'd exchanged the customary pecks on the cheek. The laugh that followed was self-deprecating, as if Judy were thinking something she shouldn't. "I hate to say this about someone who's been exposed, but was that ever coming!"

"What do you suppose Rossen will do next?" Sylvia asked.

"I've heard that he may not run next year. It'll probably be better for everyone involved—Sally, even himself. Maybe he'll do some soul-searching," Judy said.

Sylvia led the way to the elevator that would take them up to the members-and-guests-only Packer Grill on the fifth floor. "The guy could use some heavy-duty therapy," Sylvia agreed.

Two reporters—one a short man whose press badge read "Bangor Daily News," the other from the *St. Louis Post-Dispatch*—climbed into the elevator with them, flashing friendly, curious smiles.

Most reporters for Washington papers spent little or no time at the National Press Club. The *Post* and to a lesser extent the *Trib*, as Dennis once told her, were clubs in and of themselves, with enough "members" on the editorial staff to form their own cliques. In Washington terms, any paper outside the *New York Times, Washington Post, Wall Street Journal*, and, on their good days, the *Los Angeles Times* and the *Chicago Tribune*—no matter how influential on its own home turf—was a "little" paper. Many of the tiny Washington one- or two-person bureaus were housed right here in this building, each with its own fresh perspective on the Washington scene.

"Ben's spoken here twice," said Judy, "but I've never set foot in the building."

Sylvia could tell the two reporters were taking in every word, wondering if Judy was who they thought she was. Sure enough, the tall one extended his hand.

"Don Silas, *St. Louis Post-Dispatch*. Are you Judy Fincastle?"

Judy said yes.

"I was wondering if I might interview you sometime," he asked, pulling out his business card.

"I can't say just now," Judy said, "but you can reach me at the Peace Links office Tuesdays and Thursdays." Peace Links was the political group Judy headed, and she'd suggested the lunch today to discuss possible coverage of it in the *Trib*.

Sylvia showed Judy off the elevator and into the First Amendment Lounge, with its inscribed photos of speakers from Winston Churchill to John F. Kennedy and Indira Ghandi—a virtual Who's Who of famous politicians of the twentieth century. They climbed carpeted stairs to an upper level, the Reliable Source, as it was called, and looked in on the Harry Truman Lounge, where a black woman reporter was interviewing a man in a three-piece suit.

The Packer Grill was just down the hall, a cozy hangout with a bar, dining tables, and a view of Lafayette Square and the White House. Hundreds of brass plaques, each bearing a provocative quotation about journalism, adorned the walls.

Lighting on one particular quote, Judy halted in amazement. She read it aloud: " 'In the great cathedral of serious American journalism, the Washington gossip writer must skulk in a dark nook somewhere between the candle ends and the confessional. In the quiet chapel of polite society, he perches self-consciously in the back pew.—Diana McLellan.' Hmm," she said. "Colette Daniels excepted, of course."

Sylvia winced, reminded of what she knew about Colette and Ben. She quickly pointed to another. "My favorite's this one."

Judy read it aloud: " 'I ain't no lady. I'm a newspaperwoman.'—Hazel Brannon Smith."

Laughing, they fell into line at the buffet and returned to their table with plates of steamed vegetables, curried chicken, and grilled swordfish.

"Max Ridgway," Judy said, zeroing in on the subject most on Sylvia's mind. "Do you keep up at all anymore?"

Sylvia's heart started pounding. She wondered what Judy

knew, if maybe she were going to reveal something about this Nicole. "Actually I just ran into him Sunday at a Redskins game. He's moving to Washington, I understand."

"I never thought it would happen, but he's talking to Ben again," Judy said. "About joining the campaign." Sylvia knew that Judy had always liked Max, had been sorry when he quit her husband's Senate staff four years ago, but thought it best for him.

"Doing what?" Sylvia wondered.

"Fund-raising, probably," said Judy. "That's the biggest job right now. Ben is beating Dan Tison three to one in nailing down campaign dollars. It's just that people are reluctant to shell out for any Democrat. Ben thinks that Max would be great working Virginia, Kentucky, and Tennessee. Southern aristocrat, you know. One of their own."

"Does Max want that kind of job?"

"So it seems."

Sylvia picked at her broccoli, hoping Judy would say more. It was hard for her to picture Max working for Ben Fincastle again, particularly after he'd quit in disgust, fed up with politics, as Judy had told the story. But this was the new Max, the Max she had not called after two days of anxious procrastination. She would call him later today, she promised herself.

Judy turned the subject to the *Trib* and Colette Daniels, whose recent sniping column had embarrassed Sylvia and, quite frankly, amazed her for its sheer nerve. ("Judy Fincastle, wife of the oh-so-handsome senator, was spotted dining with a group of like-minded congressional wives that plans to eliminate nuclear weaponry worldwide. Good luck, gals.") Sylvia had hoped against hope that Judy hadn't seen it.

"I can't understand it. Who is this woman?" Judy asked. "Why does she need to take potshots at me?" Never in her husband's career had criticism been directed at her personally.

"It was a cheap shot," Sylvia agreed.

"You're a journalist. Do readers really enjoy these kinds of barbs?"

Sylvia nodded toward the quotation plaques. "Well," she

said, trying to lighten the mood, "to quote Edith Sitwell up there, 'The public will believe anything, so long as it is not founded on the truth.' "

Judy didn't laugh. Her distress was visible, as if she knew she were dealing with more than a mere barb here. Sylvia was in an impossible bind. To tell Judy what she knew to be true about Colette and Ben seemed only fair. But she hated being the bearer of bad tidings, delivering a poison pill and having to watch it take effect on a woman who was already hurting. Sylvia didn't have to volunteer anything.

Judy studied her intently, as if summoning the energy to ask her something important. "Have you heard anything," she started, her face stiffening, her lips moving into a tight, defensive position, "about Colette and . . . Ben?"

Being asked so directly, there was no alternative. Sylvia had to play it straight. "I'm afraid I have, Judy."

Judy Fincastle woke from her dream with a start. She had found herself locked inside the White House, those giant columns as immobile bars, blocking her way. The White House was a vault, a mausoleum, from which there was no escape. Brusque, robotic guards kept watch, and cameras recorded her every move, her every thought. She could not get out. Or breathe. Or run. As she awakened, she saw the image of Ben, holding her arms behind her, preventing her from even shifting position.

Judy wanted a life of her own, beyond just supporting Ben's campaign. It had gotten her into trouble once in 1972, and Ben had never quite forgiven Judy for that. Because of his hawkish stance on Vietnam—which she had fervently opposed—she'd spent more time campaigning for George McGovern than Ben Fincastle for Congress. It was Ben's only loss, and he'd always pinned some of the blame on her.

She'd known the last four First Ladies personally. Every one of them had been unpaid government servants, careful at choosing their words, on permanent public display. But all seemed to have had strong marriages. Judy had known since the beginning of this campaign that she'd have to work on their marriage now—before it was too late. If they moved into the White House together, there would be no chance. He'd never have any time for her.

He'd had affairs before. Three that she knew about. Deep down, she'd refused to forgive him, playing her own passive part in the downward spiral of their marriage. It made no sense—if she could not forgive him, she should get out. She knew this. But, like a stereo needle skipping on a record, she'd gone over and over this groove. Well, now she had no choice. She had to confront him on this one. She threw the covers back and got out of bed. She was in the living room pouring out a scotch to strengthen her resolve, when Ben walked in the door.

She got right to the point. "How do you think a divorce would sit with your image manager? B. D. Cole?"

"Judy, it's three A.M. Don't start this."

"You choose the hours; I merely take my time with you when I can get it."

"What are you talking about?"

"Colette Daniels."

Ben didn't deny anything. He was too tired for that.

"Do you know what an ultimatum is? If you don't, look it up, because that's what I'm giving you. It's Colette or me. Let me put it another way. Please assess the damage a divorce would have on your campaign and decide if she's worth it to you."

Ben realized that Judy was serious, and, to be truthful, he had to agree with her. She was right about his campaign—it couldn't afford a quake of that magnitude. How did she find out, he wondered momentarily, but was too tired even to pursue this thought. In Washington, a city of leaks, it was useless even to speculate.

The thought of Dan Tison—the homely, squeaky-clean senator from Missouri benefiting from any misstep of his own just about killed Ben. It was almost worth giving up Colette to prevent this from happening. Ben always shook the rafters with his Tison jokes, and his contempt for the man was great. "We ought to add a surcharge to his Senate fees for the toilet-lid covers he uses in the Senate john" was one of his favorite off-color lines, reserved for good ole boys. Ben was determined to win the race, if only to whip Tison's sanctimonious ass. Judy always was a smart woman. But after tasting Colette, he was certain of this much: Ben Fincastle didn't want his wife anymore.

Nonetheless, he went over and put his arms around her, stroking her back as she sobbed. "I'll give her up," he whispered. "I promise."

# CHAPTER
## 20

Max had been reluctant at first to talk. About the farm, about any of it. "What sort of story?" he asked sharply when she called upon returning to the office.

Sylvia had prepared herself for that question. "People have an image of the Virginia horse business as stuffy and staid. I'm looking at stereotypes versus the real forces and issues in the nineties. Financial strategies. Adaptations of various kinds. The impact of new developments on old cultural patterns."

"Is this a newspaper piece, or a lecture to be delivered at the Smithsonian?"

Sylvia flushed. Leave it to Max to slice right through her pretty words.

"You left out sex," he went on, an edge to his voice. "Aren't you going to investigate sex scandals among the horse set? Think of the possibilities. There's always bestiality, that's very de rigueur these days. Who knows, Rossen may have done it with a horse."

"Max," she snapped back, startled by his ugly sarcasm.

He was silent a moment. "That was uncalled for," he conceded finally. And then, "I'm a bit short for help tomorrow morning. If you can help me move, I'll give you a little time.''

So she found herself at seven A.M. Saturday morning—Max had always been a fanatical early riser—pulling onto Prospect Street, not far from the Potomac River between Georgetown University and the Key Bridge. She was dressed to work up a sweat in slacks and an oversized hooded sweatshirt, a rose-colored turtleneck underneath. Yet after an almost sleepless night in which she could think of nothing but seeing him again, she had not neglected a little makeup, nor had she failed to check herself out thoroughly in the bathroom mirror before leaving Adams-Morgan.

A small Jartrans rental truck straddled the sidewalk between the apartment building and the street. The inside was packed with boxes, chairs, lamps, and furniture.

Max was already in the midst of moving, wearing faded jeans and the same pair of boots she remembered from UVA, a little dustier and more beat up, but familiar to Sylvia and tinged with old sentimental associations. A tan suede jacket hugged him like a second skin, and a touch of a smile crested his lips. He and his friend, a short, muscular guy named Keith Sanders, hoisted a couch upward toward the stairs. She was relieved that Nicole was nowhere in sight.

''Could you get the doors?'' he called out.

Max's new place was on the third floor, and Sylvia rushed to get ahead of them.

The men worked quickly, almost manically, transporting something heavy from the van, then racing down the stairs at top speed to fetch the next item. Max hardly seemed to breathe, he was in such good shape. So intent was he on getting the job done that he gave her not even a moment's notice, and she looked around for something to do.

Sylvia started up the stairs with a pair of table lamps when Max spotted her. Apparently judging her efforts feeble, he nodded toward an open-topped box. ''How about getting some of those boxes of books?'' he asked. ''I don't want this truck sitting here into midmorning.''

As if paying penance for long-unpunished crimes, Sylvia

compliantly returned the lamps back to the lawn and tugged at a box of books. It must have weighed fifty pounds, but she managed to cart it up the stairs and into his apartment. It was an efficiency, small and spare, the carpet mustard yellow. The kitchen was microscopic, with a tiny stove, refrigerator, and sink. The image of Max knocking around in this sardine box was ludicrous.

"So," Max said, turning a dining table on its side with Keith to angle it through the door. "Why don't you start the interview. This is an interview, right?"

Sylvia didn't like this. Not only was there Max, with his new take-control attitude, there was this Keith, blocking any chance of intimacy. Sylvia knew from long experience never to let a third party listen in on an interview, not PR people representing a client, not friends, no one. She told Max as much when Keith was out of earshot.

"Maybe you're right," he replied. "Then again, maybe I really don't want to see my name splashed all over the *Washington Tribune*."

Sylvia held her ground. "So why did you agree to this?"

"Maybe I made a mistake."

"A deal's a deal. At least," she added pointedly, "that's the way it used to be, Max."

Their eyes locked; then Max turned to his friend. "The reporter here says you gotta go. We've got all the heavy stuff anyway." He squeezed Keith's shoulder. "Thanks, buddy."

Keith eyed Sylvia warily before he replied, as if looking for a way to protect his friend. "Any time."

After they heard his footsteps fade on the stairs, Max said, "More to carry. Fire away."

"First question," said Sylvia when they arrived back at the truck. She hoisted a stereo. "I understand that many horse farms, Ridgway included, are syndicating these days. Why is this necessary at Ridgway, for example?"

Max froze. "You didn't tell me you talked to Dad."

"Is talking to your dad a capital offense?"

"Where's your notebook?" he said shortly. "Aren't you going to take notes? A good reporter's got to get all the exact words, right?"

She started up the stairs. "Words as golden as yours will be hard to forget. You want your stereo moved, don't you?"

Max came behind her with a coffee table. "Okay, I'll answer your question. Why is syndication necessary at Ridgway Farm? Because Colin Ridgway says so."

"Meaning what?"

They came into the apartment. "Meaning," Max said, "whatever you take it to mean."

Sylvia set down the stereo. "You don't think it's necessary?"

"I didn't say that," he said, lowering the coffee table. "You did." He wheeled and marched down the stairs.

Sylvia stared down at his retreating form. Not exactly off to a roaring start here. Still, testy as he was, there was something about Max that pulled her toward him. Something in his voice, an emotion, that belied his standoffish words. She followed him down the stairs.

Max watched her from the truck. "Here she comes," he intoned, the slightest suggestion of a smile flickering in his eyes. "In her never-ending quest for truth, justice, and the American way."

She watched him lug a huge box up the stairs, packed with she knew not what. There was a story here, all right—something powerful had happened, something that had torn the Ridgway family apart. Beneath his surface, she already knew, were fierce emotions, pride and pain that made her want to reach out to him, to draw close and protect him. Guarded though he was, these emotions might even spill out if she did her job well. It could be a great story. But was a great story what she really wanted?

She brought up the lamps she had set down earlier at his request. She wanted to convince herself she was being fair to this man. "Max, look. If you don't want to talk about this, we'll just forget it."

"No, I'll talk." Then he smiled. "Just don't ask me any questions I can't answer."

"Can't? Or won't?"

He laughed. "I can't answer that." Then he sobered. "Maybe you can help."

From her face, too, the smile faded, and they were looking at each other, their friendship deep as it was old, both feeling a conflict that needed resolution. Enough of the old Max was here, Sylvia knew, that old warmth in his eyes, for her to guess that he wanted to tell her everything that had happened. Tell Sylvia, the woman he'd once loved. And that feeling that he needed her, this man who had once kept no secrets, gave Sylvia a thrill as sharp as it was sudden.

Then, when she made no reply, his expression changed, his voice went cold, and it seemed to Sylvia that what had just happened between them had only been a mirage.

"I need to get that truck back," he said, sitting down on the couch. "Ask your questions, and we'll be done with it."

Sylvia felt a chill. She sat down on a chair, taking pen and notebook from a sweatshirt pocket. If she was going to do the interview, she would do it in a professional manner. "All right. My question about syndication. Is that your answer—that it's necessary because Colin Ridgway says it is?"

"Yes."

She stared at him. "That's it? One word."

"You got it."

She thought of closing her notebook right then, thanking him for his time, and making her exit. But something held her there. "All right, then. Perhaps you can reveal what your father would not. What percentage ownership will the Ridgways retain of the farm?"

"Is this article about Ridgway Farm?" he said fiercely. "You said when you called that it was about the Virginia horse business."

"I have to start somewhere, don't I?"

"You're good," he said without inflection.

"Then maybe you'd answer my question."

"I'm sure if my father stonewalled you, he had good reason."

"What would that reason be?" Sylvia shot back.

"Oh, Dad has his reasons. You'd better ask him."

From Max's sarcastic tone, Sylvia could only surmise that Max and his father were not on the best of terms. "Your father said that you were, quote, not happy on the farm. Why not?"

Max shifted his weight on the couch. "This isn't getting any better, is it?"

Sylvia closed her notebook. "I made a mistake by coming over here. I'm sorry to have taken up your time."

He rose stiffly from the couch, watching her.

"Good-bye," she said.

"Good-bye."

They looked at each other. Was this all there was? Then Sylvia lowered her eyes and started down the stairs.

"Sylvia?"

She turned.

"Look, I know a fair bit about the business. Maybe I could give you some more general stuff that might help your story."

This was, she knew, in its own peculiar way, a reaching out. He was leaving the door open, telling her he wasn't such a jerk after all.

But, at this moment, feeling that her powers over him were no more, feeling a grief over the loss of the Max that she'd once known so well and had been nourishing in her imagination, she wasn't about to humor his desire to make token amends, to let him become just some background source in her life. Without realizing it, Sylvia Loring wanted all of him again—or none at all.

"Thanks," she said. "But no thanks."

It seemed the longest day of her life.

By the time she returned to Adams-Morgan, the edge of her anger and disappointment had worn off, leaving Sylvia with the strange and haunting feeling that she had missed her one opportunity for happiness. All morning she cleaned her apartment, trying to drown her thoughts in work and easy-listening, mellow-rock radio music. Sylvia could not shake the feeling that Max, for one moment, before it had all turned sour, had wanted to talk, had wanted to draw close again.

Misery wrapped around her like some giant tourniquet,

squeezing the air out of the day, making her increasingly frantic. She had made such a colossal mistake. If only she had abandoned all her pretensions and simply said, "Don't worry, I don't care about the story, I just want to talk." The story, after all, had started out as a scheme to "purge" Max, as Pam had said, to put her feelings about him to the test. Was it pride that made her go on with the masquerade? Had she wanted to impress Max with her skills as a newswoman? Was her only identity, as B. D. had suggested, that of reporter—a role from which she was incapable of breaking? Max had opened the door, and, for some reason, she had been reluctant to step through it.

Even now, it was her pride, she knew, that kept her from picking up the phone to ask for a second chance.

She felt like such a zero. And her apartment, once a cozy haven from the stresses of the world, had never seemed more depressing. The place was filthy. Dirty dishes were piled in the sink, and stacks of unread newspapers and magazines were scattered everywhere, the debris of a media junkie, of a woman with no existence outside of her work, not even at home.

Grimly attacking her apartment with broom and brushes, scouring powder, and toilet-bowl cleaner, Sylvia realized that she could only guess what Max had been through. A man who had always dreamed of running his own horse farm, of bonding with horses, of feeling an almost parental need to nurture them and a gambler's need to race them, had to be losing his soul in the loss of his home, his horses, his inheritance.

And there was the shell shock of divorce. It had hurt her deeply as a young child—what was it like for him at this age? To have your parents split up after thirty-odd years of what had appeared to be a happy marriage? In her case, she'd barely known her father when he left: She was only five years old at the time. Sylvia saw Alec Loring every two or three years when she was growing up and, at Christmas, he sent a card and a check. Even though she followed his footsteps into a writing career, she felt far away from him.

But most of all, Sylvia knew, there was what she herself had done to Max. It was there at his apartment, draped like a black flag around him every moment he looked at her with accusation in his eyes, every time he spoke. She had left him, she reminded herself, because she needed her own life, her own accomplishments. But what about his life? How could she ever really know what it felt like, year after year, to have been rejected by the person you loved and wanted to marry?

Sylvia was at her bathroom sink, scrubbing feverishly, when she felt the tears. God, she thought, it must have been incredibly hard for him even to decide to see me.

She stood up, crying, staring at herself in the mirror.

It was 4:15 P.M. She went into her kitchen, picked up the phone, and dialed.

Max answered.

"Hi, it's Sylvia. Can I come over and talk to you?"

A long pause. "Didn't you get what you wanted?"

"No. I mean . . ."

He cut her off. "Look. Two things: I don't like being used, and I don't want your paper hurting the farm." She could almost feel him starting to hang up.

"Max!" she said frantically. "That's not it," she said, groping for words. "Max . . . I just want more time."

"I don't understand."

"More time with you."

His silence was agonizing.

"This doesn't have to be the story," she said desperately. "Off the record is fine. Maybe I could buy you a drink?"

"Look, Sylvia, I have plans tonight," he said finally before hanging up. "I don't know about you, but I've got a life going here."

# CHAPTER
## 21

For the better part of an hour, Hale Gardiner and Lyons Smith, Ben Fincastle's campaign manager, talked politics and sipped sherry by the fire at the Ritz Hotel bar. He praised her fine work at the *Trib* and told her how delighted he was to have her—a fellow southerner—at the helm. Then he brought up Colette Daniels.

"Straighten something out for me. Is Colette covering the Fincastle campaign? Some of us wanted to know."

"Oh," said Hale, trying to sound casual. "What makes you think so?"

"Well, of course, we all enjoyed having Colette up in New Hampshire the week before Thanksgiving, but we couldn't figure her role up there. Was she working? Was she visiting?" Then he added, maybe just for laughs, "Is she a political junkie?"

The week before Thanksgiving, Hale thought, Colette had been skiing in Banff. She knew it for a fact.

"Colette was in Canada skiing all week," Hale said definitively.

Lyons's words did not contradict her, but his steadfast gaze did. "There's talk that the senator and your columnist are quite chummy."

"It's not true," Hale asserted. She thought of Colette's lush, apricot sweater. "Her boyfriend is British."

"Oh?" Lyons said. "Well, I suppose that settles that."

Hale could tell from his ironic tone that Lyons didn't buy it for a second. Strange, she thought, was it possible that Colette had lied to her? And if so, why?

"Exactly what is it you're suggesting, Lyons?"

"Nothing," he replied. "Nothing at all. It's just that, as one of Ben's supporters, I'm sure you'll do what you can to protect the campaign from gossip."

Hale steered her Sterling onto the Georgetown cobblestone street where Colette lived. There was no hint of a breakthrough on the Hookergate story, and it had been almost a month. More than once, it had crossed Hale's mind that her detractors in the Style section might be making hay of this impasse. And her conversation with Lyons Smith added impetus. It was high time to confront the situation head-on.

She rapped on the door and rang the bell for several minutes until she heard footsteps padding toward her.

"Who is it?" came Colette's voice.

"It is me," said Hale.

A long pause followed without a word passing one way or the other through the ornate, double-bolted door. Hale noticed the buttonhole of light in the peephole blacken, a sign that a wary eyeball was peering through at that very moment.

"Give me a minute," Colette said. Hale could hear the footsteps retreat and after a short while return. Colette opened the door wearing nothing, it seemed, but a satiny, rose-colored, full-length bathrobe.

Then she was there, sitting on Colette's cluttered couch. Stacks of newspapers and copies of *Interview, People*, and *Paris Match* littered the coffee table. The smell of stale smoke hung heavy in the room. Hale's eyes searched for clues of Ben Fincastle. Could there have been an assignation here?

"I'd offer you some coffee, but I've just run out," Colette said, regal in her robe.

"Not to worry," Hale said. "I've already had mine. I know I've come at an awkward time," she continued, waiting for Colette to contradict her. "But frankly, it's been almost a month since you started on the call-girl story. Digby and I are concerned. Is something the matter? Personal problems?"

"Oh, no, that's not it at all," Colette said, flinging her hand through the air dismissively. "I've run down a number of leads, and none of them are conclusive. . . ."

"That's what I'm here for, to help you nail the story down," Hale responded.

Colette ran her fingers like a giant comb through her cascading hair. It was true she'd been avoiding Hale because she had nothing to report. The story wasn't happening, and somewhere inside she feared it was because she wasn't up to it. If Hookergate had stayed with Sylvia, she'd have brought it home by now. *If* there were anything to bring home—which she'd come to doubt more than once.

Those eyes, which remained fixed on Colette when she looked up again, made her feel exposed, like the poseur she sometimes believed herself to be. Colette bit her lip, fighting off an overwhelming feeling of panic. She had to get a grip on herself. Ever since she'd first met Hale, Colette had aspired to her status, to her inherited standing in society; in order to achieve that, she sensed, to do what was expected of prominent people, she was going to have to push herself.

Then, in a flash, Colette realized that if she let this story defeat her, she would have a hard time proving herself as a respected journalist. Instinctively, she knew this was a test she must pass, that if she failed, word would spread all over town. Worst of all, she thought with a shudder, Ben would hear about it and think less of her.

"It will take some more time," Colette said firmly, "but you'll be very pleased with the final result."

Hale took in this beautiful, confident woman who had long been her one true friend at the *Trib*. Now, though Colette's words reassured her, the openness between them seemed to have vanished. Only a short time ago, Colette would simply have told her everything. After covering a party and writing her copy, Colette would call and deliver all the tidbits she couldn't put in print. She would say the juiciest things about the men she was seeing—the secrets they divulged, how they performed in bed. And now it seemed Colette was shutting her out. Could it be that the rumors were true?

Hale carved her next words carefully, with grave intensity.

"Colette, I must ask you something. Is there anything to the rumor that you've been seeing Ben Fincastle?"

Colette smiled mysteriously. She reached for an emery board and began filing a nail. "Hale, you really think my life is that exciting?"

Hale persisted. "Then it's not true?"

"Are you asking as a friend or boss?"

"Both."

Colette sighed. "Where would you get an idea like that?" Then, suddenly, agitation growing in her voice: "Don't tell me Sylvia Loring has been telling tales."

Though Colette quickly composed herself, she realized she had given herself away.

"You can be honest with me. I'm your friend," Hale persisted.

Colette nodded. "Of course I know Ben, and the word is he's keeping his pants on at least until the election." The casualness in her usually mellifluous voice sounded forced to Hale.

"Yes," Hale said slowly. "That would make sense." It would make sense, but she didn't buy it. It was obvious to Hale that Colette was covering up right now. But she would play along on the hopes that there would be a time when Colette would pour out her heart. Hale rose to leave. "This has been lovely." There was a catch in her throat. "I really do miss our talks these days."

Perhaps, Hale thought, maneuvering the Sterling through downtown traffic, she had failed to do her duty in that last moment before departure. Perhaps she should have sliced through the evasion and warned Colette directly about the folly of sleeping with Ben Fincastle. No doubt he was seducing her with false promises, having a fine time at the expense of Colette's future.

On the other hand, there was always the danger of such a strategy backfiring. This was an exceedingly delicate matter. Blunt talk, particularly with a creature as sensitive as Colette, could make her rebellious, drive her deeper into Fincastle's embrace. Perhaps, Hale considered, she had been a master of restraint.

As she arrived at the *Tribune*, Hale decided that something more must be done, something that went beyond her injunction to Colette to get on with the call-girl story. She would ponder her next move. Hale had always had an inordinately high regard for her own instincts; whenever she'd listened to them, they had been infallible. In this case, her instincts told her to lie low for a few days, to monitor Colette's work and see what she could produce. Then Hale would act.

Sylvia appeared without warning at Max's apartment Monday night two days after he'd moved in—to apologize. She'd realized finally what she should have known from the first: the story was a land mine from which there was no good escape except a graceful exit. She would tell him she'd been out of line in pursuing it to start with, and that she planned to drop it. She would apologize for any discomfort it had caused.

A loud racket sounded from inside his apartment, an argument on TV, she guessed as she rang the bell. Max flung open the door. He was wearing jeans and a plaid flannel shirt, sleeves rolled up to his elbows. He looked her over in surprise. "You reporters will go to any lengths to get a story," he said.

Sylvia did not know what to make of this greeting. Was it possible he had become this cynical?

"I am impressed," he continued. Under a coating of sincerity, she detected a hint of mockery. "You get hold of a story and won't let up on it. Isn't that the definition of 'heroic' these days? One man—excuse me, person—fighting a battle against all odds? I suppose by now you've gotten the dirt on the Ridgway divorce from Mother. Of course, you already know about her gift shop in Middleburg."

His decibel level was high for a hallway conversation. "Max," she said, flustered. "May I come in?"

"As you may have discerned, I'm not inviting you in."

Sylvia flushed. As insulting as he was, it still amazed her that they were talking to each other again. God, he was handsome. At six-three, he was the only man she'd ever dated who didn't make her feel too tall.

"Max, listen, forget about the story. I came over to apologize. Can we talk?"

"Off the record?" he said, being impossibly obtuse.

"About other stuff. Your life."

"But what if you gained information in the course of this talk that pertained to the story? That would put you in an impossible bind, since your first loyalty is to your job. Right?"

"Come on."

"In fact, it would be fair to say that you love your job."

Sylvia stared back.

Max smiled. He would have made a hell of a lawyer. He used to say so himself, except that he hated the law, the big, greedy business it had become that bore virtually no relation to the pursuit of justice.

"You want to talk? You have your car? Let's go and talk." Max backed into his door, careful to obstruct Sylvia's view inside. Was Nicole there? she wondered. He needed to get a jacket and would be back in a minute.

At her car, he hatched a plan. "I'll drive, so your hands will be free to take notes."

With his taking the story so seriously, it was hard to admit that she wanted to drop it.

Max climbed behind the wheel and shot across the Key Bridge at a clip that made Sylvia grip the edge of her seat.

"Now, then," he said. "Bring on the notebook. Deep Throat is ready to speak."

"On the record?" she said, taken aback.

He smiled, his eyes searching her startled face.

"Actually," she said, "I forgot to bring a notebook."

"The moment of truth, and the star reporter forgets her notebook?"

Abruptly, Max veered off course into the suburban wilds of northern Virginia, not content until he'd located a People's drugstore where stenographers' notebooks were in plentiful supply. "Better hurry," he said, letting her off and waiting curbside. "The Source may dry up like horse dung in a drought." His tone was so exaggerated and his language so coarse that Sylvia was all but convinced he was putting her on.

"Max, I'm serious. We don't even have to do the story. I can just can it right now."

He ignored her. "Go buy the tools of your trade," he retorted, waving her out of the car.

Standing in line at the checkout counter, Sylvia was so rattled that she felt her hands trembling. What was he up to? Then, returning to the parking lot, she saw that her Nova had disappeared.

"Damn it!" she cried out, frantically searching the parking lot.

A horn blared behind her. It was Max, braking the Nova sharply two feet from where she stood. He leaned out the driver's window. "A good reporter has to stay on her toes!"

Unamused, Sylvia climbed in.

"Just checking your brakes. We may need them."

As Max continued south, she wondered where they were going, but decided not to ask.

Max snapped on the overhead car light. "You'll have to see what you're writing. Now, to answer your leading question of the other day. No," he said briskly, without emotion, "it is not necessary to syndicate Ridgway Farm. Other measures could be taken to keep the farm in our hands." He drummed his fingers on the steering wheel. "As you may infer, my father and I have rather divergent views on the matter."

"What measures?" Sylvia said, scribbling, playing the role he apparently desired her to play.

"We're in debt, of course. Up to our ears—thanks to a few royal snafus, my own included. Ridgway the Elder believes that the only way to extricate ourselves is through syndication. He thinks there's little chance that things will improve; more than that, the money crunch is so bad that we can't afford to wait any longer, says he. Ridgway the Younger, in his infinite—some might say hopelessly optimistic—wisdom, believes that by taking a chance or two, our star might rise again."

Sylvia looked up from her notebook. "This is all very

interesting. But why do you suddenly want to see this in print?''

"Draw your own conclusions," he said mysteriously.

There was only one conclusion to draw, Sylvia realized. Just as his father was trying to use her story to help put his syndication together, Max had decided to use it to sabotage Colin Ridgway's plans. It was a strange feeling to be caught in what appeared to be a power struggle between father and son; it was strange, too, to feel "used," the very word Max had invoked against her the other day. She wasn't sure how much she liked the feeling.

"Time's up," Max said. "Figured it out?"

"I guess you're not the only one feeling used."

"You are?" he retorted. "Seems to me this is a pretty juicy piece of meat for a newshound like you."

Sylvia was silent. It was true, what he said; but to hear him say it, to know they both had entered this new adult round in their relationship with ulterior motives, made her suddenly feel despondent.

"I figure if Dad's going public to hock his wares, I deserve to get my licks in, put across my point of view." He turned to her, eyes gleaming. "All in the family, right?"

In a flash, she saw through his bravura to what she felt sure was his deepest motive. "You must love your farm a great deal."

His silence flooded the car, a silence so intense it seemed to beat at the walls that enclosed them in their intimate space. Sylvia knew she had scored a direct hit.

Then, making light of it, he said, "It's not the farm, but some kind of hormonal imbalance. Why do you think I liked bashing heads on a football field? I'm always looking for any excuse for a good fight."

"If you say so."

Max turned at the wheel, annoyed that she didn't believe him, and snapped, "Aren't you going to ask me any more questions?"

Sylvia could feel herself struggling. It wasn't only about Max's decision to go public, using her as his conduit; it was also her recognition of the emotional harm this story might do to him. It was possible that in his passion for the farm, he was blind to the damage the story might do to his father, to the Ridgway name, to himself.

As if reading her mind, he said, "The truth's going to hurt some of us. If you don't want it, I'll turn around right now and take you back to town." He slowed down sharply, as if to make good on his claim.

The truth. Wasn't that what she was here for? Wasn't that what all reporters spent their careers in search of?

Sylvia got her story. As they continued south, then veered west onto Route 50, Max told her in a strikingly dispassionate tone how one misfortune after another had put the Ridgway fat in the fire. During the boom years of the late seventies to the mid-eighties, Max explained, the farm had been on a "sleigh ride" in which sales had increased thirty to thirty-five percent each year. Colin Ridgway, until then a cautious businessman, had inhaled the giddy atmosphere of the time and begun doing reckless things. He'd started buying expensive shares in syndicated stallions and mares, "glamour horses," Max called them, intending either to resell at great profit, or garner huge payoffs by breeding or racing them. For the first time in his life, with a number of banks courting him, Colin, like many of his peers, had borrowed large sums of money. Unfortunately, a critical number of those horses had not panned out. Too many $400,000 mares had $20,000 yearlings; too many million-dollar stallions lost too many races. The value of many of Colin's investments dropped precipitously. By the mid to late eighties, when the market for horses declined generally and breeders were having trouble finding buyers at any price, banks were calling in loans and alarming numbers of Colin's fellow horse breeders were going belly-up. But despite his losses, Colin—with an infusion of youthful energy from Max—hung on.

Hung on, Max said, until the divorce. The settlement with Betsy had forced Colin to sell more than half of his two hundred horses, among them some of his best racehorses and brood mares. He'd even sold off a portion of the farm, almost a hundred of his five hundred acres, to a real-estate developer. Known throughout the conservative old guard of the horse country as one of its most honorable men, Colin had tarnished his reputation by divorcing Betsy. The divorce, which he'd instigated, had created a major scandal. Not only had Colin been ostracized by many of his old friends, but he had damaged his business, heretofore predicated on integrity. Whether from moral disapproval or from the suspicion that a man who would leave his wife of thirty-five years could not be trusted to sell good horses, many of the old buyers no longer appeared.

The divorce was, Colin Ridgway had admitted to his son, "the biggest financial and personal mistake of my life."

Writing down the last of this, Sylvia wondered whether she should ask Max why his father had divorced his mother. But he was already on to a big mistake of his own.

Less than a year after he'd returned to the farm from the Fincastle staff job, Max—who by then owned a half-interest in the Ridgway mares—went against his father's judgment and insisted on selling a prize filly, undefeated and with record times in its races, to three New York buyers who had part interest in a Virginia horse farm. They were the kind of people, Colin had said, "who saw a story in the *Wall Street Journal* about how much money you can make with horses, and that's the most they ever knew about a horse." To Max, however, the deal had looked good: their million-dollar offer was dramatically higher than any bid they'd ever received; and, after thorough scrutiny, it appeared that they were good for the money, which was to be disbursed with a down payment of $100,000, followed by regular installments.

But the sale had been a disaster. All the Ridgways ever received was the down payment. Soon afterward, according to the veterinarian, the filly had caught what was probably a treatable disease, was neglected, and eventually died. Claiming they'd bought damaged goods, the owners refused to pay the $900,000 balance. Before the Ridgways could force payment, the farm owned by the New Yorkers had gone bankrupt and they successfully dodged their obligations through a series of slick financial maneuvers that Max was too disgusted to detail.

"Not very pretty," Sylvia agreed, grimly picturing what Max's self-critical story would look like in cold newsprint.

Yet there was something terribly bracing about these revelations—a blow for the truth, bad as it was, that seemed to electrify them both. Max was worked up now, his powerful upper body hunched over the wheel of the undersized car like some fighter pilot trying to land a smoking plane. Except for the divorce, he appeared to be sparing no details, and Sylvia wondered whether this was cathartic for him. She felt strangely honored, sharing these intimacies in the darkness of the hurtling car with him, and sensed that together they were reaching some new plateau, forming new bonds in place of those that had been destroyed.

So focused had she been on the interview, only now did Sylvia notice that they were entering the toney streets of Middleburg, one of the few places in rural Virginia, as Max had once noted, with chandeliers in the Safeway. Along Washington Street were gift shops, pubs, tack shops, and antique stores sporting names like "Thoroughbreds" and "High Horse."

Max braked at the one traffic light in town, alongside the famous Red Fox Inn, where Nancy Reagan had complained bitterly about Donald Regan to George Will, where the likes of Jackie Onassis, Paul Mellon, and Bertram Firestone could regularly be seen. "Gotten so damn congested they had to put a stoplight in," Max muttered.

When the light turned, he shot forward, wheeling west out of town in the direction, she knew, of the farm. It seemed as if the farm were towing him toward it like a riptide. A brilliant moon sailed out from under a cloud, and Sylvia watched the rolling landscape rise to meet them and rush past on both sides. She felt displaced, disquieted, yet strangely excited, the shadows of the huge, bare trees that lined the highway strobing eerily across the windshield.

Short of Upperville, Max made the familiar turn, climbed the narrow paved road to the crest of the hill and the "Ridgway Breeding Farm" sign she had seen in broad daylight only last week. Now, the whole place, so familiar as she came onto it then, looked hauntingly different. Was the difference because of what she'd learned about tonight? Was it Max's brooding force, casting a giant shadow down the lane with its twin columns of oak trees, like giant soldiers at attention? Or was it merely a trick of the moon, shedding its cold and spectral light on what had once had so much life, so much color and warmth?

Max turned off the headlights and drove slowly, in first gear, up the lane.

In the tall house, one amber light burned in an upstairs window. It was Max's father, Sylvia realized. She felt his presence, and wondered how it felt to be divorced and alone in such a large old house with Christmas coming. Beyond the house, beyond the silhouettes of the old brick springhouse, beyond the barn, the sheds, the labyrinthine stables, was the ancient swell of the Blue Ridge, mystical in the moonlight, like a pale, frozen wave. This was a place, Sylvia thought, where the past flowed into the present, where the echoes of previous generations, on a night like this, could still be heard in the deep country silence.

Sylvia glanced at Max, studying him for a moment. He was heir to all this, the strong, sensitive boy who had come into manhood here. Now, alert as a hawk and swinging the car past the house toward the stables, he was stealing back home as if he didn't belong.

"Let's go," he said, killing the engine. "Quiet with the door."

Sylvia shut hers softly, feeling the chill of the outdoors invade her jacket. Max beckoned, moving swiftly across the frozen earth toward the stables. She followed.

They stepped out of the moonlight into an enveloping shadow, the ripe odor of manure and the sweet smell of hay so familiar to Sylvia. A horse whinnied in the dark. Max stood without speaking, his face dark, inhaling the air of the stables and breathing it back out in frosty jets. Sylvia remembered their times together here, Max proudly showing her the horses, the two of them feeding and stroking them, taking rides across the fields and through the woods. It was Max who had first taught her, an awkward, half-frightened suburban college kid, to ride, and Max who'd kissed her in the leafy autumn woods, pulling her tight against his chest, smelling of leather and soap and sweet masculine sweat.

Suddenly his voice, low and commanding, rang out in the frosty air. "Now I've told you what I'm going to say on the record. What's here is strictly under wraps. From here on out, it's all between you, me, and our dark friends here."

"Why are you showing me this?" she asked.

"For old times' sake," he said quietly. "There's a line from Roethke: 'I knew a woman, lovely in her bones. . . .' This is for what sinks in to those lovely bones of yours."

Then he strode away, slicing rapidly through the darkness. Sylvia could feel goose bumps prickling her skin—whether from the night air or this moment with Max, just passed, this magical Max of old, she didn't know. Her eyes had adjusted to the dark, and she saw him, deep inside the stables, halt beside a stall and reach his hand inside. She followed him, aware of the many empty stalls and, too, of the black, breathing bulks on both sides.

"Double Reverse," Max said when Sylvia came beside him, "meet Sylvia K. Loring."

"Just Sylvia," she corrected. Inside the stall, a huge dark shape pressed its long head against Max's outstretched hand. Sylvia extended her hand, and the head turned slightly, nuzzling its sleek, satiny hide against Sylvia's cold fingers.

"Hello, sweetie," Sylvia whispered, seeing the shine of its eye. "Double Reverse, where did you get that name?"

"Tell her," Max instructed the horse. "From Max's stupid football games. 'Double reverse' is a trick play in football. A real game-winner, like this beauty here."

"I guess he's stuck with it, then."

"She," Max corrected. "The finest mare we have. How many races have you won, girl? She's won some biggies in her time. Had some pretty good foals, too. She's good. She'd better be. The future of Ridgway Farm may well be riding on this gal."

"Why?"

"She's with foal," Max said. "Two months away. Aren't you, girl?" As Max vigorously stroked, Double Reverse pressed against him, eating it up. "Nine months ago, she was bred with the best stallion season we could buy. Money and hope, I should say. When this girl drops her foal, we may just be looking at a future Derby winner."

"You'll sell the foal?" Sylvia said in alarm.

"Got to. Got to get this place back on its legs."

Sylvia gazed at the horse. "You mean one foal could bring enough money to prevent you from having to syndicate?"

"It's a shot," Max said. "Not our only shot, but maybe our best one. If we play our cards right, with her bloodlines we could be talking a million and a half here. Maybe more."

Sylvia whistled in the darkness. "I don't understand. Why isn't your dad with you on this?"

"Doesn't want to take the chance. Anything could happen. She could lose the foal. She could birth one that doesn't impress. She could have a flawless little foal and the buyers might not materialize. The Japanese aren't spending big bucks on horses these days. The Arabs have gone back to breeding their own. It's a risky little game you have to play. Meanwhile, the creditors are breathing down our necks. And the expense of running this place . . . you wouldn't believe it. Besides," he added ironically, "after what happened with that filly, he's got doubts about my judgment."

"So Colin says, 'Let's syndicate.' "

"Horse farms are up for sale all over. Virginia. Kentucky. Maryland. Florida. You've got to have nerve to keep your own place. You've got to have an appetite for taking risks. It comes with the turf." Max paused, and his voice changed its pitch. "Dad's lost heart. The divorce has just about put him in the ground."

"Max," Sylvia said. A moment passed. "What happened?"

His answer took him forever, and when it came it brought all the darkness with it, wrapping his voice in a chilling shade Sylvia had never heard in him before. "He'd been cheating on Mom for twenty years."

"Oh, Max. Betsy knew?"

"She found out." A half minute passed. A horse whinnied.

''She didn't want the divorce. He wanted it because he felt he could no longer live with her knowing.'' A few beats more. ''He paid a very high price.''

Sylvia looked at him in sympathetic silence. Whenever she had thought about Max Ridgway—from the very first at UVA and all during the years when she hadn't seen him—she thought of him as having it all: the ideal family, loving parents, an adoring older sister. He had brains, looks, drive, and money. He was the perfect one, and she was the one who didn't fit in, who needed adjustment. But now for the first time she saw that his struggle had been every bit as tough as her own.

''Are you angry?'' she asked finally.

''I try not to be,'' he said. ''But I am, too much of the time.''

Sylvia glanced out of the stables, through the square of moonlight toward the house as if Colin himself would appear suddenly. ''Max . . .'' The spark of doubt she'd had earlier suddenly ignited in her now. Her voice was a half-whisper. ''Maybe I shouldn't do this story.''

''It's a good story.''

''Yes.''

''Then do it.''

At that moment, Sylvia knew that she would.

# CHAPTER
## 22

As Sylvia and Max drove back to Washington late that night, it seemed to Sylvia that they could easily fall into their old roles, picking up where they'd left off five and a half years before. The intimacy of truth had brought them together again, had turned back the clock.

But then, at the door of his apartment building, the intimacy seemed suddenly to vanish. He stepped out of her Nova lightly and surrendered the car keys without a hint of regret. No suggestion of a kiss followed, no inkling of any personal interest. He was again remote as a stranger.

Max looked at his watch, glanced up at the windows to his apartment, and said, businesslike, "So when do you expect the story to appear?"

It was the question she was asked most often, asked by almost everyone whom she interviewed. Rare was the person who would simply grant an interview and deliver it into her hands, unfettered by interest in the resulting publicity. Every third person asked if she would read the story back over the phone—"just so you'll get it right"—a request that never failed to diminish her impression of the requestee. never failed to sting for the implicit no-confidence vote in her abilities.

This line of questioning always brought home the naked reality of the exchange between journalist and subject. After every quip, every half-truth, every perception had been uttered, after the interview subject had done his job, sidestepping her questions here, owning up to the truth there, now it was up to her to do hers. And that was always the most important thing between them. The story.

She had never expected it to come to this with Max Ridgway. But here it was, as cold and apparent as his involvement with Nicole.

"I don't know, but I'll try to let you know when I find out," she said. And then, to protect herself from exposing the blow that was spreading like a tremor to every part of her body, she added, "If I forget, I'll save you a copy of the paper."

It was eleven o'clock at night when Max left her, but Sylvia was too hopped up to go home and sleep. Unless it were a real emergency, she had no business calling Pam at this hour and risk waking Jesse. Her mother was out of the question —Jan Loring was simply incapable of being a confidante, of following her line of thinking. If she hadn't learned that lesson about her mother after their blowup in Cleveland, she never would.

There was no one to talk to and nothing else to do, Sylvia thought as she found herself driving through the dark, deserted streets of Washington like a homing pigeon toward the *Washington Tribune*. She had embarked upon this Ridgway Farm story for the most selfish of motives: to purge herself of Max Ridgway. But the net result had been just the opposite. He seemed to have taken possession of her.

Ever since she'd seen him at the Redskins game, she had been unable to concentrate on anything else. She'd spent hours analyzing the nuance of their encounters, trying to figure out where he stood, who the man was now.

And up to now, she had been able to sell herself on the most favorable explanation for his standoffish behavior: he still loved her but had been so shattered by her rejection of him, he dared not let his feelings out again. She'd half convinced herself of this, and the thought had given her courage—and power.

But tonight, when Max got out of her car, something was different. What was it? Not impatience exactly, but he'd seemed distracted, spent. His mind was not on her. His mind was somewhere else. On someone else.

She had stuck out her own neck about as far as she could, appearing at his door with apologies, offering outright to scrap the story. How much more direct could she get? No, it was clear: her plan had backfired. She'd used her position to get back in touch with him, and he'd taken her offer at face value. He'd decided he wanted the story for his own reasons, and that was all he wanted. Only a fool could read signs of love into their parting. And that was one thing Sylvia Loring had long ago vowed never to be.

Setting up shop at a computer terminal, Sylvia spread her notes out around her. If all she was to Max was a reporter he knew, once quite intimately, once loved, at least she owed him one hell of a story.

Once she got it going, Sylvia banged out a biting, truthful story about the problems faced by an old Virginia horse farm and family trying to cope with the economic realities of horse-breeding in the nineties. The piece was not for tomorrow, not scheduled to run till the following week. But Sylvia wanted to finish a draft tonight, while she was so obsessed. She stayed at work till six in the morning, straining, pushing, groping for the reality of life at Ridgway Horse Farm. She tried to imagine, conjecture, fit together the pieces of Max's conflict with Colin and how their situation stood within the larger context of changes in the industry.

On a pad of paper, she jotted down names of people to call to further bolster her story: the president of Saratoga Horse Sales for statistics about yearling sales generally, the man behind Virginia's pari-mutuel betting operation, which was passed as a referendum by the state's voters in 1988 after years of unsuccessful tries. It was ironic, but she could already feel it. This story would be the best of its kind, because it was about feelings, real feelings that she'd almost been able to touch.

In her effort to get the story out, she had distracted herself from what she'd have to face on her drive home: the knowledge that Max was lost to her, that she must move on. But even with the pain, the pain of feeling for the first time the finality of their separation, she knew it was for the good. When you drop someone, she thought, you always think deep in your heart that he is still there waiting for you—even after years apart, even in the face of conclusive evidence to the contrary. But now, having seen him and spent time with him, no more could she nurture this illusion.

It was the Friday before Christmas when Sylvia's big story, "Hard Times in Horse Country," appeared on the front page of the Style section, surrounded by enormous photos of the farm. Even a shot of Double Reverse grazing in pasture was included. Max had gone out to the farm to meet the photographer and appear in the spread.

The many compliments she received on the story renewed Sylvia's feeling of confidence in her profession, that she was once again a force to be reckoned with at the *Tribune*.

The weekend came and went, and there was no word from Max about the story. Sylvia told herself this was to be expected, that his behavior when they parted had been a harbinger of his silence. Still, she had to admit disappointment, even moments of anger, that he had not called in appreciation of her work. That would have been the polite thing to do. She read the story over several times, trying to see it from his eyes. Perhaps it had been harsher than he'd anticipated. Perhaps he'd expected her to airbrush reality in places. She even considered the possibility that she'd unconsciously done a hatchet job on the family. But no, that wasn't it. The piece was solid. She'd bent over backward to be sure of that, being especially careful when treading on sensitive territory, such as the divorce.

Christmas came and mercifully passed. With Nana gone and her mother's cheer forced, it had seemed as if Sylvia were just going through the motions. But, on New Year's Eve, there was a bounce in Sylvia's step as, holding B. D.'s hand, she entered Elect Fincastle Headquarters, across the Potomac from the capital, determined to enter into the spirit of change. Max was lost to her; she'd let that part of life pass her by. She was older and wiser now, and damned if she was going to let any more of it fall through time's sieve without taking hold.

Necks craned to catch a glimpse of the celebrated B. D. and his date.

Sylvia had seen surprisingly little of B. D. lately. He'd been out on the campaign trail most of the time, calling regularly to check in with her, apologetic about his absence. Several times on the phone, though, he'd promised a romantic evening she'd never forget. Looking out over the jam-packed headquarters floor, it seemed to Sylvia that tonight might just be that night.

She wanted so much to believe him, and had convinced herself that B. D. was just the right man for her. B. D. was even better suited to her than Max, she insisted; they had similar backgrounds, both having arrived in Washington with no advantages—social or financial.

Sylvia had also come to see that a man can't be perfect, or perfectly in tune with your needs. You had to work with him. She had lost Max because she had seen things in absolute terms. She'd believed when he'd made his play for her that she had to be ready just then. Since she wasn't, she'd discarded the whole ball of wax. Which had been a foolish mistake.

B. D. was pumping flesh as if he were the candidate himself. Sylvia had to admit a certain excitement, being on such close terms with the new ruling powers. Everyone was here, drinking, dancing, and ringing in the election year of 1992 with a giddy confidence that Ben Fincastle, before the New Year's end, would beat the unpopular incumbent and become the President-elect.

"Hello, Mike," B. D. said with a handshake, introducing Sylvia to *Post* reporter Michael Paradyne. Just then, B. D. spotted someone across the room, leaving Sylvia alone with a man whose byline she knew well.

"Are you enjoying the party?" she began, then noticed his attention was elsewhere. Colette Daniels, strikingly dressed, was several yards away from them, obviously seething.

It had been three weeks now since Colette had seen, touched, or tasted Ben Fincastle. Ten times every day, she had stopped herself from calling him. He had instructed her never to call; he would be the one to make contact. Now she would corner him and find out what was wrong. Something had happened. Someone had gotten to him. Judy. Or maybe it was B. D.; maybe he'd found out and persuaded Ben the risk was too great.

There he was in a crowd, his hand gently steering Judy at the small of her back. Resplendent in a velvety mauve dress, gathered at the waist, and matching low-cut silk jacket streaked with festive colors, Colette planted herself in front of the couple and reached for the senator's hand.

"Senator," she said without acknowledging Judy. "I need a moment with you alone."

Colette couldn't believe what she was hearing. Without a hitch in his expression, Ben delivered a vacuous line, as if to some nobody voter out on the hustings. "On behalf of Judy and myself, we wish you the happiest of New Years."

Incredulously, Colette watched him move on to the next handshake, Judy at his side. Michael and Sylvia, the two reporters, stood together watching the scene.

"You're a *Trib* person," Michael started, with just a trace of condescension in his voice. "You must know Colette Daniels pretty well. What's she really like?"

It was peculiar. Despite all her problems with the *Tribune*, with Hale Gardiner and Colette Daniels, Sylvia felt a fundamental loyalty to the paper, and wasn't about to help out the competition. Sylvia said nothing.

"How long have you been working there?" Michael asked. Sylvia knew his technique. You start with an innocent question, to warm things up, to get someone talking about herself, then use that information to dig deeper.

"Ever since college," she said. Then, before he could slip in a follow-up question, she turned the tables on him. "How long've you been at the *Post*?"

"Two and a half years," he said. "Was Colette there when you started?"

"We started together."

"So you know her pretty well."

"That's fair to say," she said, looking around for an escape hatch.

"Do you think she's sleeping with Fincastle?"

Sylvia didn't feel like being cagey, so she just came out with it. "Why should I tell you?"

"I'm somebody you should get in good with," Michael said. A soapy smile crossed his face, as if to pass his remark off as a joke.

B. D. returned. "You two must have a lot in common," he said, whisking Sylvia away. She glanced back at the *Post* reporter and noticed that he was jotting something in a notebook, the same smile still on his face.

Sporting festive holly-green suspenders with his tuxedo, Ben greeted B. D. "So this is the famous Sylvia K. Loring?" Ben said. "I read your story just the other day about my staffer, Max Ridgway."

"You did?" Sylvia replied, pleased and surprised.

"B. D," Ben said, "may I have the pleasure of a dance with Sylvia?"

"Just bring her back before midnight, will you? I want to start the New Year right."

As Ben reached for her arm, she spoke to Ben and B. D. at once. "Wait. How about asking me?"

Judy smiled at Sylvia's rightful indignation.

But B. D. looked chagrined. "Touchy, touchy. She gets this way sometimes. . . ."

Brushing B. D. aside, Ben made a gallant show and half bowed, asking Sylvia directly for this dance.

B. D. took Judy to the dance floor as Ben led Sylvia. They danced to an old Guy Lombardo–style tune, played by a live band.

"That story of yours was really something," Ben said.

"Thank you. I'm amazed you had time to read it."

"I was curious about Max. You certainly captured the fighting spirit of that young man."

"Did Max mention it to you?"

"Not to me." A knowing gleam sparkled in Ben's eye. "B. D. tells me you once knew Max rather well."

Sylvia was caught off guard. "True," she said lamely.

"As a matter of fact, Max is here tonight." Ben gave her a twirl, then nodded toward the center of the crowded dance floor. The man loved a good soap opera, that much was clear. "There he is now." Ben smiled wryly. "Likes them young, doesn't he?"

A knot gripped her stomach as she took in Max and Nicole. Max was a sensational dancer, gliding effortlessly across the floor, his supple athlete's body not in the least obscured by his tuxedo. He whirled Nicole, her curvy body emphasized by a low-cut dress and the pouty suggestion of sexual heat. Sylvia glanced away quickly.

"Yes," Ben replied admiringly. "He's a dynamo, isn't he? Going to raise a hell of a lot of money for us."

The senator and Sylvia finished their dance. As the emcee called "Ten minutes till midnight," Ben squired Judy to the center of the floor, with B. D. and Sylvia in tow. In a simple but elegant black crepe dress, Judy was aglow in the arms of the senator. Sylvia had never seen her look so radiant. With flashbulbs popping, there seemed to be no one else in the world for Ben but his wife.

Suddenly, Colette swept into orbit behind Judy. As Sylvia watched in disbelief, she tagged Judy on the shoulder to take a turn with the senator.

To the astonished Judy, Colette winked and said, "Just a whirl with the hubby, darlin'!" Her nerve was astonishing.

Heads turned. Surely, as the cameras recorded his every move, the senator would not indulge this voluptuous young woman. But, catching Judy's eye, Ben shrugged, as if powerless to control this boldness. As he took Colette into his arms, it seemed to Sylvia that he could not resist her.

"What the hell is he doing?" B. D. muttered. B. D. steered them closer to the senator, as if wanting to physically block his man from the harsh judgment of the cameras. Just inches away from the candidate, Sylvia heard Colette's breathless whisper: "Tuesday at my place. Eight o'clock."

Ben's face was a mask.

Wouldn't Paradyne like to have heard that, Sylvia thought as she watched the scene play itself out.

Squeezing the senator's hand, Colette lanced him with her eyes. Then she turned to Judy, who was still hovering awkwardly nearby. "Thank you," said Colette with a knowing smile. With that, she disappeared into the swell of partygoers.

It was almost midnight. With B. D. at her side, Sylvia glanced around the makeshift ballroom for Max. The thought of his ringing in the New Year with Nicole was enough to ruin her evening, but she'd been prepared for this. She wasn't going to let it get to her. The moment came. Horns blared, balloons swirled toward the ceiling, champagne flowed, couples kissed.

Ben seized the photo opportunity and kissed Judy.

B. D. drew Sylvia close and planted a passionate kiss on her lips.

"To B. D. and Sylvia in 'ninety-two!" he toasted, taking a swig from the bubbly.

The band struck up "Auld Lang Syne" and they joined

the mob on the dance floor. It was not until she almost bumped into him that Sylvia realized she was dancing next to Max.

"Happy New Year," he said.

She looked at him, aware that B. D.'s eyes were taking in everything. "Max," she said, her heart thudding madly as if it were about to fly from her chest. She stared at him, wondering if he could still read her mind, wondering if he even tried anymore.

But Max wasn't watching her. "Hello again, B. D.," he said. "See you tomorrow, huh?"

"Right," B. D. said. "Work to do."

"Until we meet again, then," Max said, speaking to B. D., but raking his eyes across Sylvia's as he swirled away with Nicole into the enveloping crowd.

This will be wonderful. This will be just right, Sylvia said to herself again and again as she settled into B. D.'s leather couch at four that morning. The highs and lows of the party, the tangle of conflicting emotions combined with glass after glass of champagne made her head a whirlpool, void of clarity.

B. D. stepped toward her and took her hand. "Come on babe."

The moment had arrived. And she would go through with it, just as she hammered out a story she didn't want to write. She was a trooper who did her job. But wait, Sylvia thought, suddenly picturing herself in B. D.'s bed, suddenly picturing their lovemaking that evoked no sensation. This wasn't an assignment. This wasn't work, or a task to be completed. And if that's how she felt, she just couldn't go through with it, no matter how fickle she might appear.

The moment had arrived, but she hadn't. Her heart was holding out on her.

Even he could see something had changed. "What's wrong?"

"Nothing," she said.

"Tell me."

All right, she told herself. If this is going to work, I've got to let him in on my thoughts, whatever they are.

"I don't like the way Ben asked you to dance with me."

"What?" B. D. said, apparently not remembering. "Oh, that, that's nothing. Nothing. He liked you."

"I'm saying that, on principle, he should have asked me for the dance. Or you should have suggested he ask me instead of telling him I'm touchy."

B. D. appeared totally lost. "It's not important," he said, putting his arm around her.

"It is to me," Sylvia said, breaking free of his grasp.

B. D. squared up, suddenly seeing she was serious. "Loosen up," he said.

"Don't you see? You're setting the terms here. You're deciding what's important."

"You're too uptight," he said, losing his patience. "That's your problem."

Sylvia looked at him hard, seeing as if for the first time the essence of her relationship with B. D.: she was trying to force something that wasn't there. She stood, gathering her coat from the couch. "Don't tell me about my problems without first looking at a few of your own."

"Like what?" he snapped furiously.

"Like your ego." She was at the door now, making her getaway.

# CHAPTER
## 23

Colette sat at her desk one February afternoon in quite a tizzy. Now the heat was on. What to do about the story? Really, it wasn't her fault: Sylvia's single source had dried up, and her own contacts—old reliables on the social circuit—if they knew anything weren't talking.

January had passed too quickly, its winter chill thawed by

the renewal of her bedroom fires with Ben. She'd made good her New Year's Eve promise to herself and snared him again. Judy would never be the wiser, and they'd been so careful not to be caught. Ben always came to her apartment at different times—once at six in the morning! And he parked his car in different spots around Georgetown, always at least three blocks from her place, always arriving at her door in sunglasses, like some Hollywood stud.

Conjuring up their rendezvous tonight had made her vanquish all worry about the story, and Colette had left the *Trib* in a delicious state of anticipation.

Eight hours later, at quarter till eleven, Colette was fuming. Ben had been due at eight. True, he'd been campaigning in Iowa earlier in the day for the upcoming February caucuses. But he'd been scheduled to arrive in the city late that afternoon. If his plans had changed in Iowa, the least he could have done was called. Ditto if he'd somehow got hung up at home with Judy. Now it was almost too late. Daring as he was, Ben wasn't about to spend the night with Colette unless he had a solid alibi.

The doorbell rang. It was Ben. It was also B. D. Cole, barging in right behind him. They'd been drinking and were as giddy as boys out of school; she could smell the whiskey on them both.

"Damn it, Ben," she said. B. D. knew about their affair—he was the only one Ben had told—so she didn't have to keep up any pretense around him.

Ben kissed her on the mouth, then strode to the liquor cabinet, B. D. trailing behind. Ben poured two glasses of whiskey and waved the bottle at Colette. "Join us?"

Colette did not reply.

"We knocked 'em dead in Des Moines!" Ben exulted. "They're eating out of our hands." He plopped down on the couch with his drink. "We got the corn vote, the hog vote, the cow vote—we got every raggedy-assed farmer in Iowa in our corner!"

B. D. joined in, perching his bottom on the armrest of the couch. "Tison's practically waving the white flag; he's down by twenty percent."

"Do you think he's going to get out early, or slug it out till the bitter end?" Ben asked B. D.

"He probably wants veep, so he might stick around, collect some delegates, on the assumption that . . ."

Ben roared out with anticipation of his first act as nominee designate. "I'd sooner name Jesse Helms!"

Colette wasn't amused. There was nothing she liked less than coming in second—in this case a distant second—to the campaign. For just an instant, it crossed her mind that Judy might have a case against Ben. On top of that, these two adolescent drinking buddies, lacking only the pimples, had been out on the town celebrating their triumph.

She looked B. D. square in the eye. The man's attitude toward her was no longer one of friendship. Now a guarded, suspicious edge had risen up in him. "Who invited you?"

B. D. turned abruptly to his boss. "I want to hear you say it."

Ben smiled lamely. His lips parted momentarily, then closed again.

"Say what, Ben?" Colette demanded.

Ben turned to B. D. with a strange, almost pleading look. "Do it, Ben. Get it over with."

Still, Ben's words didn't come.

"Look, if we have business to discuss," Colette said, "I'm not doing it with this jackass here."

"Ben," B. D. commanded, throwing Colette a withering glance. "We made a deal."

"Oh, I get it," Colette said slowly. She gripped Ben in an icy stare. "Who's running the show here?"

"Okay!" Ben snapped, wheeling on B. D. "Out of here, sucker!"

B. D.'s voice was shrill. "So what are you doing, Ben? Spending the night?"

Ben exhaled. "The lady's right. I've got to do this alone."

"Smart. Real smart," B. D. said acidly. "You're gonna tell her you have to break this off, then she's gonna eat you alive."

Ben's arm jerked toward the door. "Out!" he shouted.

Picking up his coat, B. D. stormed into the hallway. "I'm no Judy, Ben. Don't think I'm going down with the goddamn ship."

The door shut heavily behind him. Ben and Colette listened to the footsteps retreating down the stairs.

"He's right, Colette," Ben said miserably.

Colette saw his expression. For the first time, she could feel how difficult it was to be Ben Fincastle.

She came to him slowly, running her palm up his forehead until her fingers reached into the dark thickness of his hair.

"Darling," she said gently, and Ben slipped into her arms and they fell together on the couch.

Ben was quiet at first. Then, "He's brilliant, you know," he began. "He reminds me of Billy. Even now, probably the most important person in my life." He was silent, his mind seemingly far away, deep in the hills of North Carolina. "I'd give my right arm to have him back."

Once before, Colette remembered, and in this same faraway tone, Ben had mentioned Billy. A rich kid—the son of the owner of the factory where's Ben's father had been a shop foreman.

"What happened to him?" Colette said.

After a time, Ben said, "He died."

"How?" Colette said.

A longer time passed and, puzzled, Colette turned and gazed into Ben's eyes.

"In a car wreck," he said at last in a plaintive tone Colette had never heard in him before. He drew the words out slowly, as if picturing the wreck in his mind.

Once outside, B. D. kicked a discarded pop can so violently that it made a loud, tinny racket careening down the street. God dammit, he thought to himself. The man is on a destruction course because he won't listen to me. Charisma, political street smarts, the best consultant in the business—Ben had everything going for him. But if recent history had taught national politicians one thing, it was that the public would not tolerate philandering. It was impossible for B. D. to dismiss the idea that this damned self-indulgence, this vain weakness for female flesh, could be the very thing to bring him down.

Searching the street for his car, B. D. thought of the sacrifices he'd made for the man. In the beginning working for no fee, helping carve and craft his campaign, the hours, the weeks, the months of work. And now Ben was free to blow it all if he chose to. It just wasn't right. A man's political career didn't belong only to him. It belonged to everyone who had invested in him. And, of all those people, B. D. had sunk in more of himself than had anyone else.

As he drew his key out from his wallet, his eye caught on something flickering inside a sedan two cars down. A moving light. And a man sitting inside. Instantly, he recognized the occupant. It was that sneaking, sniveling son of a bitch, Michael Paradyne of the *Washington Post*. Staking out Colette's apartment, like some two-bit hack for the *National Inquirer*.

Wheels raced inside B. D.'s head. So as not to arouse Paradyne's suspicion, he would go ahead and crank up his car. He would drive the short distance to Colette's building, double-park in front of it, then collect Ben and something from her apartment, like a punch bowl or box that would cover them in case Paradyne inquired what they were doing there.

Some piece of work, Paradyne. But then, B. D. wasn't really astonished. Paradyne had kept his distance from him, accepting what B. D. could give him, then wrapping himself in the sacred flag of a journalist, acting as though he owed nothing at all in return. From now on, this prune was on the shit list. And damned if B. D. was going to keep covering for Ben Fincastle's ass.

# CHAPTER
## 24

"You probably don't remember me, Sylvia," came a stranger's voice on the other end of the telephone line. You're right, Sylvia thought to herself before the caller identified herself as Kokoh's roommate, Shana.

Shana had gotten Sylvia's answering-machine messages, she said. She was calling because something was amiss. Sylvia quizzed her on this point and that, extracting as much information as she could before the inevitable turnover to Colette Daniels, who, sad to say, was there at work, putting in more hours lately than anyone could remember her doing in years.

Yes, Shana was still living at the same place, and no, she wouldn't give her last name, "not now, anyways." Kokoh had disappeared that afternoon after the story about Bob Rossen came out, Shana blurted out, and she'd intended to keep her mouth shut except that she was starting to worry that something awful had happened.

"Please deposit fifty-five cents for the next three minutes," the operator's stentorian voice interrupted. "Fifty-five cents, please."

Sylvia quickly jotted down Shana's pay-phone number and dialed back.

No one had heard a word from Kokoh, Shana continued, and she knew that Kokoh wouldn't just run off and leave all her clothes and her modeling portfolio, especially since she'd just forked over $189 on a leather case for it. "Kokoh was too into money to do something like that."

It seemed that Shana had had words with the managers of the escort service today, and that when, in anger, she brought up Kokoh's name—saying "Am I the next one to go, after Kokoh King?"—somebody had slapped her like an unruly child. They'd told her never to mention "that name" again. "I know I'm breaking the law," continued Shana, "but taking money from men for sex and taking somebody's life are two different things."

Even though it was no longer her story, Sylvia jotted down the substantive points, scrawling her notes over an assortment of sheets and pillowcases advertised in a white sale ad in the *Post*. It was always the case: when your most important calls came, there was never a notebook handy, not even scratch paper.

"You think they might have killed her?" Sylvia asked, incredulous, and with that, Sylvia saw Colette across the room cock her head and seem to listen in. Reporters have some kind of sixth sense, Sylvia thought, especially when you're treading on their turf. Colette seemed to know, could tell probably from her own excitement, that Hookergate was at issue here.

"I'm not saying that," said Shana. "Maybe she got hit by a car. It's just that they never told us. They owe us that much. I wondered if you could help us find Kokoh."

Reluctantly, Sylvia explained that Shana would have to talk with Colette Daniels, who was now the reporter on the story. She hoped that Shana would not know that Sylvia had violated newspaper etiquette by grilling a source for a story that she had no license to write. Especially when the reporter was sitting right there, giving you the evil eye.

"Look, I don't have all day," Shana protested. "You want me to talk to someone I don't even know?"

Shana was begging for reassurance. Although Sylvia's own regard for Colette was not high, the story was too important to betray her true feelings. "You'll like talking to Colette," Sylvia said. "I'm going to transfer you right now. Could you hold just one minute while I explain to her who you are?"

Colette burst into the four-thirty editorial conference proclaiming her forthcoming scoop. She was going to meet with

Kokoh King's roommate this very evening, and the story would break right open.

"Sylvia herself," said Colette, standing before the assortment of editors munching on melba toast and critiquing the merits of this story and that, "has met this woman and vouches for her and said this was just the break we needed."

Hale Gardiner, who was sitting at the head of the long table, wanted no mention of Sylvia Loring to mar this shining moment. It was her push that had gotten the story rolling again, and she could think of no better timing! The *Trib* circulation figures had been flagging this first quarter. Even *Trib* loyalists were reading the *Post* for its extensive advance coverage of the Iowa caucuses—and with good reason. The *Post* had sent seven people up there, and all the *Trib* could afford was Frank Glover. The *Post* had an advance team working in New Hampshire, and Frank would have to move his tired show up there next. Hale had even cut the rather unorthodox deal of sending Wanda Glover to New Hampshire to help with the legwork. "Won't cost you a dime," Frank said of his wife, a brisk, efficient former Miss Black District of Columbia. "If you'll pay her airfare and expenses up there, she'll work for free."

Aside from Glover's voluminous filings, the bulk of their primary news had to be picked up off the wires. Wouldn't it be a fine surprise to the *Post* for the *Trib* to scoop them in town when all their aces were up in Iowa covering boiler rooms and Methodist women's teas in Cedar Rapids?

"You're meeting with this Shana today?" Hale asked. "What time?"

"Six sharp," said Colette, flushing with anticipation.

"Can you have the story on my desk tonight by say, nine-thirty, quarter to ten?" In Hale's mind, she calculated that would mean she'd see it at ten-thirty, quarter to eleven. It would be a late night. What the hell! It was worth it. She'd order out for dinner.

Colette had not anticipated writing the story so fast, having so little time. A column was one thing—but a hard news story? Hale's question sounded more like a command, though, and Colette couldn't very well voice her doubts in front of all these hard-news professionals.

"Well, sure, but I don't know how many inches I can give you on such short notice."

"Splendid!" Hale exuded. "Give us what you can. Inches don't matter, it's substance we're looking for. I want a nice follow-up to what happened to that girl Kokoh, and any hint of the vast network operating, whatever she can give you about its scope."

Though the front page had been dummied out for tomorrow's editions, Hale took the large sheet with its penciled-in stories and photos and slashed a dramatic red line through it. After Colette exited the room, Hale announced to her audience of editors, with unsuppressed excitement, "This page will have to be completely reworked." Before they started discussing its probable reconfiguration, she ceremoniously called the press room and warned the foreman he might have to "hold the presses as late as eleven P.M."

They were to meet at Peggy's on 15th and L, a place where by day *Washington Post* staffers had lunch, but by night was overtaken by a more seedy bunch—including, Colette understood, some members of Shana's profession.

Colette ordered a pitcher of Margaritas and waited. She felt like a Girl Scout tonight, prepared with her notebook and several spare pens. Being conscientious was something she never was much good at. Her strengths were in people skills, hunches, taking chances others didn't.

She'd brought along, too, a mini tape recorder, with extra tapes and batteries. She'd also packed a line of cocaine and tucked it in her pillbox—just in case.

Colette really couldn't say, even now, exactly what this story was about. Shana thought that Kokoh's disappearance was mysterious, and suspected she may have been harmed—that was part of it. Sylvia had said it was okay to print Kokoh's name now, but Shana's only if she agreed to give it. But the heart of the story, so Hale seemed to say, was the extent of the operation. How many people?

How much money? Who was involved? Despite her jitters, Colette reassured herself, the story would work out; they always did. At the beginning of the Society beat, she'd been nervous about those stories that were now a piece of cake to write.

Time passed as Colette waited in the dim light, thought fragments materializing in her mind, but vanishing before she could carry them to their logical conclusion. She thought of Ben and how proud he would be of her story. It amazed her how closely he read the papers, even the *Tribune*, and lately, all his comments had been about other people's work: Frank Glover, Andy Ferraro, Sylvia Loring. Luckily, she'd remembered her cigarettes tonight, and as she waited, she went through a third of the pack.

Minutes turned into a quarter of an hour, then half an hour, and still Shana did not show. This was not unexpected, Colette thought as she licked the salt from the Margarita glass rim and downed glass after glass of the sweet, sticky stuff. Perhaps she'd had a last-minute appointment and had to be late.

A worn-down blonde in desperate need of a dye job—her roots were a thin black comb of hair at her center part—appeared to be walking toward her.

Colette stood, her feet feeling a little wobbly, and raised her arm. The woman looked at her blankly. "Shana?" Colette called out loud.

"I don't know what your trip is lady, but I'm not on it."

It was well after seven-thirty, and Colette retreated to the bathroom and locked the door. The toilet lid was wet with urine, leaving no place to sit. She fumbled in her bag for the cocaine, snorting it from the underside of her long fingernail. Shana would show up; she had to. Otherwise, how could she face the humiliation of having nothing to deliver?

It was between nine and ten P.M. when Colette staggered back to the Tribune, and though no one else could tell—which gave her a kind of private thrill—she was high as a kite.

Hale was waiting for her like an anxious parent. Digby

was staying late, too, over concern for this story, as was the best copy editor. Ray from Photo was working now on getting art together for the piece, Hale explained.

Hale squired Colette to the private office that sat between hers and Digby's. It was a place where Colette could write without distraction, without a phone ringing, without having to see anyone's face. "I knew we'd be a bit later with this than projected," Hale said in a tone that told Colette not to worry.

Everything, it seemed, was laid out for the genius at work. A fresh pot of coffee sat heavy on its hot plate with Half 'n' Half and sugar cubes to dress it. A six-pack of Tab perched atop a mound of ice in a plastic cooler.

An enormous smile of pride played on Hale's face as she reviewed the appointments in Colette's room. "We'll just leave you alone," she said. "If you need us, we're right outside."

Then Colette was alone, facing a computer screen and a one-hour deadline. Her mind was blank as the green screen. She couldn't think. Why didn't she go out this minute and call it off? She could say she needed time and then think this through. It wasn't too late to beg off the story entirely.

Colette's eyes lit on Sylvia's Bob Rossen piece, which had been pulled from the library and was sitting for her reference on the table. All this service, Colette marveled. This must be the way it is in the White House, everything all laid out for you, your every need anticipated.

Her eyes glanced over the story. This hooker, now commonly known as Kokoh King, Sylvia had called an "unnamed source." For a minute, Colette wondered why Sylvia hadn't named her. She knew who she was, everyone knew. Kokoh this, Kokoh that. She'd identified her in a photo a week or so before, throwing a drink at Bob Rossen. It was all so arbitrary. Colette had never understood the rules of journalism. One time you put someone in; one time you leave the name out. Maybe Sylvia did it so that she could make up quotes. That was easily done. You didn't remember what you said yourself ten minutes after you said it, so how could someone else remember? At a party, at a bar. The noise was loud. You might say one thing and think another.

Colette's mind swam.

A knock sounding on the door boomed in her ear. Ray entered. "Colette, I hate to disturb you," he said deferentially. It seemed that the whole world was waiting for her to perform at the keyboard. He held out two black-and-white glossies, both of her. "Which do you want to run with the story?" One was a glamorous Colette in her fur coat. The other was more sedate. She was wearing a jewel-neck sweater and looked lovely but serious. She chose the latter; it looked more like the pose of a serious journalist.

The story reached Hale's desk at exactly 11:14 P.M. As her eyes sprinted through line upon line of dot-matrix type, she flushed with pleasure. It was working, hanging together! Only now, upon seeing its success—Colette's command of language and image—could she admit to herself she'd had some concern. This would have been a tough assignment for a Frank Glover or an Andy Ferraro, hard-newsers to the core. But Colette had done it. She'd come through in the end, lacing her delicious writing style and eye for detail together with solid reporting.

Hale took in the whole story in one decisive sweep.

It was extraordinary, outlining a multimillion-dollar prostitution operation masterminded by a ruthless, German-born madam. Colette's months of reporting were paying off. And Shana was the crowning interview. She'd spilled her gut, detailing the sexual favors that unnamed senators, a Supreme Court justice, two Cabinet members, even a former vice-president had preferred from the working girls. Shana wanted to go by the name Melynda Ravenel.

Hale lifted her phone and called production. "We'll have it ready to film in thirty-five minutes," she promised. She remembered Digby, who'd specifically stayed late tonight so he could see the story. It was a mere formality, of course, but she'd have to get his okay.

Looking up at Colette, Hale was carried away by her own

excitement. "Now you're going to be famous on your own," she exuded, "without Ben Fincastle!" The words "without Ben Fincastle" stung, but Colette had learned long ago to let people think what they will without bursting their balloons. Besides, she liked the part about famous. Fame was something she'd always felt a sense of predestiny about achieving, even as a little girl. Being special, standing out. Grandpa had always called her his little princess.

"Do you have anything to drink here?" Colette asked.

Hale motioned toward her refrigerator. "Poor thing, you must be exhausted. Help yourself, dear," she continued. "I have to go see Digby for a minute. Make yourself comfortable."

Hale entered Digby's commodious domain—with its prominent photo of Phyllis Reeve, its red leather chairs and couch, its photo of the publisher with the previous president at the White House—and handed him the story.

She waited as Digby sat behind his massive antique desk and read the story page by page at what seemed to her a glacial pace. He turned to the last page and read deliberately, his eyes narrowed behind the ream of pages. At long last he finished, his fingers plucking at his red plaid tie, his eyes not quite engaging Hale's.

"Well, Reeve?" Hale prompted. "Stunning, isn't it?"

Digby leaned back in his chair and exhaled a sigh. "Hale, why don't we hold this one for a day? She, uh, she might have the chance to smooth out a few things."

Hale's mouth fell open. "Digby, it's an extraordinary piece as is."

Digby leaned forward, drumming his fingers on the desk. "I don't know. It seems a little . . . ."

"A little what?" She glanced significantly at her watch. "We're losing time. I told production we'd be ready shortly."

Digby rose ponderously, opened his liquor cabinet, and extracted two glasses and a bottle of scotch. "Join me, will you?"

"Digby . . . ," she said, about to cut him off, then stopped short. She reminded herself to humor him and accepted the drink.

Digby clinked her glass with his. "To Hale Gardiner," he said, and drank. "Sit down," he said, gesturing toward the couch.

"I don't have time," she declared, interpreting his toast as a celebration, a green light for the story. "I've got to write the headline."

"Not yet." To her amazement, Digby gripped her arm and sat her down on the couch. He sat down beside her—not close, but not far, either. He looked at her soberly. "There's something about Colette's story that's sticking in my craw. Didn't the business about the German madam seem a bit . . . melodramatic? And the descriptions of the operation, the way it reaches into every corner of government, every bureaucracy in town." He shook his head slowly. "A bit extravagant, don't you think?"

"What are suggesting, Digby? That Colette made it up?"

"No, no," he said quickly. "Not at all. But I think it's possible Colette's source exaggerated. . . ."

"No," Hale said flatly. "Colette is too much of a professional to be taken in by a source. I know her, Digby, perhaps better than you do."

He drank his scotch, swilling it around in his mouth like mouthwash. "Still, it's a big chance. Lord God, Hale, if she's wrong, just picture it: I'd be the laughingstock of this town."

You already are, Hale thought. "Digby," she said, remembering what might just be her ace in the hole, "I've already torn up the front page. You want a paper tomorrow? We must go with Colette on page one; we don't have another one."

Digby glanced at his watch. "No," he said urgently. "We still have time to put that page back together."

"At this hour! Do you know how much that would cost?"

"We've done it before." He swallowed hard. "We have to do it. I'll see to it myself."

Hale examined him a second time, as if sizing up someone

she'd just met. Looking at him carefully, she saw how serious he was, how concerned about not wanting to make a misstep. She remembered her own doubts about running Sylvia's story about Bob Rossen—but it had all worked out so well. Quickly, she reconstructed Dennis's argument.

"Digby, this source Shana is a loose cannon about to go off. If we don't go to press tomorrow with her story, she'll take it to the *Post* tomorrow. And we will have gotten nothing—*nothing*—for all these months invested in it."

"How do you know that she'd go to the *Post*?" he asked, seeming uncertain for the first time.

"She's ready to spill, and she doesn't care where she does the spilling. If we move now, we catch the *Post* totally off guard. We recapture the market share lost to their political coverage."

"Hmm," he said, weighing her argument.

Hale brightened. "You know, I had the same problem you're having with Sylvia's story on Bob Rossen. Quite frankly, I didn't want to run it. I didn't want to get into the man's sexual closet, but I overcame my doubts and every paper in the country followed us. Do you remember the numbers we did that week? They helped make that quarter profitable. I'm convinced that there are times when we must rise above our fears. This is one of those times."

Digby appeared finally to cross over to her side. Slowly, he nodded his head, then dialed production to tell them to go ahead with the page.

"Bravo," Hale said in the spirit of celebration, feeling a keen sense of vindication in the knowledge that she had persisted, had cracked the whip when necessary with a talented writer, who'd rewarded her efforts by giving herself utterly to the story. And now, she'd emerged victorious from a second, unexpected skirmish.

"Let's write the headline together," Digby suggested, picking up on her mood. He astonished Hale by coming up with a clever grabber of a head, then shipped it downstairs with a command of the keyboard.

Digby got up and poured them both another drink. He sank into the couch next to her and looked at her not as publisher to editor, but man to woman. Hale had long understood that one of her strongest cards was Digby's unspoken attraction to her. But what surprised her at this moment was her feelings for him. Though she'd ultimately brought him around to her way of thinking, the obstacles Digby had raised reminded her of her own father's high standards. Robert Gardiner was always a tough fish to reel in, and his obstinacy had made her rise to her best heights, challenged her to excel.

Once he came over to her side, Digby gave her everything she wanted, including color, graphics, and an over-the-masthead, banner headline. And he agreed to use Colette's magnified byline wrapped around her photograph. The future had never looked better.

# CHAPTER
## 25

Colette's story, Sylvia thought after she had read the last word early the next morning in her apartment, was engaging in its way. She read the piece again, combing through it this time. There was much to admire: it had an intriguing story line, lively, often witty use of the language, a larger-than-life quality that made it a compelling read. Of course, she noticed that the story seemed to lack the nuts and bolts of a good investigative piece. It named no prominent Washingtonians by name; Colette had struck out there. There was no expert commentary, no reference to the body of research about prostitution. But she had certainly gotten everything else: information about the madam and how she started in the business; the women who worked for her and what they were like; the scope of the operation, which the source claimed covered every political and business corridor in

Washington. Colette had sure struck it lucky—talking to a woman who had no inhibitions about spilling the beans. And most impressive, Sylvia realized, was that Colette had overcome the handicap of working under right-at-deadline pressure.

It hurt, every word like a blow to Sylvia.

Yes, she had to admit she was achingly, searingly jealous; only jealousy could account for that raw feeling in the pit of her stomach, that tensing all over her body as she took in not only the story but the banner headline, the huge photo, and the byline. If only her grandmother hadn't died, it would have belonged to Sylvia K. Loring.

But it didn't. That it was not, but might have been, was the ceaseless echo haunting Sylvia's brain as she went to work that February morning. Her own role in this saga was already forgotten. Colette Daniels, with her late arrivals to work and her Tabs and her gossipy phone calls, was the star. Sylvia's only solace was the grim realization that she'd been right: if she hadn't stuck with the Rossen scandal back when, there would have been no story today.

As Hale had couched it to Colette, this cool, crisp Saturday afternoon at the Gardiner estate—just seven miles northeast of Ridgway Farm—was also a chance to discuss strategies for "building on" the Hookergate story: not only potential follow-ups, but submitting the present story for the Pulitzer Prize, exploring book and movie rights. "Let's take the bull by the horns," Hale had said.

For the moment, however, the subject was horses. "It's been some time since I've ridden," Colette was saying as she strolled with Hale and her parents, Robert and Jane Gardiner, toward the stables where the Gardiners kept their horses for their favorite pastime, foxhunting.

Colette was stretching the truth a bit. The fact was she'd never set her bottom on a horse in her life, and was mortified at the prospect. Mortified and somehow exhilarated. After the success of the Hookergate story, she felt she could take on any challenge. And she had a personal reason for accepting Hale's invitation to the farm. Ben had recently dropped a hint: could he count on the *Tribune* to get behind his candidacy?

A short, middle-aged man, one of the Gardiners' many servants, stood at attention outside the stables. "George," Robert commanded, "bring out Powerhouse for Hale, of course. And," he said, turning with a thin smile to Colette, "do fetch Canterbury for this lovely young creature."

"Canterbury?" Colette said doubtfully when George had gone.

"Our finest quarter horse. Very responsive. He'll give you precisely what you ask for."

Colette nodded knowingly to Hale's tall, trim father with Hale's Roman nose, his thinning, reddish-brown hair streaked with gray. She had no idea what a quarter horse was, but said, "Thank you. I do prefer quarter horses."

"Do you?" he inquired in his cultivated tone.

"I much prefer them to other sorts of horses."

"Indeed?" Robert said, looking at her curiously. "But you have ridden thoroughbreds, I assume?"

"Oh, yes. My grandfather breeds thoroughbreds in Missouri. He has an enormous, twelve-hundred-acre horse farm west of St. Louis."

Colette smiled, pleased to see that the recently retired judge was visibly impressed.

"You never mentioned that to me, Colette," Hale remarked, as impressed as was her father. Here, she thought, it had happened again. Colette's grandfather would be one of the preeminent breeders in the state, and Colette had never bothered to mention it. It startled her, how much she managed to keep to herself. "You're much too modest."

Colette simply smiled; but the smile faded as George led out an unimaginably huge black creature, followed by a teenage boy leading an equally immense brown horse. Colette could hardly imagine how she was going to mount either one of these beasts, much less ride one.

Robert strode commandingly to the brown horse. "I trust the English saddle will be acceptable?" he said to Colette, patting his hand around the flat saddle, with its short stirrups, as if to make sure it was properly mounted.

"I never use any other kind," Colette assured him.

"Good! I'm sure you ride well." He turned proudly to Hale. "Perhaps even as well as my daughter! A Virginian teaches his sons to ride, shoot, and tell the truth." A slight grin prefaced the punch line. "In that order."

His petite wife, Jane, who'd heard this joke innumerable times, laughed the heartiest of all.

"Of course," Robert went on, inspecting the saddle on Colette's black horse, "it rubs off on some daughters, too. Ready?" he said to Hale.

Colette studied every detail of how Hale mounted her horse. Colette had never seen her so physically masterful, deliberate, poised, as if mounting a horse were an Olympic event. The way she approached evenly, without sudden movements, facing Powerhouse's shoulders; the way she gripped the stirrup with her left hand and the pommel of the saddle with her right; the way she put her left foot in the stirrup, her left hand low on the horse's neck, and sprung up from her right foot; the way she straightened her left leg and stood upright, elegantly balancing herself on her hands, like a gymnast, then swung her right leg, knee bent, over Powerhouse's back and settled smoothly into the saddle, hooking her right foot in the stirrup.

Holding the reins loosely in both hands, Hale sat high and erect in her long black riding boots that reached just below her knees. In her black jacket and white blouse, buttoned at the collar, she looked severe, almost masculine, and utterly in command.

Then it was Colette's turn. Imitating Hale precisely, she managed to mount without any serious hitches, slipping the black boots the Gardiners had lent her into the stirrups and settling onto Canterbury at an alarming height. The ground looked a long way away, and she hoped to God she wouldn't fall. She gripped the reins in both hands, as Hale had done, and felt the brown mass beneath her, shifting slightly, ready to be converted at a moment's notice into frightening speed.

"Ride well!" Robert said, briskly patting Canterbury's flank.

"We'll be back before dinner, Papa!" Hale trumpeted.

Then she was off. Dear God, Colette thought, watching her trot through a gate into an open field, aware that the Gardiners and their two employees remained below her, scrutinizing her every move. But she did as Hale had done—squeezed Canterbury's flanks with her calves—and was amazed to find herself in motion. Holding the reins loosely, she followed at a fast walk into the field, where Hale had pulled up short, waiting.

"I've never seen anyone look so good on Canterbury," Hale said, admiring Colette in her cardinal red wool coat. "Is he giving you trouble?" she said then, noticing how Colette seemed a bit tentative with the reins bringing the horse to a halt.

"I really am a bit rusty."

"Of course you are," Hale said sympathetically. "However, I'm sure it will come back to you. Tell me," she said, pointing toward a forest, "there's a lovely path along a stream, continuing to a little church at the top of a hill, with a perfectly marvelous vista. We have enough daylight to make it there and back. Would you like to go that way?"

"Lead on," Colette managed.

"We'll take it slowly at first, then pick up the pace."

Ducking under a branch, Hale led into the woods, Colette following at a walk. At this pace, and with the horse seeming to know what he was doing on his own, she felt reasonably secure. As the path twisted through the woods, with its fine old oaks, she even began enjoying herself. She liked the feel of the horse beneath her, the sensual rhythm of his gait. From time to time Hale pointed out features along the stream and recalled childhood adventures she'd had in these woods. More than she'd ever realized, this was Hale's element perhaps even more than the *Tribune*; and she had never looked better, her cheeks flushed from the chill, her body at ease yet proudly erect on the horse.

They emerged from the forest into a long, narrow meadow that sloped upward toward a stone church, barely visible at this distance. "Shall we pick up a bit of speed?" Hale said, a coy smile betraying her deliberate understatement.

"Might be fun," Colette said doubtfully.

"See you at church!" Hale called out. Powerhouse broke into a trot, then was quickly at a gallop, Hale leaning her head far forward above his neck, her head high, her shoulders back, her buttocks raised from the saddle, charging up the hill in her black coat and boots like some cavalry officer hell-bent on victory in battle.

If Hale were showing off, she certainly had the skill to back up her display. Then, caught up in the excitement, Colette did her best to emulate her, urging her horse to a trot with pressure from her legs, then bringing pressure again and leaning far forward.

Canterbury responded. Before Colette could think about her next move, she was tearing up the hill at a terrifying pace, trying to keep her butt above the saddle, clutching at the reins and hugging the horse desperately with her legs. Unlike Hale's, her body had tilted back on the horse until she was certain, if this kept up, that she was going to be left behind by its forward motion and fall off the horse backward. Frantically, Colette tugged at the reins, trying to regain her balance, and saw the church rushing toward her at a dizzying speed, and Hale motionless on her horse, tracking her in alarm.

"Don't let him take control!" Hale shouted.

"How?" Colette screamed.

"Lean forward! Rein him in—gently! Not all at once!"

Colette obeyed; Canterbury slowed and, with Hale riding to meet them, halted.

"As I said," Colette got out, her heart pounding in her ears, "I'm a bit rusty."

Hale drew a deep breath, enormously relieved. "I'm sure it's just unfamiliarity with this horse." She shuddered visibly. "I'm sorry. I should never have galloped ahead of you."

Hale changed the topic abruptly, not wanting to dwell on what might have been a tragic mistake. They were at her parents' church, Hale said, pointing to the old graveyard where generations of Gardiners were buried.

"My brother is buried here," Hale said.

"Your brother?"

Hale beckoned Colette to follow. They passed through a

wrought-iron gate into the cemetery and walked slowly past slanting, lichen-covered headstones. Hale halted before a relatively new marble stone with a delicate angel carved on top.

"Robert Porter Gardiner," Colette read softly. "Born August seventh, 1963. Died December twenty-third, 1974."

"Just before Christmas," Hale said.

"He was only eleven."

"Yes. Leukemia. A lot of retarded children contract it; no one quite knows why."

Hale dropped to one knee and tugged at a vine that had started to climb the tombstone.

"He was my younger brother, my only sibling. It's funny how I live with him even to this day. You'd think a retarded child wouldn't affect you. But I spent so much time with him. Played with him. Mothered him. . . . Daddy was so happy when he was born, to have a son. But Bobby was never right." Hale ripped the vine from the ground and flung it from the grave. "So I became the son Bobby never was."

Colette was silent.

"I'll be buried here, too, one day," Hale said in a strange tone. Her eyes, plaintive, vulnerable in the rosy light, found Colette's. Behind Hale, the setting sun was melting into the Blue Ridge that had turned into a deep violet blur on the horizon.

"But first," Hale said then, her voice as emotional as Colette had ever heard it, "I want to live!"

They showered in the elegantly appointed guest house, Hale first. Wearing only a robe and slippers, Colette strolled leisurely around the place, waiting for Hale to finish. She flapped through a dated issue of *Town and Country* for a few minutes before realizing that she was looking at a sumptuous spread of the Gardiner Country Manor. A half-page photo depicted this very guest-house bedroom, with its Colonial canopy bed, antique dressers, and fireplace.

"It's yours," announced Hale, draped in an enormous Turkish towel.

"I'm soaking up this place," Colette replied. "It's exquisite."

"Do take your time," Hale said. "Enjoy!"

In the shower, Colette heard the bathroom door swing open. "I've made you a scotch," Hale called out. "Will you take it here?"

"Thank you," Colette said. Hale parted the shower curtain and thrust the drink into Colette's hands, not averting her eyes. For a moment, Colette thought the woman was going to step into the shower with her.

When she was dressed and had joined Hale in the library, her hostess was nursing a scotch and talking grandly about the Pulitzer Prize.

Colette drank her scotch and for a few transcendent minutes absorbed all of Hale's projections: the book, the movie rights, the follow-up stories. Then Colette's scotch ran dry and she fell back to earth.

"What do you think?" Hale asked excitedly. "The possibilities are endless."

Colette sighed. "I don't know how much more of this story I can take."

Sitting by a roaring fire in the huge manor-house fireplace, the Gardiners were curious about the Hookergate story. Artfully, Colette steered the conversation elsewhere. She was not unaware that Robert Gardiner was a former Virginia state chairman of the Republican party who'd grown disaffected with his own party, blaming it for the enormous federal deficit, duplicity in government, wastefulness, and failure to protect America's national interests. Hale had told her about his recent conversion to the Democratic party.

"When Jimmy Carter was driven from office, I thought America had made a turn for the better. But I was wrong. Jimmy Carter was at least an honest man. Decent. Driven by moral values. His two successors, by contrast, have been washouts."

Colette was pleased to hear this. She had hoped she could enlist Robert Gardiner's support for Ben's campaign. It seemed likelier now that she would be able to report to Ben a highly successful visit. She couldn't be too obvious about it, though; she'd have to tiptoe around Hale's suspicions.

"Who do you favor among the Democrats this year?" she asked innocently, munching on an hors d'oeuvre of venison sausage from a deer Robert Gardiner had shot himself on the estate.

"Dan Tison," he replied without hesitation.

She stole a glance at Hale. "You'd prefer Tison over Fincastle—a fellow southerner?"

"A fellow southerner, yes. An honest southerner, no. Ben Fincastle's crooked as a snake. Not his record, but his character, his moral fiber. At least Tison is honest." He sliced another piece of sausage. "And you?"

Colette noted the thin, triumphant smile on Hale's face. For some reason, she felt provoked. "Well," she said, "whether one likes the man or not, I think it's important to get behind a winner. Ben . . ." Colette flushed at the mistake of her familiarity. "Fincastle," she said recovering quickly, "is going to win. He'll win big in Iowa. New Hampshire's coming up—he'll win up there hands down. There's no stopping him once he gets to the South. It'll all be over. So why not get behind him now? The Democrats haven't taken the White House since 'seventy-six! We desperately need a candidate with appeal to more conservative voters."

Robert Gardiner fell silent. "You may be right," he said finally.

Colette smiled broadly. Hale's stony expression was not lost on her as they adjourned to the dinner table.

Afterward, the air still a little chilled between them, Colette told Hale that she really had to return home to the city that night.

"But can't you stay?" Hale replied. "We have acres of room."

"I really must go. I have so much to catch up on tomorrow—you had me working overtime on the story!"

Hale walked Colette to her car, a sleek, red Alfa Romeo purchased only last year. "Colette," she said, "I don't want you to take this personally. But . . . I do hope you think about what Papa said. It is true, you know."

Colette knew what she meant: Ben's dishonesty. Not finding words for a reply, she said nothing.

Then, to her astonishment, Hale embraced her. For a moment, arms tight around her in the dim light reaching from the porch, she thought that Hale would not let her go.

Then Hale stepped back. "Good night, Colette." Before Colette could reply, she turned smartly and marched a straight line toward the light.

# CHAPTER
## 26

Monday afternoon, when Colette arrived at the *Trib*, a spectacular, three-foot-high banner hung across the nape of the newsroom, strung from one obsolete (but intact) pneumatic tube to the other. The banner read: "You bet, it's Colette!" Beneath it was a long table dressed with bottles of champagne on ice, great mounds of catered fruit, cheese plates, and a huge cake.

The honoree gasped. Not so long ago, there was a time when she'd wanted to outdo the impromptu celebration for Sylvia's story on Bob Rossen. But now, it seemed, the last thing Colette wanted was a big in-house fuss over her Hookergate story. As much as she loved a good party, her first inclination was to turn and exit the building before anyone noticed her.

But it was already too late: per instructions, Patricia in the Style section had picked up the phone at sight of Colette and called the chief. Now Hale was approaching rapidly, summoning staffers to the event.

From all sections of the *Trib*, Hale's underlings obeyed. Many of them reluctantly shuffled their way toward what at least would be some nice snacks and a taste of the bubbly. Each had found in his or her mail slot that morning a memo requesting—in no uncertain terms—attendance at the surprise party. Now all converged at "Celebration Central," as Andy Ferraro had sarcastically dubbed it, to take a look at Hale's anointed one, who stood awkwardly before them at an uncharacteristic loss for words.

With Digby following from his office, Hale smiled proudly at Colette, clapped her hands for silence, and declared that the official *Washington Tribune* celebration "in honor of one of our own" would now begin.

Like Dennis Berman, who remained stubbornly at his computer terminal, Sylvia had intended to skip Colette's fete. Seeing that banner go up, she'd never felt more alienated from her job or less inclined to give it her all. Lately, she'd come to think of the *Tribune* not as the noble, scrappy underdog, the people's paper, but as a kind of banana republic where small-minded dictators ruled fawning, flea-bitten serfs.

But at the sound of Hale's ringing voice, some kind of morbid, writerly curiosity summoned Sylvia to the scene. On her way, she passed Dennis, who turned to telegraph a look of ironic distaste before resuming his work.

Telling herself not to get angry, Sylvia reached the edge of the crowd. There was Colette, standing between Hale and Digby, a lame smile tacked onto a face that looked essentially miserable. This wasn't like Colette, Sylvia thought, who normally loved attention. There was Digby, awkwardly clasping his hands together as he listened to Hale's speech that sent Colette on her way to a Pulitzer. There was Hale, mouthing words like "courage" and "distinction" as she glanced adoringly at Colette. Sylvia ached with the feeling growing inside her, a kind of cancer of the spirit, a sense of injustice. First Hale claimed moral objections to this kind of story; now she'd decided it would win a Pulitzer.

As Hale finished and Digby began making a speech, Pam whispered to Sylvia, "Counting our little chickens, aren't we?"

One of the downstairs guards ambled into the party, right toward Sylvia. For a moment, Sylvia assumed that the word had filtered down that there was pink angel's food cake for the taking, but the guard stepped up to her.

"You Sylvia Loring?"

Sylvia nodded yes.

"Visitor to see you in the lobby." The guard took in the party fixings. "I tried dialing your extension," she grumbled, "but no one answered. Not even the secretary."

Sylvia handed a piece of cake—a flimsy plastic fork spearing into the icing—over to the guard. "Here, have mine. I haven't touched it." A perfect excuse to break away, she thought.

Sylvia wondered for a moment who the visitor might be. No one ever just dropped in on you here. Interview subjects always made appointments. Maybe it was some pushy PR person whom she'd turned away. Or Max, she thought, hopefully.

Sitting sprawled out on the ornate gilded couch in the lobby was none other than Kokoh King. Sylvia's heart jumped. Kokoh was alive! Colette had insisted Shana didn't even mention Kokoh in the interview. This had perplexed Sylvia, forcing her into morbid speculation: could Shana have learned something so heinous that afternoon between the time she'd called Sylvia and met with Colette that she couldn't even speak of it?

Unpainted, Kokoh looked adolescent, more like a ninth-grader than a woman of the night. The canvas strap to an overstuffed, oversized duffel bag ran a dent into her shabby coat shoulder. As Sylvia got closer, she detected fatigue and wariness in Kokoh's eyes.

Sylvia rushed toward her to offer a hug. "Where have you been?"

Kokoh resisted her embrace and tossed Sylvia a look she'd never seen before: hard and steely, as if buffering herself from personal contact. Gone was the giggly-girl stuff, the yogurt-loving future-model act. "I'm not saying a thing," she said. "Not until we make a deal. And I know a lawyer, too."

"Did you go back and see your folks?" Sylvia asked. "We've all been worried about you. Shana called me worried, too," Sylvia blurted out, but immediately wished she could take back this last remark. You never knew who was in with whom or what was going down in a business. Like her own at the *Tribune*. What outsider would ever guess the politics involved behind just one story? What she just said could get Shana in trouble if Kokoh happened to be indiscreet.

Kokoh stared at her, right through her. Sylvia could see that the girl had gone through something since she'd seen her last, might still be going through it. Kokoh's fingernails, once long and tapered, were bitten to the quick.

"You all right?" Sylvia asked.

Kokoh glanced down at her scruffy body. "I'm one piece. That's the best thing I can say. Where I've been and what I've been through," she said, her lips curling up into a vomitous scowl, "you would not believe. I have been through shit that would make your hair stand on end. But like I said, I'm not saying a thing to you or anyone else. I want fifty thousand dollars for the rights to my story. Cold cash. Or else I'm gonna sell it to someone else."

"You mean there's more than before?"

"You ever heard of white slavery?" Kokoh said. "I'll tell you that story. But I don't do nothing for free." This was crazy talk about money, but someone just might pay it to her.

Sylvia couldn't let her get away. She'd have to think of some way to stall her. "I guess you saw Colette's story last week."

"That piece of . . ." Her voice trailed off. "I thought the *Washington Tribune* was straight up about what it printed. Truth and justice and all that crap."

"What's wrong with Colette's story?"

"Let's just put it this way: what's not wrong with it?"

Sylvia drew a deep breath. "What are you telling me, Kokoh?"

Kokoh broke into a fit of laughter, a kind of conspiratorial laughter, stronger than anything she could say in words. "You get me the money, I'm gonna give you the real stuff, not make-believe."

"Wait a minute. Wait a minute," Sylvia stared at Kokoh,

digging her nails into her clasped hands, boggled by what Kokoh was suggesting. "Are you telling me Colette made that story up?"

"Yeah. Hey, when I want to read junk, I buy the *National Inquirer*—'Woman Has Green Baby by Extraterrestrial Lover!' "

"What do you mean it was made up?"

Kokoh answered in breathless indignation, making it plain that she had at least read the story carefully. "You believed that German madam shit? You believe she's from some rich family that was friends with Hitler and all that shit and came over here with no money? You believe she's got some thick German accent?"

"It's possible," Sylvia said.

"You don't know shit! The real madam talks American, just like you and me."

"You mean she's American?" Sylvia said.

"Cut it right there, babe!" Kokoh said, leaning forward on the couch and pointing an accusing finger. "This information don't come cheap."

Sylvia sat down opposite Kokoh on the couch. "How do I know you're not making this up?"

"Go ahead," Kokoh answered coolly. "If you wanna believe one of her girls is a fifty-year-old, ex-movie star that dyed her hair, go right ahead. The real madam only uses girls in their twenties or younger. If you wanna believe she's doing business with some judge from the Supreme Court, be my guest. It's not like that. I mean, the real madam's got some big names—but a judge on the Supreme Court? I would have heard about that."

Sylvia had to admit that she herself had been amazed to think that a man of that stature was among the clients. Still, in this city of Wilbur Mills, Watergate, Gary Hart, Irangate, Oliver North, Jim Wright, the list went on, anything was possible; and the steel in Kokoh's voice, the intensity in her eyes convinced Sylvia she was telling the truth. Either that or she possessed Oscar-winning acting potential.

Sylvia shook her head slowly. "I don't know," she said.

Kokoh leaned toward her, close. "Look. Did I lie to you last time?"

Sylvia had to admit Kokoh had not.

"It all checked out, that stuff about Rossen. Right?"

It had checked out—everything Kokoh had told her.

"I may be a lot of things," Kokoh said, her nostrils flaring, "but I don't make things up." She leaned back on the couch, her expression so inflamed it could have given off smoke.

Sylvia's thoughts raced ahead of her ability to process them. Maybe it was just that she wanted to believe Kokoh. After the way she'd been bumped, after all the hurt and jealousy, to find out that Colette was a fraud would be unbelievably sweet. Not only in the way she felt about Colette, but also about Hale. She had to be careful not to let her feelings color her judgment.

Still, what Kokoh was saying made sense. When you added up all the extraordinary details of Colette's story, it amounted to a total mass of improbability.

Then Sylvia flashed on Colette's thinly disguised misery, her discomfort at the celebration upstairs. Not like Colette. And no wonder!

"What are you gonna do?" Kokoh said impatiently.

"I'm thinking, okay?" she snapped. Sylvia glared at Kokoh, but her mind was on Colette. Sometimes you just have to go with your gut feeling. She was having an irrepressible intuition about that expression she'd just seen upstairs. Could the unthinkable really have happened? Could Colette have completely fabricated the story?

Kokoh seemed to assume that Sylvia could just get large, unmarked bills in no time, like on TV. As if there were a bank upstairs in the editorial offices. In fact, the *Trib* didn't pay anyone. Even models for their fashion shoots worked for "exposure" and sometimes for glossy prints to add to their portfolios.

Sylvia would have to think of a way to stall her, to check it out. She searched her mind for something she could offer Kokoh. She thought of Shana. She'd already done the damage of mentioning her. She might as well continue.

"When Shana called, she said you'd left your lizard modeling portfolio. Assuming you're not on speaking terms, I could go pick it up for you and also your clothes." Another benefit of this plan would be checking Colette's story with Shana.

For the first time, Kokoh's ice melted. "Would you really do that for me?"

In a few moments, Kokoh was accepting Sylvia's offer to stay in her place, where she could find a temporary safe haven from whatever it was she'd been through.

What would her next step be? Sylvia wondered as she escorted Kokoh to a shop down the street from the *Trib* to make copies of Sylvia's apartment keys. This must be how an espionage agent feels, carrying around time-bomb information not generally known that, if true, could change the course of relations between nations, affect the balance of power globally. If Kokoh were on the level, Sylvia had something under wraps that could disgrace the *Tribune* and maybe even cost Colette her job. But better they should get hold of it than the *Post*. Certainly her contention deserved checking out.

"Four dollars, ma'am," the keysmith muttered.

Sylvia handed over a five.

"You interested in a key chain?" he asked, pointing to a revolving stand from which brass and cowhide chains dangled.

Kokoh nodded her head vigorously. "I need something to put them on, or else I'll lose them for sure." She selected a brass chain that was inscribed with the Rolls-Royce insignia. Sylvia wondered for an instant what she was getting herself into by taking Kokoh in.

"Nine-fifty altogether," the man said before she could object.

"You and Shana were close?" Sylvia asked as they exited the shop.

"If you're thinking she's some saint, she probably only called you because she lent me some money that I never paid back," said Kokoh.

Sylvia hailed a cab, gave the driver her address, and prepaid the fare.

When Sylvia returned to the newsroom, the party had dispersed and an assistant copy editor was busy cleaning up. Sylvia plunked herself down in the anteroom to Hale's office, waiting for an opening to have a word with the Big Boss. The door to the office was wide open, and from where she sat she could hear a conversation in progress. "I really feel as if I'm coming into the height of my powers," she heard Hale say.

Sylvia knew that Hale wasn't going to like what she was about to tell her. She'd try to couch it in as tentative terms as possible, suggesting that Kokoh certainly needed a hearing. But if something as serious as an allegation of a false story were at stake, Hale would have to give it its due. Nonetheless, Sylvia felt nervous. When she finally heard Hale end the call, Sylvia stood, poking her head inside Hale's door. "You have a moment?" she said, as friendly as she could muster.

Hale looked up at her, a now-what-do-you-want look on her face. It was obvious she did not want to lose any more time from her busy day.

Sylvia sat and spilled the goods. Kokoh King had just appeared at the *Tribune* lobby, she said, pausing for a reaction but getting none. Kokoh insisted that Colette's story was not on the up and up. "I wanted you to be the first to know," Sylvia said.

Before Sylvia could continue—relaying the supporting details and Kokoh's demand for money—Hale shot her a look she'd never before seen. Her face appeared dotted all over in red darts of blotchy anger.

"Knocking down a star makes some people feel good about themselves. Sylvia Loring, I've had it up to here with you and this story."

"Do you want to hear what I have to say?"

"Jealousy is not pretty," said Hale. Evidently, the answer was no.

Despite her determination to stay calm, Sylvia found herself pouring the cumulative frustrations of the last three months into her retort. "Neither is taking away a story that you didn't even want to begin with and giving it to someone who may not have been equipped to handle it."

Hale said nothing, but sat there looking as if she would have pulled the trigger had there been a gun in her hand. "I decide who does what, what runs, how it's played, and," Hale said, pausing for effect, "who works here."

Sylvia stormed out of Hale's office and blindly returned to her desk, not seeing or hearing anyone. Dennis, she thought. She wanted to talk to Dennis. But he wasn't at his desk. "Out meeting someone," Patricia said.

"Well, I'm gone too!" Sylvia almost shouted.

Mystified, Patricia watched as Sylvia headed for the stairs, slamming the door behind her and taking the stairs three at a time. She was just about at the point of leaving this stupid paper, typing a curt memo to H. G. saying that she was through. But without a job, what could she do? Public relations was the most common alternative for burnt-out or out-of-favor journalists, but not for her. It was bad enough to sell a story to her editor, who in turn had to sell it to his editor, but trying to peddle trumped-up stories to newspapers and magazines, sucking up to journalists like they were gods—that was about the size of public relations, and it wasn't for her.

Free-lancing was the other route, she thought as she steered her Nova home toward Adams-Morgan and Kokoh. But that was so speculative, so uncertain, so iffy. You could sell a couple of pieces for three or four thousand dollars, but you had to wait for months until the check arrived. And there were so many pitfalls. The story could fall through. The editor who'd assigned the article could leave the publication and the piece—through no fault of the writer's—could hit the circular file. If it hadn't been bought and paid for, there was no incentive for a replacement editor to act honorably if he or she had no plans to run it. The most you could hope for was a kill fee. No, the best way to free-lance was to do it in conjunction with a job. To collect your regular check and then write extra stuff on the side.

Unlike Hale, Sylvia had no trust fund. She swiftly turned

over in her mind the people who might help her. Dennis was not influential enough with Hale to be of real help. Pam would always lend moral support, but moral support wouldn't pay the rent. B. D. would probably say that she'd be smart to quit and look for another job. The *Tribune* in his mind was a second-rate paper. Max was a stranger now. In her mental Rolodex she flipped to the name Judy Fincastle. Here was a person with—just maybe—enough clout to really help.

# CHAPTER
## 27

Judy Fincastle was determined to lead as ordinary a life as possible, despite Ben's anticipated landslide in the Iowa caucuses. And though she was aware that some found it odd that she wasn't out stumping for her husband, she knew that others admired her for continuing with her own work. Certainly staying on at Peace Links—putting in fifteen hours a week performing ordinary office tasks; she'd been answering phones and mail this very afternoon—was one way of drawing attention to their work. Every article about the candidate and his family inevitably gave at least a paragraph to Peace Links.

Judy was looking forward to the Indian vegetarian dinner their son Arthur was planning for her and Ben at his place that very night. It would mark Ben's first visit to Arthur's urban homestead. Ben had cleared his schedule, he told her this very morning. A meeting at five downtown was his last appointment of the day.

Things had gone better with Ben ever since she'd given him the ultimatum. Not that there'd been any overnight transformation into the model husband. But when he hadn't been in Iowa or New Hampshire or on his preliminary swings through the South, Ben had spent his nights in her bed. Occasionally, he'd even made love to her—not with the heat of the old days, but with a certain proficiency for which Judy could only be grateful. She despised having to reduce their marriage to the level of realpolitik, but the strategy seemed to have worked. The cost of Judy's blowing the whistle was simply too high for him to pay. Colette Daniels, she noted with some satisfaction, had ceased her sniping remarks in the *Trib*; their affair was apparently on the shelf. Besides, with Ben campaigning as hard as he was, she hardly saw how he could find time for any monkey business, even if there still was lust in his heart.

As for their conversations, they too lacked passion; but at least they were respectful. And Ben had promised her more time—maybe a vacation together—when he'd locked up the nomination. Seeing his exhaustion when he arrived home, she knew the campaign posed an almost inhuman physical strain, and she made allowances for that, extending him every courtesy. If she could not have much of him now, she held out hope for a time later when there would be more of Ben to give.

Judy was just preparing to leave for home—to dress for her dinner with Arthur—when Sylvia Loring called. Though it wasn't clear exactly what had happened, she had never heard Sylvia so upset. It surprised and secretly pleased Judy that someone as beautiful, gifted, and young as Sylvia could have any problems at all. She needed to be reminded of other people's trouble sometimes to keep from feeling sorry for herself. "Come over to the house," Judy said warmly. "We can talk while I get ready to go to dinner." But really she couldn't imagine how she could help.

It was only Sylvia's second visit to the stately Fincastle residence, and if she had been in another frame of mind, she would have taken great interest in exploring the house of the likely future president. As it was, she merely wanted help in an hour of outrage and need.

Because Judy didn't have much time, she invited her distraught guest upstairs, offering Sylvia a seat on the chintz-covered divan in her bedroom. Leaving her closet door open so they could talk as she selected a more casual outfit, Judy said, "Tell me what's on your mind."

Sylvia related what had happened at the *Trib*, from the day Hale had taken the Hookergate story away from her, to this afternoon, when Hale had stonewalled information about Colette's story and then threatened Sylvia's position at the paper.

Like every other person in town, Judy had devoured with salacious interest Colette's story about the German madam running an undercover operation on the Hill. It had crossed her mind as she read that Ben might be one of the guilty but unnamed participants. Now, hearing Sylvia's version of events, Judy sat on the edge of her bed in astonishment, holding her selection of wool slacks and a matching hand-knit sweater in her lap. What astonished her as much as Sylvia's account itself, was that she'd come to her, a friend but not exactly a bosom buddy. "You're asking for my help?"

"I don't mean to be forward about this, but I know you know some people at the *Post*." The next sentence was even harder to utter: "Maybe you could help get me an interview there."

"A job interview?"

Sylvia nodded, convinced that she'd just overstepped her bounds. But after all the swirling thoughts of the afternoon, this, in the end, seemed her most promising option.

Judy glanced at her watch. "I'd better change."

Sylvia's eyes followed Judy into the adjoining dressing room, where she half closed the door for privacy. This was not going to be her day; first she'd come to within a fraction of an inch of losing her job; now she was antagonizing the future First Lady with an overly aggressive approach.

"I'm thinking about this," Judy said, her thoughts racing. The implication of Sylvia's story was beginning to dawn on her—if her suspicions were true, Colette Daniels would be hung out to dry in this town. How could Ben ever sleep with or in any way associate with a woman who'd fabricated a banner headline story in the *Washington Tribune*? She couldn't wait to see Ben's expression when he learned the news.

Judy emerged from the dressing room, pulling the sweater down over her head. "You really think she made it up?"

"It's hard to be a hundred percent sure."

Judy slipped on her shoes. "If your life depended on it, yes or no?"

Sylvia tugged at a strand of hair behind her ear as if it were a lifeline. "Yes. She made it up."

A smile exploded on Judy's face. It was not hard for Sylvia to guess what she was thinking. She, too, had pondered the rather awesome fact that she just might be in the early stages of destroying Colette Daniels.

"Listen!" Judy said, the excitement obvious in her voice. "Why don't you drive me over to Arthur's. That way we can keep talking."

"How do you get back?"

"Ben's meeting me there. He'll bring me back."

They headed south in Sylvia's Nova down Massachusetts Avenue. "Why don't you go to the *Post* with your story?" Judy blurted out. "A story like this needs maximum exposure."

"You mean go there with the story about Colette—and also apply for a job?" Sylvia wasn't sure she was thinking all that clearly, that she really knew what she wanted. Going to the *Post* with the story about Colette was a different thing from going there looking for a job.

"Listen," Judy said, as if sensing she'd confused the issue for Sylvia. "You do what you want about Colette Daniels. What I'll do is call my friend Len Haber at the *Post*. He's the assistant managing editor."

"I know the name," Sylvia said.

"Then when you call him, you can do whatever you want. How does that sound?"

Sylvia smiled gratefully.

"Of course," Judy said coyly, "I have no interest whatsoever in the outcome of all this for my good friend Colette."

No comment was needed. Sylvia wheeled bravely through Dupont Circle—the closest thing in Washington to the chariot race in *Ben Hur*—and steered southeast a few blocks down Rhode Island. Sylvia was surprised to recognize the Adams and First Street address Judy gave her as belonging to a poverty-stricken, crime-infested neighborhood.

"Arthur's very brave," Judy said. "Too brave, thinks his mother."

In another couple minutes, the Nova was navigating dimly lit streets where, even in the February cold, men and children were hanging out in impressive numbers, some selling what she took to be drugs in the streets. Sylvia began to wonder if Judy did not have an ulterior motive in asking to drive her here: fear of coming to this place alone. From her own experience as a reporter and Washingtonian, Sylvia knew all too well how it felt to make this kind of journey unescorted. As a woman going solo, it was possible in a certain frame of mind to see every stranger on the street as a potential rapist or mugger especially here where drug shootings and robberies were so common.

Judy was going on now about Arthur's carpentry skills with obvious maternal pride but at a nervously rapid clip, about how he'd found this house all on his own and decided to buy it, about all the things he was doing to fix it up, about his apparent lack of discomfort about being one of only a handful of whites in the entire neighborhood. Sylvia wondered what Ben thought of his son's move, but thought better of asking.

They pulled onto his block on Adams Street, which was lined with two- and three-story brick row houses. "That's it," Judy said, pointing at one address that was indistinguishable—except by its number—from all the others. "Park here," she said, her voice a little jittery.

Judy asked Sylvia if she would come in for a minute and meet Arthur. It was obvious she did not want to cross this street alone.

"I tell you what I'm going to do," Judy said. "As soon as we get inside, I'll call Len. He works late—I'm sure we'll catch him."

Arthur Fincastle greeted them at the door wearing drawstring pants of unbleached muslin and sandals and socks, despite the cold weather. The only sign of affluence was his oversized fisherman's-knit sweater, but even it was soiled at the collar and cuffs.

The house inside was unheated, little warmer than the outside. He kissed his mother on the cheek and turned to Sylvia, as gracious as a southern host. "You with Peace Links?"

"No, Arthur. This is my friend Sylvia Loring. She drove me down. Listen, Arthur, dear, could I make a call for Sylvia? Is there somewhere we could talk?" Judy said.

"In private?"

She nodded her head yes.

"I'll just go upstairs and hang out while you conduct your business." With that, Arthur sprinted up stairs that had neither banisters nor railings.

Judy got Len Haber on the line immediately. "I've been talking to Sylvia Loring about a little problem she's having over at the *Tribune*," she started. "She's an excellent person and friend, and I'd like to know if she could call you some time."

Judy held her hand over the phone and whispered enthusiastically. "He knows your work! He can talk right now."

Sylvia hadn't thought her situation through, hadn't considered all the consequences of blowing the whistle. Had she done so, she might have been more restrained, but in the moment, having spilled her gut to Judy, and with Judy standing right there in front of her, so agreeably assuming the role of patron, Sylvia felt hypocritical holding back.

So she made a chess move without studying the board.

After talking briefly with Len Haber—conveying both that she would like to be considered at the *Post* and also touching on the possibility that Colette's story may have been a fake —Sylvia held as he transferred her to someone else. A reporter. Suddenly, she was the interviewee, and someone else was asking the questions.

John Lester Coggins was a hard-nosed guy who sounded a whole lot like a white, New York version of Frank Glover when he was conducting an interview. She told him she had reason to believe the second Hookergate story wasn't true.

No, she didn't want her name used, she said, realizing how quickly the stakes can change when you're on the other side. And no, she couldn't provide him with any evidence. (She wasn't about to tell him Kokoh was sitting in her apartment right now and offer up the story on a silver platter.) He asked for her home number, as all good reporters always did. And like many interview subjects, she demurred; the thought suddenly occurred to her that if he tried calling her at home and got Kokoh, she might spill the whole thing to the *Post*.

"Listen," she said. "I'll call you tomorrow to check in. But this is really a tip more than anything else."

As soon as she hung up the phone, it rang again. It was Ben Fincastle.

"Judy?" he said, puzzled.

"No, this is Sylvia Loring," she answered.

"Oh, Sylvia, Sylvia," he said, as if trying to place her. "Is Arthur there?"

She called to Arthur up the stairway, and he appeared as quickly as he'd vanished.

"Dad-o," he said cheerfully. With that, Judy whirled around from staring out the back window, which was covered with bars. She twirled white wine around in a jelly glass, her attention riveted on the telephone.

"You can't. Don't be sorry about it," Arthur said with exaggerated politeness. "We all understand that it takes every bit of your waking time to do something as momentous as you're doing."

Sylvia could tell Arthur was angry, very angry, but that somehow this last-minute cancellation was not unexpected.

Then Arthur seemed to hang up the phone without any parting remark.

"Count on Dad to be the life of the party," Arthur said.

"Did he say why?" Judy said.

"Does Dad ever say why?" Arthur said.

It was cold in the house, and Sylvia realized that she'd better be going. Judy seemed numb, as if unable to put two thoughts together. Then, as Sylvia got to the door, Arthur said, "Hey, why don't you stay? You can fill in for the senator. Table's all set." She could see that it was, that her presence was welcome, and that what was needed here was a note of cheer.

She could afford to be compassionate. Judy was in the doldrums, but Sylvia had scored a victory of sorts. She'd acted boldly, she'd taken a chance, and it had paid off. The *Post* seemed almost to welcome her call. There was life outside of the *Washington Tribune*!

"Arthur," she said, "if your food tastes as good as it smells, I'll fill in for the senator every night!"

# CHAPTER
## 28

John Lester Coggins reached Colette Daniels the next afternoon at work. After identifying himself, he brought up the Hookergate story. It was unorthodox, of course, to ask a reporter at a competing paper for her sources, he admitted, but this was different. He had information that something wasn't right about the story itself. He was hoping for a comment—or would she prefer to meet in person to discuss this?

Colette said nothing. Then she started laughing. The higher she climbed on the totem pole of Washington society, the more ridiculous it all seemed. Everyone took themselves so seriously—especially these guys at the *Washington Post*—when the people themselves weren't any different from the folks at the Esso station back in Herrin where she'd hung out as a kid. Back there, you could steal money from the cash drawer and get yourself a Coke or an Orange Crush, and if you got away with it, even the Esso owner had to laugh. What the hell, it was only money.

"So you have no comment, then?" Coggins was asking

her in this most serious tone. He probably had a master's in journalism from Columbia. He probably read the *Columbia Journalism Review* in his spare time.

She had to tell him. She had to let him know how absurd all this bullshit system was. She had to shake him out of his little self-important cubicle of power. Colette did the incredible.

"You want my sources?" she said. "Are you a brain surgeon?" she joked. As she talked, she could hear his fingers punching her words into a computer. "'Fraid I can't provide them. I made that silly thing up."

Only later, the phone back on its hook, amidst the normal clatter of newsroom voices on the phone, fingers slapping keyboards, did Colette fully awaken to what she had just done. Only then did she think of Ben's reaction and feel a cold shudder pass down the length of her body.

"I can't believe this," she said out loud. Her body, always the picture of languid contentment behind her desk, was drawn up stiff in her chair, as if suddenly struck by a sharp pain.

She had wanted this to happen, she thought, imagining what she would tell her analyst in their next session. Without having any idea of just how deep her desire went, she must have wanted to break out of here!

Frantically, afraid that she would lose him in one fatal stroke, she tried to think of what she would tell Ben. This would be splashed all over tomorrow's *Post*. He would read it before she had a chance to talk with him,

Then she hit on an idea. She retrieved Ben's travel itinerary from inside her French clutch. She'd carried the precious sheet with her for days now, and, in an uncharacteristic exercise of self-control, never once succumbed to the temptation of calling him. Not until now.

Her heart racing, she dialed his Des Moines hotel. She knew that the odds were that he'd be out pressing voters' flesh.

The sound of Ben's voice on the line gave her a start.

*Tell him now*, she told herself. *Get it over with.*

Briefly, she described her story fabrication and subsequent confession to the *Post*.

"Jesus," Ben said. "Why'd you do a thing like that?"

"Oh, every reporter does this kind of thing," she said. "Besides, I thought no one would ever find out."

"I can't believe you did this, Colette," he said, the tone of voice chilling her. "Just like that, you told the *Post*?" Colette could feel him pulling back from her in judgment.

"Ben," she retorted, "you love boldness as much as I do. Taking chances. That's why we're made for each other."

She could feel his silence.

"You know as well as I do you don't get what you want without taking big risks," she said.

Suddenly, a derisive laugh crackled over the line, a laugh that was distinctly not Ben's. The voice that followed belonged to none other than B. D. Cole, apparently on an extension line the whole time. "Christ almighty, Ben," said B. D. "You don't buy this crap? This is what I call pouring gas on yourself and lighting the match."

"I won't stand for three-way conversations," Colette screeched into the phone, slamming down the receiver.

She was aware of reporters looking at her, distracted from their work by her vehemence.

Colette held her body still and stared down at her desk. She was not a vindictive person, but she'd had enough of B. D. Cole. Ben was letting himself be pushed around by the man, and she would find out a way to take care of him.

Then she thought of Hale Gardiner.

Even at this moment, that *Post* guy might be dialing Hale to tell her, to get her reaction. Colette sprang to her feet. Hale would hear it from her first.

But Colette's resolve weakened as she approached the office. Hale was on the phone, talking to someone in Boston, Colette could tell, making final arrangements for a speech to be delivered tomorrow night. Colette was relieved it wasn't the guy from the Post. Hale, turning in her chair, saw her and was beckoning her into the office enthusiastically as she signed off the phone.

"Sit down! Sorry to keep you waiting. Just finalizing the

plans for my speech to the American Society of Newspaper Editors. I'm to make the keynote address. I can't imagine how I was selected.''

''Hale,'' Colette said hastily, ''I've got some news.''

''News? So have I! I was going to call you in. Sit down, let's chat.''

Colette obeyed. Funny how when the moment of truth comes, she followed her instructions like a little lamb.

Hale seemed almost giddy with glee. ''I must tell you we're closing in on that book deal! Just got off the phone a few minutes ago. The latest is that they're discussing it this very day, in-house, at the highest level. Let me assure you, they're a-titter over the prospect. Our agent says a bid should be in by the end of the day.''

''Hale, the *Post* got a tip about my story.''

Hale thumped her pen, once, on her desk. ''What are you talking about?''

''I mean someone tipped them off and they called me about it. Hale,'' she said. ''My story was false.''

Apparently, Hale had not heard. ''A tip from whom?''

''I don't know.''

Hale speared the tip of her pen into a pad once, twice, three times. ''I know,'' she said.

''You don't seem to understand,'' Colette said, amazed at her sudden display of courage. ''I told the *Post* I made up that story. I told them the truth.''

This time, if Hale heard, there was no acknowledgment. ''This is it,'' she said in a voice so low that Colette almost missed the words. ''Sylvia Loring is out of here.''

''He didn't say anything about Sylvia.''

Hale picked up the phone and dialed Sylvia's number in Style. She got Patricia, who reported that Sylvia had not been in all day. Hale slammed down the phone, then picked it up again and dialed Sylvia's home number. ''She's not going to sleep tonight,'' she said to Colette as the phone rang.

Evidently, the answering machine picked up. ''Hale Gardiner. You've really done it this time. Be in my office tomorrow at nine sharp.''

\* \* \*

Sylvia did not obey. One act of defiance led to another, and she did not rearrange her schedule to appear in Hale's office the following morning. Instead, she carried out her plan to do some grocery shopping for Kokoh, the result of an agreement of the previous evening in which Sylvia said she'd try to find some money to pay for Kokoh's story. Just give her a little time. Sylvia had no idea how she would find it, but knew that she would do whatever was necessary to keep this source in her corner. In her increasingly cocky mood, Sylvia liked the way she was operating. Maybe some of Kokoh's brassiness was rubbing off. One thing she was sure of was that Kokoh, despite her blustery talk, trusted Sylvia and remained impressed with her credentials. Later, after work, Sylvia would contact Shana and follow through on the promise she'd made Kokoh to retrieve her prized possessions.

She had not even bothered to look at the papers that morning before she came in, not until she passed the coin-slot stand of machines on the street in front of the Tribune Building. Then, as if by force of habit, she glanced at the color graphics of *USA Today*; the somber, serious *Wall Street Journal*; and the *Post*. Some of the headlines had to do with next Monday's caucuses in Iowa, Fincastle's wide lead, and the President's inevitable win on the Republican side.

But there it was on page one of the *Post*! "*Trib* Reporter Admits to Fake Story." Sylvia could hardly believe it. For a moment she wondered if some tricksters had dummied up a fake paper and put in the machine for her benefit.

But no, it was no trick. The *Post* had acted so swiftly. The story started just above the fold. Sylvia read the first four lines, and then, her heart racing, dashed into the building and upstairs, straight for Hale's office.

It was 10:45, and even without stepping into the newsroom, she could feel excited anarchy in the place. The reporters were buzzing.

She knew that seeing Hale would be anything but pleasant. Hale's "you've really done it this time" could mean nothing else. She must have gotten wind of her tipping off the *Post*. Sylvia knew it was her right to have done so, and would tell

Hale where to go, if necessary. It was an extraordinary feeling, not being the least bit intimidated by the prospect of Hale's wrath. She'd had no idea that taking matters into her own hands was so incredibly liberating.

Hale wasn't in, Luanne said. She'd left only a few minutes before to catch a flight out of National for Boston. Ever the loyal foot soldier, Luanne appraised Sylvia with a critical eye. "Didn't you have an appointment at nine this morning?"

Sylvia responded coolly. "Hale asked for an appointment then, but it was never confirmed." No longer would Sylvia Loring play anyone's pawn!

The phone rang. "No, Mr. Klein," Luanne said. "Miss Gardiner is en route to the ASNE meeting today. She'll be staying at the Copley Plaza, if you want to try her there for a comment."

Sylvia reached her desk, and a memo from Hale was propped publicly into the carriage return of her typewriter. For all to see. No doubt some already had.

> S.K.L.:
>    Your unprofessional behavior causes me to reconsider the terms of your employment here at the *Tribune*. Due to your unethical behavior, we must terminate you effective immediately.
>
> H.G.

There it was, in black and white. She was terminated. Canned. Axed.

She sat at her desk—now her former desk—and tried to scan the *Post* story on Colette, but she couldn't concentrate. All the confidence and verve of twenty minutes ago had been replaced by a churning in her stomach. Hale's blow had had its desired effect. She felt as if the life had been knocked out of her. She had cursed the paper, hated it these last few months ever since Colette had been given her story, but she could never have guessed how bereft she would feel at the thought of leaving it.

Nothing seemed to make sense anymore. Maybe Judy was right. She could try to sell the Kokoh story to the *Post*, free-lance or—if she were deliriously lucky—on staff. Her appointment with Len Haber was set for the day after tomorrow. The *Post* had infinitely greater financial resources than did the *Tribune*. Perhaps it might be able to cough up some money for Kokoh. Or maybe the interview would be a mere formality, granted her in deference to Judy Fincastle. She reminded herself grimly that being fired rather than quitting enables you to collect unemployment.

Sylvia got up and walked over to Dennis Berman, who was sitting at his desk with the *Post* opened to the page where the story jumped. Suddenly, he seemed like a stranger. So much had transpired without his having been clued in.

"You were the tip," he said so no one else could hear.

She had no reason to deny it, so she did not. She held the memo from Hale in her hand. "And I've been convicted without being tried."

Parked inside Digby's office, Dennis was waiting when the publisher returned from a midmorning business meeting.

Digby looked worn and drawn as he sat at his swivel chair. He could find no satisfaction in having been wary of Colette's story. What rankled him most was that he'd been too weak to stop it. This was the great trap of a publisher. You had to pay for the mistakes of your subordinates. In his efforts to be liked by Hale, in his efforts to get ahead of the *Post*, he had blundered.

Still, he felt no bitterness toward Hale. If this were hard for him, he thought, it must be triply hard on her. She must feel recrimination and self-doubt. He wished she hadn't run off to Boston, that Hale were here with him so he could reassure her of her brilliance, of his continued admiration and respect for her. He wished that she would let down her hair and cry into his arms.

"What can we do?" Digby was saying, sadness in his voice.

"About the fake?" Dennis shrugged. "The only thing we can do is go to press tomorrow with an editorial retraction and apology. And of course we'll have to collect Colette Daniels's resignation."

"I guess that's my job," Digby said reluctantly.

Dennis didn't object. "I'm sorry for you, for us all." Turning to another matter, Dennis laid Hale's memo to Sylvia on Digby's blotter. "You must be aware of this."

Digby read the paper slowly. "No, I wasn't."

Dennis had always liked Digby, but never quite respected him. Digby was slow to grasp things, where Dennis was quick. And here was a case in point: he did not immediately see what was unprocedural. Quite frankly, Digby seemed lost, as if not knowing where to turn.

Dennis saw that he would have to suggest a path for Digby, a way to react. He saw, too, how Hale Gardiner could have gained so much leverage with him, filling the vacuum in Digby's psyche that begged for direction.

"Hale fired Sylvia without consulting you?" Dennis said with just enough surprise in his voice to hint at indignation. When it came to Hale, he had to tread lightly. Digby was her greatest champion.

Digby nodded grimly.

Dennis had heard Digby previously express concern about lawsuits, and so he mentioned today's litigious climate where so many lawsuits issue from employee to employer. Sylvia would have a damn good case against the *Trib*, Dennis pointed out, should she choose to pursue it. She had not even been warned or placed on probation.

Dennis studied the effect of his words on Digby. Digby's eyes squeezed shut. He breathed heavily, and his large palm stretched protectively across his tormented face. Dennis wondered if, this time, in light of the worst crisis ever to hit the *Washington Tribune*, the man would draw into himself and rise to the occasion.

# CHAPTER
## 29

Hale had just begun her speech to the black-tie audience at the Copley Plaza in downtown Boston when Digby arrived, an uninvited guest. He squeezed into an unclaimed seat at one of the rear dining tables, making apologies to his neighbors, and riveted on Hale. Her voice strong and assured, her hair trimmed stylishly short for the occasion, she cut a magnificent figure in her bold choice of attire, black wool-crepe pants, a black wool-knit jacket, and a long, stunning challis scarf, in a damask-and-gold pattern with matching earrings.

"What is an editor?" Hale asked rhetorically. "What are we at our best?" She paused dramatically, moving from one face in the audience to another as if demanding an answer. "What makes an authoritative newspaper lies in the breadth of its coverage and the editing of its report. Walk with me, if you will, through the halls and byways of the *Washington Tribune*."

Despite his urgent mission to take the situation in hand, Digby could hardly get his breath. The woman was positively awesome; she wasn't merely standing at the dais, she was a queen holding court. His heart went out to her for her courage to get up before this audience of peers on the very day the *Post* story broke about Colette Daniels! Everyone in the room knew by now. Yet, if there were a trace of self-doubt, it was not apparent in Hale's voice or in the almost intimidating gaze she trained on her colleagues in the audience.

Hale threw what seemed her very soul into her message, rousing what was surely a skeptical audience with her concept of editor as conduit for social change, as "a sometimes lonely voice in the wilderness" against those who would sabotage the free press, as the "champion of the cutting edge of ideas, no matter how disquieting, how unpopular those ideas may be."

Digby jumped up as Hale finished, adding his applause to the standing ovation of her peers. When a short congratulatory speech was completed at the dais, Digby pressed forward toward a corner of the banquet hall, where coffee and drinks were being served, where Hale was surrounded by what he took to be an admiring crowd.

Then he grasped her situation: she was fielding questions from sharp-witted newshounds about the Hookergate fake. Half her audience was gathered here, like wolves for the kill.

But Hale's mastery astounded him. Rather than shrink before the crowd, she had gathered herself magnificently erect, a radiant smile turned toward every new interrogator, as if she were basking in glory, not enduring public shame. Poised in her left hand was her drink; her right hand jabbed toward the crowd as she made her points with her scalpel-like use of the language, the way JFK had once done at his press conferences.

"But Miss Gardiner," a bookish, bespectacled man protested in a doubtful tone. "Surely you must have some regrets."

"Absolutely none, Bob," Hale declared. "These things happen. It's important to refrain from making ad hominem attacks on editors in such situations. In my view, it's far better that we as editors assume a risk on a story than merely submit to sanitized, press-release journalism."

To Digby's delight, there were shouts of "Bravo!" and "Hear, hear!" from the crowd. How could anyone be this good!

"What about sex-scandal stories?" a short, rotund man asked. "Don't you have any qualms about those?"

"Now, Irwin," she began, with just the right amount of coyness in her smile, "here we had not only a sex scandal, but a prostitution story." Keeping Irwin in her sights, she sipped her drink, not even remembering that the following words came almost verbatim from Sylvia. "Irwin, we all know that prostitution is a prickly affair. However, while I am by no means convinced that it should be against the law, as long as it is, we must make every effort to cover it.''

Digby stepped up next to her to make a show of support.

Hale turned to him in surprise. "What are you doing here?"

She nodded hastily to the crowd. "Thank you. And good night."

Digby came right up to her, his resolve quickening. "I want to talk to you."

"How could you barge in like that?" she spat out.

"Hale," he said, following her into the lobby. "You were splendid, absolutely splendid, but we have urgent matters to discuss."

She turned to him. "Digby, this is hardly the time or place. Business can wait till we get back to Washington."

"No, it can't. We must talk now. Either we go to your room and talk in private, or we take a table at the bar. You decide."

Without a word, Hale stepped into the elevator, her silence stony. She led the way to her room and shut the door firmly behind them. Without inviting him to sit, she demanded, "Now, what is it you want?"

"Let's get right to the point," Digby started. "In order to prevent loss of morale and general chaos, we must cut our losses immediately. I've instructed the editorial page to draw up a retraction and apology to our readers for Colette's story. Glover has written a news story for page one."

"My God, Digby," she exploded, "can't I even be away from the paper for one day without this sort of heavy-handed overreaction? This is the editor's prerogative, and the publisher has no business interfering."

"Even if that were true, you relinquished control when you chose to leave in the midst of a crisis," he said calmly.

"I accepted this invitation six months ago," she said huffily. "I was hardly in a position to renege at the last moment."

With a look of dismay, Digby brushed past her and strolled toward the window and gazed out into the street. "Hale, your speech did us proud. It disappoints me, however, that you're unwilling to face the consequences of our mistakes." This was the most difficult moment in his mission to Boston, but he'd rehearsed it carefully. He turned to face Hale directly. "There are two things we must do now. First, you acted hastily and unilaterally in your dismissal of Sylvia Loring."

"Does loyalty mean nothing to you, Digby?" Hale said icily. "That woman is our Benedict Arnold. What you call a crisis would never have arisen without her betrayal."

"We will reinstate her," he said simply. "Secondly," he continued. "We must terminate Colette Daniels immediately."

Hale's lips began to tremble.

"It's the only way we can regain our respect," he said.

"A talented performer like Colette Daniels did not have to fabricate a story," said Hale, who appeared to be regaining her composure. "Please, I apologize for being so rude. Have a seat. I've talked with Colette Daniels, and this was done as a bid for our attention, a cry for help. To put her out on the street would simply destroy her, Digby."

Digby drew a breath. He knew himself well enough to recognize his soft spot for young women—not excepting this dynamic editor who, flushed with feeling, seemed so alive, so magnetic.

Hale settled into a plush demicouch, patting the cushion beside her. "Here, Digby. Please. Let's talk."

Little time had passed since she'd convinced him with her charm to go against his better judgment and run that blasted story. This time he would not yield.

"Hale," he said. "I have a plane to catch. I'll see you as soon as you get in tomorrow morning."

Now the ball was firmly in her court. It was up to Hale Gardiner to prove she was every bit the editor she presented herself to be.

# CHAPTER
## 30

Sylvia appeared on the ground floor of Elect Fincastle Head-quarters and searched the room for Judy, who was proving to be a foul-weather friend. Her efforts on Sylvia's behalf had redoubled with her plight. If it didn't work out at the *Post*, she'd said over the phone when Sylvia called her with the news of what had happened, she had other contacts and hinted that there might even be something for Sylvia in the new Fincastle White House. Judy had insisted that she buy Sylvia lunch that very day so they could talk over develop-ments. "Meet me at headquarters," she'd said.

Judy didn't come right out and say it, but Sylvia suspected she felt a kind of righteous vindication seeing Colette publicly humiliated. Sylvia had also been surprised at how readily (after yesterday's *Post* revealed Colette's fake) Judy had been enlisted in making plans to help Ben's campaign. It was as if Ben's candidacy were some centripetal force into which she could not help being sucked. Perhaps after all, Sylvia thought, Judy did want her husband to go all the way.

Sylvia gave her name to a receptionist at the front desk and asked if Judy was in.

"Judy Fincastle, a Sylvia Loring here to see you," the woman spoke into a public-address system that made Sylvia cringe. She motioned Sylvia toward a low-backed Naugahyde couch. The formality seemed artificial, since people were wandering in and out of the front door carrying fast-food bags and other materials. A couple of college-age students walked in off the street inquiring where they could sign up for vol-unteer work.

Sylvia hoped that Judy would hurry. She did not want to

bump into B. D., whom she'd managed to avoid since New Year's, or worse yet, Max. She did not want to see either man until she could regain her sense of self. Without her job, she had no direction, felt stripped of purpose, uncertain of what lay ahead. Uncertain even of who she was.

The inside room was configured something like a newsroom with an enormous floor of desks and more telephones it seemed than in the *Trib* newsroom. As if anticipating their victory five days away in the Iowa caucuses, staffers buzzed excitedly about. There was an abundance of pasteboard boxes filled with supplies that nobody bothered to unload. Rather, they stood as makeshift furniture. Just a few offices in the back had doors that you could shut for privacy.

Then she saw them approaching her from outside, walking up the sidewalk together. Max and B.D. Each carried a brown bag and a large paper cup. Tall and handsome as ever in a stylish tan overcoat, the wind whipping his hair into a wave, Max walked curbside.

They were so deep in conversation, it occurred to Sylvia that they might walk right past without catching sight of her. She tried looking away, so her concentration on them would go undetected through the airwaves.

This was one of those moments when Sylvia believed in telepathy. She saw Max look her way, at the glass-paneled door. He did a double take, then rushed through the door.

"Sylvia," Max said, striding right up to the couch. A broad smile betrayed his genuine delight, a reaction that might have delighted her had it been any other time but the present, had things not ended so inconclusively between them, had she not just been fired. "We meet again."

Sylvia had always loved this about him—the way Max could turn a platitude into something fresh and amusing. But now all she could feel was how wrong this was, for him to see her in such sorry shape.

"I guess so," she said weakly, remembering how beautiful she had felt, how handsome he looked the last time she'd seen him, on the New Year's Eve dance floor in this same place.

"What brings Sylvia K. Loring"—theatrically he emphasized the "K."—"out to Crystal City? Might you be doing a story about our little operation?"

Catching up with Max, B. D. was plainly annoyed. "Sylvia," he said, "I called you this morning at work when I got back from Iowa, and the woman said she'd pass along a message but from now on, I should try you at home. What's going on?"

She was sitting, and they were both standing at attention before her. She hardly had the energy to stand. What could she say?

Max seemed to read her—which made it worse, made her feel more like crumbling. There was an unmistakable note of concern in his voice. "Sylvia, what is it?"

Throwing all her effort into keeping herself from breaking down right there, she put her lips together, firmly, and took the plunge.

"I've been fired."

"What?" Max said, his voice outraged and incredulous at the same time. "You're kidding."

"Let's move into my office," B. D. said, directing his remark exclusively to Sylvia, glancing at Max as if to shake him loose.

Sylvia stood, and B. D. took her elbow, moving her toward the elevator. As the doors started to close, Max managed to squeeze his large frame through.

B. D.'s face took on a distinctly reddish tint, and the two men eyed each other like strangers in a poker game. B. D. looked away irritably, watching the ascending floor numbers light up. Then, when the doors opened, he quickly moved Sylvia away, down a corridor into a sparsely furnished office and started to close the door. Again, at the last moment, Max slipped through, walking right into the office.

"What is this, Max?" B. D. snarled.

A cool smile spread slowly from Max's lips outward. "Wasn't I invited, B. D.?"

"If you don't mind," B. D. said to his colleague. "I'd like a moment with the lady."

Sylvia stared at Max, who moved not one muscle. There

was a cool, iron strength about Max Ridgway that gave her a sharp, sudden thrill. The contrast with B. D., who was fidgeting with his hands, clearly on the verge of losing his composure, could not have been more striking.

A knock sounded on the door, and in walked Judy, surprisingly cheerful as she took the three of them in. "I saw you all come in. Guess you heard what happened to Sylvia," she said. "Isn't it outrageous?"

"Actually," B. D. interjected, "they've done her a favor." He went to his desk and started flipping through the Rolodex. The circumstances seemed not to matter to him. Only taking action.

Judy came over and hugged Sylvia. "How're you holding up, sweetie?"

With that, Sylvia burst into tears. It had always been easier for her to maintain her composure amidst hostility than kindness.

Judy held her. "There, there," she said brightly, obviously embarrassed. "We'll go to lunch and feel a hundred percent better."

Sylvia's eyes cleared slowly, and over Judy's shoulder she saw Max, standing near the door with an expression she had seen only once, at UVA, when his fumble lost the game against Virginia Tech.

Max reached for the doorknob. "Call me, Sylvia," he said, "if there's anything I can do."

The words echoed through her night. It wasn't just what he said. It was the way he said them. It was the way he said her name—an exquisite, deep, masculine enunciation—that made her shiver when she heard it in her mind.

Sylvia lay in her bed. It was late, ungodly late, and there was no sleeping, not with the *Post* interview tomorrow, not with Kokoh snoring on the couch. And not, most of all, with Max. He was here, filling the dark room, making it throb with his presence.

There was so much she wanted to ask him. About his reaction to her story about the farm. About his father's reaction. About what had happened to the place: had the syndication gone through, or had Max staved it off? About whether the prize foal had been born.

Having seen him in her distress, she knew now that Max cared for her. Without that knowledge, the night would have been unbearably bleak. But it was not bleak; were it not the dead of night, the witching hour when the mind played its cruelest tricks, Sylvia could swear, could proclaim, could shout it from her window that Max Ridgway still loved her. Had always loved her. Had never given her up.

But the doubts held her back. Though he had bested B. D., toyed with her sullen lover like a cat with a captive mouse, Max had not swept Sylvia onto his horse and ridden off with her into the sunset. Only that one line, planting a few words in her mind that would give her no rest. *Call me. If there's anything I can do.*

Sylvia sat up on the edge of her bed. In her nightgown she let her chin fall into her palms and looked out her window at the streetlight. In the distance, way off, a siren wailed, plaintive, echoing down the streets, down the alleys. A lonely voice in the night. Someone dying maybe. Someone being born.

Her mind, tracking the sound as it receded to a whisper, a crossroads of the conscious and the unconscious, the past and the future, played strange, subliminal tricks. "Ask not," she flashed on Donne's line, "for whom the bell tolls/It tolls for thee." Poetry. The beautiful, haunting stuff of college discovery. Of first-time emotions. Of swept-off-your-feet college romance. Mysteriously, the line conjured that old, resonant feeling. So many years ago now it seemed forever buried—now, out of nowhere, alive! That crazy old feeling, that magical, self-contained world of old Charlottesville, where poetry and language and love for Max were one bundle of emotion. She had wanted to write then. To create. To bring out the deepest feelings of her soul.

And she had wanted Max to make that journey with her.

Suddenly, in a shivering flash of intuition, she knew the old passion was back. All of it. "It tolls for thee." Sylvia sprang to her feet and had to move, knew that despite everything that had happened, all the adult lessons, the old magic was there, lighting her up from inside out like a sky full of fireworks, painting the night a thousand coruscating colors. This was her. The core. The real woman.

Sylvia lunged back against the headboard and hugged herself tight to stop the trembling. It was so strange. What was happening to her was not supposed to afflict a cool, rational, hardheaded woman. This morning, she had broken down and sobbed, and now this.

What was it?

She knew. When the truth hits you in the night like a train hurtling out of a tunnel, there's no denying it. What they'd had, she wanted again. Only better.

It wasn't rational. But Sylvia knew, wanting to deny it, that she adored, craved, lusted after—loved that man, that beautiful man Max Ridgway.

It was another thing to tell him, to pick up the phone and beg for all of it back again. It was another thing to be the fool when what she wanted to see in him might only turn out to be his natural kindness, his natural warmth. Either that or—like the time she returned from the farm—his inexplicable cold shoulder.

She was proud. Why did she have to make the call? Why did she have to put herself in the position of asking him for something?

She knew she wouldn't do it. She knew she had come too far, accomplished too many things on her own, to go crawling back to a man. Any man. Even the one she wanted.

She lay down in her bed and told herself to get some sleep. But no sleep came.

Walking past the Soviet Embassy on a bitterly cold Thursday morning, Sylvia arrived at the entrance to the *Washington Post*, red-eyed, wired with caffeine, deeply shaken by the revelations of the night, yet determined to make a strong showing at this interview.

Many times she'd passed the entrance to the *Post* at 1150 15th Street, with its window display of an old linotype machine, its famous *Post* editions in bronze—"President Kennedy Shot Dead; Lyndon B. Johnson Is Sworn In''—but this was the first time she had actually been invited to come into this sacred temple of American journalism. She walked past the guards in the lobby, onto the elevator with its elite cargo of silent personages, onto Len Haber's floor, with its thick carpet, its modern, antiseptic work stations, its surprisingly hushed atmosphere. Even the clatter of fingers on VDT keyboards seemed subdued, as if the writers and editors were reverentially wearing white gloves as they solemnly, importantly, produced the copy that would be read and revered in capitals the world over.

Sylvia halted, looking out over the vast room, picturing herself here, wondering if the "velvet coffin''—as some had dubbed this prestigious newspaper—was what she really wanted. The *Trib* was ancient and musty, it was understaffed and underequipped, it was a battered ship helmed by a female Captain Bligh, but it had soul.

Then Sylvia remembered, with a jolt, that she had been ''terminated.'' She was acting as if she already had in hand a job offer from the *Post*, but the truth was she was incredibly lucky even to be considered.

She felt suddenly lost, and looked all around her for Len Haber's office.

''Looking for something?'' came the voice of Michael Paradyne, sitting at his desk.

''Yes, Len Haber,'' she said. ''I'm running late.''

Sporting an ironic smile, Michael directed her to her destination and then added, ''Didn't I predict you'd jump ship first chance you got?''

Soon Sylvia was at the threshold of Len Haber's corner office, waiting for his secretary to send her on in.

She shook Haber's hand. He was a burly, balding man in his mid-fifties, with thick eyebrows, horn-rimmed glasses, and an owlish, professorial face. He courteously offered her a chair in his spacious office and sat down behind his desk, tamping tobacco into his pipe and peering curiously at Sylvia.

''Mind if I smoke?''

What was she supposed to say—yes? To the assistant managing editor of the *Washington Post*, in his own office? She smiled and shook her head no.

He lit up with a wooden match, puffed, and looked her over, as if examining merchandise. Then, in a rumbly voice, he sidestepped the preliminaries. "Would you like to work for the *Washington Post*?"

Was this a job offer or the kind of get-the-ball-rolling question asked of all applicants? It was hard to tell. Would she like to work for the *Washington Post*? She wasn't quite sure if she would. Working for the *Post* had never been her professional goal, unlike so many of her colleagues. But Pam and Dennis had advised her to be positive and definite no matter what. To bag an offer and agonize and deliberate later. Len Haber, she thought, would doubtless make her jump through a series of rhetorical hoops, of which this was just the first.

Sylvia set her head steady, firm but friendly. It was a posture she'd learned to adopt when interviewing prominent people around whom she didn't feel comfortable but wouldn't dare let it show.

"It is something about which I'd given very little thought until the day before yesterday. I've enjoyed my time at the *Tribune,* and hadn't planned to leave; the *Trib* has given me a chance to develop as a writer." Even as she spoke, she ran her words back through and realized that she must sell herself, offer something that she could do for them. "I think I could bring a great deal to the *Post*. I'm dedicated, hardworking, and know the city almost as well as Frank Glover!"

Haber puffed on his pipe, considering her answer for a moment. "Your work is very good, Ms. Loring. Top drawer." He paused for a moment, then fired. "Ms. Loring, I want to offer you a staff position as a reporter at the *Post*."

Sylvia's breathing stopped, then came in short bursts.

"It would be in the Style section, of course. I, uh . . ." He lit his pipe again, which had apparently gone out, drew on it more deeply this time, emitting an impressive cloud that hovered like a wraith over his desk, and resumed. "Before any of this came up, we were aware of your work."

She could hardly believe it. She didn't have to sell herself; they'd already made up their minds. Was it Judy Fincastle's word? Or her work? "Thank you," she said for lack of anything more original.

"Now." Haber leaned back in his chair, puffing, scrutinizing, important. "What this would mean, of course, is that you would be roughly on the same turf you've been occupying over at the, uh . . ." Here he paused slightly, as if it took effort to remember the name. "Over at the, uh, the *Tribune*. Feature stories, of course. The arts. Doings at the Kennedy Center. That sort of thing."

A thin haze of smoke was settling over them like a shroud. Sylvia nodded, deciding that if she were going to bring it up, she might as well do it sooner than later. "Uh, the story that I was working on before the . . ."

He enunciated the word with evident relish and the slightest hint of a smile. "Fabrication." He puffed. "Yes, I'm aware of your work on that."

"In addition to my other assignments here, I'd like to get back to that story. There are some new developments."

"Are there?" he said in a tone that perfectly camouflaged his reaction. "Well. You should know that we would have to assign another reporter to that story—if indeed there is a story. Normally, here at the *Post*, a Style reporter would not be assigned to an investigative story of that sort. It just isn't done, I'm afraid."

She nodded, disguising her reaction with equal effectiveness. "I see."

She was aware of the pipe smoke in her nostrils and of Haber looking at her owlishly, knowing that the next move was hers. Perhaps, like Max, he could read her mind. Perhaps he knew that she was thinking this was a terribly high price to pay, giving up her story, now that it belonged to her again, for a plush job at the *Post*.

She had to do it. She had to inquire after the salary. If she appeared indifferent to it, they would automatically drop it down.

"What could you offer?"

"Thirty-five five."

This was the moment in which to bargain upward, if she were so inclined. But she wasn't. He probably knew her *Trib* salary—if not the exact figure, a ballpark one. She did not betray that his offer represented a five-thousand-dollar increase for her. She nodded her head as if that was agreeable.

"May I have time to think about this?"

"By all means." He rose, signaling her departure, and said with a note of warning, "Just let me know by Friday. Certainly not any later than that."

She called Dennis before lunch. "Sylvia," he said wearily, "I don't care what you've got on that Hookergate story. You'd be a fool to turn this down."

"I know. It's just . . ."

"I know what it is. But don't do it. The feeling will pass, okay?"

"It won't, Dennis. I've come too far on this thing. I just want to finish what I've started."

"Sylvia," he said impatiently, "what leverage does a reporter have without a paper? Don't be a hero on this, am I loud and clear? Besides, after all I've put into you, why should I be deprived of getting up in the morning, having my first cup of coffee, and seeing my star reporter's byline in the *Post*?"

"Yeah, but if I were in the *Post*, I'd no longer be your star reporter."

It was the same story with Pam, who argued for Sylvia's "self-interest" that she take the job. Sylvia hung up from that call no more satisfied, feeling even more isolated, alone. Kokoh, as usual, was watching TV, a game show, as Sylvia peeked out at her from her bedroom. Sylvia didn't know how much longer she could keep up this posture—stalling for time, telling Kokoh she was finding the money, keeping her here—even though Kokoh seemed perfectly content to watch TV and eat Sylvia's food. One thing she had to say for the girl: she drove a hard bargain and wasn't spilling one bean without the money. But it was more than the money she wanted. She wanted to be Jessica Hahn or Donna Rice; she wanted a spread in *Playboy* or *Penthouse* and her own TV series to boot. Her fantasies knew no limit, and who could blame her? At eighteen, Sylvia had been convinced she would be the next Sylvia Plath.

She sat down on the floor, leaning back against the wall of her bedroom. For the first time since waitressing in Manhattan, she felt utterly torn in two. For most people, that *Post* job would be the reward for years of inhumanly hard work. Why shouldn't she just take it? Why should her life plot resemble some TV show she'd always ridiculed, the kind where the cop is thrown off the case but smells blood and continues his own investigation?

Then she had a thought. Funny she hadn't thought of this one before now. What the heck, it was worth a try.

Hale found Colette at home and, on the phone, they arranged to meet at a coffee shop only a few blocks away. When she appeared, Hale began circling the topic, ruminating out loud about Colette's "options." "You have so many directions in which to go," Hale said, unable to lay out the keystone fact that, professionally, she'd have to find a new one, soon.

Colette could immediately see the way the conversation was headed. She hated to see someone beating around the bush, and social niceties under such circumstances seemed abhorrent. Cutting short Hale's meandering monologue, she said, "I can't stay on at the *Trib*, I know that. I want you to understand that that's okay," as if having long ago crossed that bridge.

What had always softened Hale had been sentiment; she seemed to have a tolerance—no, an appetite—for almost lethally sentimental doses. And Colette knew how to apply it, as she did cosmetics, in pampering pats and loving strokes. "I know it's not what you would want, that it's hard for you—and even harder for me. Hale, believe me, I know what I've done; I've let you down."

Touched by empathy for this woman, who was so kind, so sensitive—that had been her downfall; so hard had Colette tried to please her that she'd made up the story—Hale had to fight back tears. Somewhere within, she knew she'd placed too many expectations on Colette. Colette had done it despite herself. In a way, Hale had thought more than once, the story was even more extraordinary, considering Colette had made it up out of her head. In just over an hour's time.

Now here this dear heart was, trying to soften a blow that was triply hard on her, by apologizing.

Colette's hand fidgeted with a paper napkin, and Hale grabbed it, and stared intently into her eyes. "You haven't let me down, Colette. I'm letting you down."

Then, as if out of nowhere, Colette said, "What I want to tell you is that I've got another job. I'm going to work for Ben Fincastle."

Suddenly, Hale shot up in anger. Once again she'd been locked out. It was so typical of Colette: having something else, separate, apart from her.

"Why should you jump at that?" With startling bitterness, she added, "Since when has Ben Fincastle known what's best for you?"

Sylvia marched directly into Digby Reeve's office and informed him of this morning's job offer at the *Post*. But what she really wanted to do, she said bluntly, was finish covering the Hookergate story, for which she now had a new lead. Since Hale had fired her in the anger of the moment—a dismissal that might not hold up under guild regulations—Sylvia was prepared to sweep the whole thing under the carpet. She was well aware that the *Trib* needed a new reporter to pick up the pieces on Hookergate, now that Colette was off the story.

"Of course, there are certain conditions I'd like met."

"You're good," Digby said finally, hunching across his desk and smiling with an air of Cheshire satisfaction. "You're very, very good. And you're back on board. I'll give you a week to turn up something on the Hookergate story." But when she mentioned Kokoh's request for money, Digby shook his head slowly. "We just can't do that, Sylvia. It would set a dangerous precedent."

* * *

After officially tendering her resignation at the Tribune—walking into and out of the building with her head held high—Colette pulled into a swanky hotel en route to Fincastle Headquarters in Crystal City.

It was fourish, a time when even respectable people could drink with impunity. Taking a seat at a table for two, Colette downed several vodka collinses. Thinking over the course of events of the past week, she had to admit she had no regrets. Mabel Stoneman had said as much. "Deep in the recesses of your psyche, you wanted to do this. Fantasy has always been your means of escape."

Ben Fincastle, she knew, was at his headquarters this afternoon. Colette had to know why he hadn't been in touch since that duplicitous phone call. She stepped into the ladies' room to prepare her face. She spent three quarters of an hour doing so, spreading out her cosmetics on the marble counter as if it were her personal vanity, oblivious of the other patrons trying to peek around her in the mirror. Finding an electrical socket, she drew the curling iron out of her pocketbook and tended her hair. Satisfying herself that the cut of her suit and fine leather accessories would head off any protest, she set off in her Alfa Romeo for Elect Fincastle Headquarters.

In fact, she had no job offer at all. But it made her feel better to tell Hale that she did, to produce in her a jolt that altered her version of reality. Manufacturing reality had always been delicious.

Lots of politicians had flings with plagiarism. The college papers of a famous Massachusetts senator, the lines of a British politician lifted by a candidate in the last election proved this. In her case, the words were all hers. She hadn't stolen a one.

When she arrived at the headquarters, she breezed right by the receptionist, preferring to strike without warning. From the New Year's Party, she knew exactly where Ben's office was positioned on the top floor.

Secretaries and staffers were no obstacle in her path. Ben, in the midst of a phone conversation, appeared startled to see Colette march up to his desk and settle herself directly in front of him. She thanked her lucky stars that B. D. Cole was nowhere to be seen and made a snap decision not to bring up that last ugly conversation. This would make her job much easier. Ben signed off his call.

"I'm here to work for Elect Fincastle," she announced.

"Oh," he said coolly, rolling his chair back away from her. "You're out of work now?"

"I was planning to quit the *Trib* anyway. I can think of nothing more important than putting you in the White House."

Despite himself, Ben flushed with pleasure. "I appreciate the sentiment," he said. "And I can think of no one I'd rather have on board." He grasped a letter opener and, for a moment, ran it along his jacket sleeve. "But, you know as well as I do how it would be perceived."

Colette folded her arms across her chest. "That sounds like B. D. talking."

Exasperated, Ben started to reply, but Colette wouldn't give him the floor. "I have a lot of friends in this town," she said.

"Yes, but you've lost credibility," he said.

"My friends are loyal," she declared with just a hint of accusation. Then, masterfully, Colette challenged him. "It's your decision *alone* to make, Ben."

Ben was silent, impressed by her strength.

"You need my help, Ben. Just watch what I can do."

# CHAPTER
## 31

"Found the money yet?" Kokoh asked, not taking her eyes from *Love Connection*, her favorite TV show, as Sylvia returned from her first day back on the job.

Sylvia sat down beside Kokoh on the couch. She had thought long and hard about how to raise the money after Digby refused. She could get a little cash from her mother. Seven or eight thousand, maybe. And she could throw in her life savings—all of $3,000. It wasn't anywhere near the $50,000 Kokoh was demanding, but Sylvia was grimly determined. Sylvia took a deep breath and made her proposal. She could pay $10,000 to Kokoh, drawn from her own personal resources—part borrowed, part financed. This much she would do for Kokoh and the story. She would pay $5,000 in advance and $5,000 upon publication of an accurate story. She detailed the risk to her, but said it was a risk she wanted to take.

"You mean I've waited all this time, and this is it?" Kokoh said after a moment, her voice tinged with alarm.

"Kokoh, it's all the money I have. Or, I should say, don't have."

Kokoh rose from the couch, crossed her arms, and stared out onto the street. It occurred to Sylvia that she had made a colossal mistake, that in less than five minutes Kokoh would be out on that street, taking her story elsewhere.

"What happens if I go to that other paper?" Kokoh said tartly.

"Try it if you want. You won't get any money."

"I could go to *Playboy*. They might pay me a hundred thousand."

Something in Sylvia snapped. Maybe it was just everything built up—the frustration, the fatigue, the seeming ingratitude of this girl she'd boarded for free, this girl whose life she was trying to protect. "Go ahead, Kokoh," she shouted with a fury that surprised even her. "Do it." Sylvia sprang from her chair and marched toward her bedroom, slamming the door behind her.

In a few minutes, a weak knock sounded.

"You think *Playboy* will do the story after you write it?"

"There's a chance. It wouldn't be fair to tell you that's definitely going to happen."

They eyeballed each other in the doorway. Kokoh thrust out her hand for Sylvia to shake. "Let's do it."

From the television in the living room, Sylvia heard the network anchorman announcing the returns from Iowa. She ran back into the room and turned up the sound as Ben Fincastle appeared on screen, handsome, smiling, waving to a crowd with his daughter, Glenda. Conspicuous by their absence from the picture were Judy and Arthur. Apparently, neither had been willing to pose for the cameras, to come to Iowa and share the victory "as a family."

Fincastle, said the anchorman, was the big winner, winning by a projected fifteen percent at this hour over Dan Tison, sending him on to next Tuesday's primary in New Hampshire with tremendous momentum in a state where he was already well ahead in the polls.

The moment the anchorman moved on to other news, the phone rang. It was B. D., in Des Moines. He would be back in town tomorrow. He wanted to take Sylvia out tomorrow night and celebrate.

"I don't know, B. D. I've got work to do."

"What are you working on? You're unemployed."

She told him about her reinstatement.

"What kind of reason is that?" he demanded. "Sylvia, we just won the damn caucuses out here." When she didn't reply, he continued. "Don't you understand? We're going all the way to the White House!"

She repeated her line about work.

"Sylvia." There was a knife in his tone. "It's Max Ridgway, isn't it?"

She said nothing.

"Are you seeing him tomorrow night?"

"No, B. D., I am not seeing him tomorrow night. Or any other night, for that matter."

"I don't believe you."

"Believe what you want." Sylvia slammed down the phone. She thought better about turning on the answering machine. He might call again, and she'd have to listen to his voice. She unplugged the phone.

"Who's the dude?" Kokoh asked.

Sylvia stared at the TV. "Some jerk."

Kokoh nodded, then hesitated and said, "What about the dude he said you were seeing tomorrow night?"

Sylvia turned her stare on Kokoh. "You don't miss a trick, do you?"

"Sounds like you got the hots for that one."

"How would you know?"

Kokoh grinned. "I got my ways."

"Like what?"

"Like watching your face when you talked about him."

Sylvia flushed, half with embarrassment, half with anger. "The subject is closed," she snapped, springing up from the couch and opening the refrigerator. Time to start cooking for this know-it-all.

Kokoh followed her into the kitchen. "I was in love once, too."

"Yeah? Tell me about it," Sylvia said sarcastically.

Kokoh was quiet a few moments. "This boy at school." She was quiet again. Then: "I was fifteen. I'd like had other lovers and stuff, but this boy, I just dreamed about him all the time. He was real strong. Black curly hair—real good-looking. Seventeen years old. Real quiet. . . . Finally, one day I asked him out. You know what he said?" Sylvia made no reply. "He said, 'What took you so long? I been wanting to go out with you for three years.' We made love a few times. He was incredible. I've been with a million guys, and he was the only one."

"Only one what?"

"You know . . . that brought me." Kokoh's eyes were misting over. "Very slow. Very sensual-like. Very . . . I don't know. Exciting. He loved me."

There was another matter to settle. The job at the *Post*. Sylvia retired to her bedroom and dialed Len Haber.

"Sylvia, you've done a good job of keeping us in suspense." He laughed. "When can you start?"

She had no other choice. At the *Trib*, she had a week. At the *Post*, she had no story at all.

"Mr. Haber, I want to thank you for your offer, but I must

regretfully decline.'' She told him she'd managed to patch things up at the *Tribune*.

When his voice returned, all the previous warmth had vanished. ''I'm sorry to hear that, young lady,'' he said, as if she'd just made the world's most foolish move.

That night, Jan Loring heard the whole story. Or most of it. Sylvia spared a few details she knew her mother would not want to hear. Sylvia asked for a $2,000 loan to add to her $3,000 savings, the up-front money. Where she would find the money at the back end Sylvia had no idea, but that was a later bridge.

''Oh, Sylvia,'' Jan said indignantly as she cleared the supper dishes. ''I just can't believe you're doing this instead of taking that job at the *Post*!''

First Len Haber, now her mother. They were probably right. She'd just blown the opportunity of a lifetime. But how about a little support for a change? ''Please don't start on that!''

At the sharp note in her daughter's voice, Jan reached for her cigarettes and lit up. She studied her beautiful daughter. ''Sylvia, just how bullheaded can you get?''

''Yes, I am bullheaded. Writers are bullheaded, or else they don't write.'' She didn't mind bringing up the term ''writer,'' though that had been a loaded one for years because of her father. Since Alec Loring was in her mother's book a failed writer, the two words were synonymous in her mind.

''You're just like your father.'' There, her mother had said it. But somehow the bite had no sting.

''Mom, I want to tell you something,'' Sylvia began, her voice calm now, sure. ''I've never asked for something like this before. Why am I doing it now? Because I'm going for it. If you hadn't taken your savings and started investing in real estate, where would you be now? I wouldn't be here asking you if this weren't my best shot.''

Pursing her lips, Jan turned away, loading a platter into the dishwasher.

''Mom, who else would I turn to?''

Jan swung back around to face her daughter. "You won't like my interest rate."

"Interest rate? With your own daughter!"

Jan laughed heartily. It was a good joke. It was a very good joke.

# CHAPTER
## 32

The next morning, Sylvia typed up a contract that included the proposal Pam had suggested for first refusal on an as-told-to book deal. She offered to have it notarized, but Kokoh, to her surprise, brushed that aside, saying that if she couldn't trust Sylvia after all this time in her apartment, she might as well "hang it up and check out" right now. After they both signed, Sylvia withdrew her savings and returned to the apartment with $5,000 cash, having first been to her mother's bank to cash her $2,000 check.

Sylvia chain-locked the door behind her.

Kokoh sat at the kitchen table and watched Sylvia count out the money in $100 bills. When it was all accounted for, in five piles of ten bills each, Kokoh slowly stacked all the money together, her eyes lingering on her treasure in unabashed delight. For the first time, it occurred to Sylvia that Kokoh was quite a poker player. She might have settled for half the amount.

Five thousand dollars, Sylvia thought, watching it disappear in one folded wad into a side pocket in Kokoh's jeans. This better be good. "Okay," Sylvia said, her heart pounding across the narrow table from Kokoh, her left hand ready to take notes on a steno pad. She depressed the record button on her Sony tape recorder. "You're on."

Kokoh certainly had a flair for suspense. She rose, strolled to the refrigerator, extracted a Diet Coke, sat down again, drank one swallow, two swallows, three, and plunked it down on the table. Sylvia felt like reaching out and grabbing her body to shake loose the goods.

"Boss Lady's name is Ellen."

"Ellen? Ellen who?"

"I don't know her last name; none of the girls do. She never gives it out." She drank Diet Coke and suddenly grew angry. "His name is Rich. The son of a bitch!" She flung the Coke toward a trash can. It missed, spilling the remaining contents in a puddle on Sylvia's floor.

Sylvia tore off a paper towel and sponged it up. With a wary glance at Kokoh, she took her seat. As if on a seesaw, Kokoh immediately got up and brought back a fresh Diet Coke from the fridge. She sat down. Her mouth opened to speak.

The doorbell shrilled in Sylvia's ears.

Sylvia went cold. During the time Kokoh had been staying here, it had crossed her mind a few times that if Kokoh's story was true, the people who had hurt her might eventually suspect she was here and come to get her. She had managed, for the most part, to dismiss this thought.

The doorbell rang again. Sylvia's eyes latched on to Kokoh's. Then she went to the door. She had never regretted more not putting in one of those one-way peepholes. "Who is it?"

"Flower delivery!" a voice announced.

Silently, Sylvia motioned Kokoh to the door. "Who?" Sylvia said.

The man repeated himself and added the name of the florist.

"Recognize the voice?" Sylvia asked Kokoh, who shook her head.

"Hey, lady," the voice said impatiently, "I got a dozen red roses out here! You want 'em or not?"

Sylvia glanced at Kokoh. Sometimes you just had to take the leap.

The door opened on a man who looked vaguely like Pat Sajak, wearing a jacket with the florist's decal. He thrust the roses into Sylvia's hands. "Sign here."

After they were back at the kitchen table, Sylvia unwrapped the roses and glanced at the attached note. Only the letters "B. D."

Sylvia nodded at the roses. "You can have them," she told Kokoh, shoving them across the table. All business now. "Tell me more."

"About Boss Lady?" When Sylvia nodded, Kokoh said, "I've heard she has some kind of studio."

"What kind of studio?"

"For photographs and stuff. I think it's like maybe a front for the operation. I've never seen it."

"What do you mean you've never seen it?"

"Like, there's no one place we go to. See, when I go to work, I go to like a hotel, or the dude's house or whatever. I don't go to where Boss Lady is. She just gives me the address and I go."

"What about when they collect the money?"

"Yeah, right, well we just meet"—she spat out his name—"Rich somewhere in the city, like at a coffee shop, and fork it over. They're so uptight that they won't let any of the girls see the headquarters."

Sylvia chewed on that one. "Where do you think it is?"

"Who knows? All I know is she takes pictures of all the girls in sexy poses. You know, like a . . ."

"You mean like for an ad?"

"Yeah. See, she never lets any of the girls in her studio. I mean, I've never seen it, I don't even know if she's got one. She and Rich take all her pictures in a motel room."

"Where?"

"Who knows? It was at night—some motel out in Maryland. She took my picture out there."

"What does Ellen look like?"

"Tall. Like you. Blond hair."

"Attractive?"

"Not bad. I give her about a six. Maybe a seven on her good days."

"How old?"

"Pretty old. Like maybe, I don't know, thirty-something."

Sylvia had to smile. Once, thirty-something had seemed

old to her too. But the smile faded when she learned this was virtually all Kokoh knew about the madam. After at least a dozen more questions, the only significant additional item she revealed was that Ellen often hung out at the Mayflower Hotel.

"What about the famous clients. Who are they?"

Kokoh seemed to rack her brain. She'd been out of commission for a while now. "Some guys with big fancy titles. One called the 'majority whip.' Also a big man at the Pentagon. And the secretary of defense." Kokoh had not actually serviced these men, nor did she remember their names. She'd heard about them from Shana and the other girls.

All of this was interesting, but Sylvia would have to have a lot more substantiation before she could use any of it. "What about Rich?"

"That fucker."

So far, Kokoh's information, though not entirely a washout, was a major disappointment with an equally major price tag. What she knew about Rich, it turned out, was even less impressive—a short but muscular man with dark, curly hair who "cussed a lot," who was maybe Ellen's boyfriend—at least she'd once seen him "squeeze her ass."

However, there was one sensational aspect of the story, if Kokoh were telling the truth—and Sylvia had no reason to believe otherwise. That night when Sylvia had flown to Cleveland and Kokoh—telling Sylvia she wasn't afraid—had reported for work, there was no client waiting for her at the address, the Westin Hotel. Instead, "good ole Rich" had opened the hotel-room door and pulled Kokoh inside. And that was only the beginning.

"He seemed especially rough that night, but I thought he was just on his usual macho trip, so I let him take me to this limo with dark-tinted windows. It was, like, the only time I'd ever been in a limo; I thought we were going to some big party. But only after I got in did I see how angry he was. Someone else was driving, and he shoved into the back seat with me. Then the dude blindfolded me and started hitting me. I couldn't fucking believe it, and when I said anything he slapped me across the face.

" 'You want to be rich and famous, bitch, you gonna get what you want.' "

"I figured out he knew I was the one who put the finger on Bob Rossen, though I never did say nothing. He kept going, 'You gonna pay for this, bitch.' "

"Then he stuck a needle in me. There's nothing I hate worse than having a needle stuck in me. There I was, blind-folded. I was sure that was it. That he was going to kill me and toss me into the Potomac. I thought about your telling me I was in danger."

"When I woke up, I was in this closet. I don't know where the hell we were, I banged on the door, and there was Rich's voice telling me to shut up from outside. Said if I made any more noise, I'd be sorry. I didn't shut up, though. I figured maybe someone could hear. Then I heard a gun go off, like right next to me. And Rich banged on the door and said if I made another noise, the next bullet would rip through my skull."

Kokoh's voice grew low and strange, as if suddenly she were back in that closet, cooped up and frightened, needing air. She wiped her face as if it were midsummer and she were outside in the heat. "Man, this is hard." She went to the refrigerator and retrieved another Diet Coke. She was utterly convincing, and Sylvia forgot for a moment her own pressing needs as she listened to this woman who had been staying in her house, a sanctuary, she could see now, a halfway house after all this horror.

"I stayed in there forever," Kokoh continued. "Like days passed before they even gave me anything to drink. I thought I was going to die. Finally, they gave me stuff to eat and drink. But let me tell you, it was no picnic." Kokoh moved from the table to the couch and drew Sylvia's throw blanket around her like a shawl. She tucked her bare feet under her bottom like a cat resting on its haunches. Then, nothing.

Sylvia remembered something Kokoh had said that day she appeared at the paper. "Kokoh. The white slavery?"

Kokoh flinched, as if not wanting to get into that.

"Yeah, that too." After a pause, she began. "Well, like

after a few days . . . I don't know how much time passed, maybe weeks. One night Rich got me out and drugged me again. And I was almost completely out of it, but I could see what happened around me. A bunch of ugly-looking dudes came in. Drug guys. I could spot them a mile away. And they tied me up, and it was like a gang rape. I was bruised bad and cut and hurt like hell for days. They treated me like shit. The thing about Rich that makes me hate him most is, he stood there and watched. Toking on something. It's the most disgusting thing that ever happened in my life. But, hey, I don't want to get into that. Do I have to? I mean, do you have to write it?''

"I don't know what I'll use," Sylvia said as gently as possible, not wanting to introduce the hard fact that every shred of information she was getting rightfully belonged to her. "It's too early to know. Kokoh, you could put this man behind bars for years."

"Yeah, I know." The tough-girl face melted just then, and the tears started to flow.

It suddenly occurred to Sylvia that prostitutes can be raped, too. Selling their bodies voluntarily and being forced against their will were two entirely different things. Sylvia rushed to Kokoh's side, stroking her hair, holding her close. No longer was Kokoh a shrewd businesswoman, but rather the victim of senseless brutality. "My God, you've been through rape. Gang rape. Honey, you need help, professional help. And you'll get it. And you're going to get your new life, too."

In time, Kokoh finished her story. As she told it, this woman started feeding her. A young black woman with a nice face, and when Kokoh asked for more food she always gave her more food. But she would never say anything to her, as if she didn't want to know what was going down. And one day when the woman came to the door, Kokoh rushed her, knocked her down, and raced out of the apartment house. When she got to the street, she was in pajamas but nobody paid her any attention. It was somewhere in northeast Washington. At first, she thought the sun was going to blind her, though it was hazy that afternoon. Then she found a raincoat in a trash can and hopped on a bus that dropped her close to the *Tribune*. "I never paid my fare," Kokoh boasted. "And the driver never said a thing."

After a smashing win in New Hampshire, Ben Fincastle emerged with Glenda from his plane at Washington National, where they were met by a throng of photographers and reporters.

"Senator," one reporter called out. "Is it true that your wife might not vote for you this fall?"

Ben smiled lamely and brushed past the reporters without comment. He was enjoying a ride with the press that seemed to portend certain victory at the convention that summer and probable victory in November—except for one hitch. It had come to be known as the "Judy Factor"; this morning, a story in the *Post* had turned remarks made by the candidate's wife into the campaign's first major crisis.

Early in the campaign season, little had been made of the fact that Judy Fincastle never went along on Ben's campaign trips. After all, she was a political wife with a family to raise, a household to run back in Washington. And there was her admirable commitment to Peace Links. But, of late, as Ben had emerged as the Democratic front-runner, his picture on the cover of *Time, Newsweek*, and *U.S. News & World Report*, the public felt a right to examine the wife. To study her picture and figure and wardrobe, to hear her speak on television and watch her with her husband, to see how warm her smile was. The Wife was part of the package. The only problem was that Judy wasn't present, wasn't even available for examination, and it had given rise to speculation that perhaps the marriage was in trouble.

And with good reason. Judy had suspected that Ben had broken his promise to her and resumed his affair with Colette Daniels. But the final straw had been learning that Colette had joined the Crystal City campaign staff and was now arranging some grand event in late March for Ben in town, a party that was intended as the celebration of his primary victories in the South. Judy felt like a female cuckold, with no face, no dignity, the object of pity.

Though B. D. had tried to twist Judy's arm to grant some tasteful interviews—or at least make herself available for photo opportunities with the candidate—she'd doggedly refused. "The only thing I'll talk about is my organization," she'd said.

B. D. had decided that any press was better than none, better than Judy appearing to be a recluse. So he'd brokered just one interview with the *Post*. He'd selected a young woman reporter, about Sylvia's age, whose work was good but not as hard-hitting as that of some others, and offered her the story. They both understood that it was a coup for her, and he figured that in return, she would be kind to Judy. And though she would have to mention it, B. D. trusted she would delicately handle the "Judy Factor."

So two days ago, Judy had granted a ninety-minute interview on the subject of Peace Links and posed for a photograph in her home. But when the story came out—this very morning—a certain offhand remark stood out in bold print.

"I haven't decided who I'm going to vote for yet," Judy had told the reporter as the woman was leaving, having already shut her notebook and stopped the tape recorder. "Because Ben Fincastle hasn't submitted his position papers to Peace Links, and I don't know where he stands on the issue of nuclear disarmament."

That was all that was needed to set off the fireworks of scandal.

The reporter had deftly woven the remark into the lead, where—concurrent with Ben's victory in New Hampshire—it hit the wires and every radio news broadcast as well. Commentators and the press were now speculating that the marriage was on the rocks.

At Elect Fincastle, a full-scale, behind-closed-doors strategy session had been set up for ten A.M. by B. D. to decide on how to exert "damage control."

Colette, secretly delighted by Judy's gaffe, believed that it was exactly the ammunition she needed to pin Ben down on something that was every bit as important to her as his candidacy: the matter of his divorce. She had run the argument through her mind more than once. He should get out now, before he reached the White House. The divorced President Reagan was the most popular president in recent history, after all, and since America loves a wedding, what a delightful way to give them a preelection show!

Not that she would ever make such a proposal in a meeting with B. D. Cole, Lyons Smith, and other top aides. It would have to be saved for an intimate moment with Ben.

"Why is she here?" B. D. said indignantly to Ben as they entered the conference room and saw Colette seated at the table. "Was she invited?"

It was yet another thorn in B. D.'s side. Since Ben had chosen to make Colette a trusted aide, there had been nothing but enmity between the two rivals to Ben's innermost ear. And it was Colette, more often than not, who had the final word.

"Keep your shirt on, pal," the candidate replied, smiling at Colette. "I want a female perspective on this thing."

"I called this meeting," B. D. fumed. "I'd damn well like to know who's going to be here."

Ben laid a hand on B. D.'s shoulder and steered him to his seat. "Just settle down, big boy." Ben winked at Colette. "Let's see you put that brain of yours to better use than picking on pretty women."

It was a less-than-tranquil meeting. B. D. was convinced that Ben's only recourse was to demand that Judy issue a retraction. "Whatever it takes to make a deal with her, you have to make it," he told Ben, throwing a significant glance at Colette. His meaning was clear: dump Colette and Judy will come around.

"I don't think that will work," Ben said. "My wife can't be bribed, I'm afraid."

"It's not a bribe, Ben," B. D. retorted. "It's a political necessity. The American people love gossip, but that doesn't mean they're going to feel secure with a candidate who can't even keep his own wife in his corner."

Ben bristled. "B. D.," he said, "I don't need lectures on what makes the American public feel secure. They've felt just fine about Ben Fincastle to this point, and my guess is that's not going to change."

"Ben," Lyons said, knowing his man, "we're not going to self-destruct. We're going to win. But we do have a problem, and it's not going to go away. The press is not going to let the voters forget it." Lyons lit a cigarette, drew on it deeply, then spoke again in his rich Tarheel accent. "Ben, I've got to agree here with B. D. One way or another, you're going to have to sit down with Judy and talk this thing through. Find out what she wants. And it can't wait. You've got to act today."

Seeing the effect of Lyons's words on her man, Colette turned to him and said, "I have a better idea."

They all looked at her warily, including Ben.

"You're all forgetting one thing: your sense of humor, Ben. JFK had nothing on you! Or look at Ronald Reagan. Americans will forgive anything if you say it with a smile. If you make them laugh. Remember what JFK said to the little boy? The little boy asked, 'Mr. President, how did you become a war hero?' JFK said, 'It was absolutely involuntary. They sank my boat.' That's the kind of touch we need to handle Judy. I mean, the way you men are talking, all those voters out there are nothing but little Puritans, all dressed in black, all the women wearing chastity belts! Come on, guys, where've you been? Everybody's got marriage troubles. They can sympathize. Make it funny, Ben. They'll adore you for it."

"Oh, spare me," B. D. snapped.

But it was too late. Colette had dropped the right acronym. Ben's face had lit up and he was already picturing himself as JFK, coming up with the clever lines that would make this problem disappear, like those early Democratic rivals who had announced but not even made it as far as Iowa.

"Ben," B. D. said, "let's get serious here."

Ben nodded impressively. Sometimes he had to humor B. D. a bit. "Oh, I'm serious. Yes," he said with a second nod to Lyons, "I'll certainly talk to Judy."

"Good. And posthaste. And by the way," B. D. went on,

"I have another idea. I can have Sylvia Loring write a 'marriage on the mend' piece for the *Trib*. That'll get the ball rolling in the press. You know how that goes—all the other media follow suit. We'll have stories all over the country on how the Fincastles have their troubles, like other couples, but they're getting through them. That's something everyone can relate to. It makes Ben and Judy very human."

"B. D.," Ben said, "that's all well and good, but what happened with that nice *Post* article you thought you had for us?"

"I delivered it," B. D. said irritably. "Your wife is the one that botched it."

"Anyway, my wife is not talking, you know that."

"But you forget, Judy and Sylvia are buddies. Sylvia has lunch with her all the time," B. D. said, aware that this was news even to Ben.

"I don't know what makes you so sure Sylvia could do it," Colette interjected. "You know, she and Hale are on the outs."

B. D. brushed that aside with the important air of the true insider. Leave it to the Great Fabricator, as he liked to call Colette behind her back, to try to spoil everyone else's standing at the *Tribune* when she had none of her own.

"Sylvia is a senior reporter; she can write anything she damn wants. If she turned in the D.C. yellow pages, they'd print it." B. D. took a swig of coffee from his Styrofoam cup and glanced at his boss to see if he was persuaded. He had just about had enough. This was an insult, having to deal with this woman. More than once now, it had taken all of his strength to restrain himself from quitting.

After the meeting ended, Ben assured Lyons Smith that he would, indeed, talk to Judy that evening. Twice he phoned his wife's private line at home, hoping to sound conciliatory while arranging their talk, only to get the answering machine. Now, arriving home at eight o'clock, he found her at the dining table, finishing a dinner of roast beef, boiled new potatoes, and brussels sprouts.

"I tried to call you," Ben said, sitting down at the opposite end of the long table, with no place set for him.

"I know," she said, spearing a brussels sprout.

Though he knew damn well what she would tell him, he had resolved to get right to the heart of the matter. "Judy," he said, "what is it you want?"

She did not look up at him, but methodically chewed her brussels sprout. Then her head remained bowed, her eyes fixed on her plate, as if in prelude to prayer. "I think you now know," she said calmly, "what I am capable of doing."

Shrugging his shoulders as if chilled, Ben rose and ventured to the liquor cabinet, pouring himself a stiff scotch. "I suppose you're referring to your, uh, interview in the *Post*."

She offered no reply. Ben added ice to the scotch and leaned against the wall. He sipped his drink and said, "I'm not sure I follow you."

Her voice was eerily flat. "It's very simple, Ben. This time, some of your 'damage control' may repair the situation. Next time, when I announce that I am divorcing you, no amount of Elmer's glue will put Humpty-Dumpty back together again."

Ben straightened against the wall, the ice tinkling in his glass. "Judy," he said, "I don't think you're being fair."

Her eyes lifted, pinning him. "Your gall amazes me, Ben," she said, still remarkably without inflection. "You assured me you would break it off. Can you now stand there and tell me you're not sleeping with Colette Daniels?"

It was his mother, Ben often thought, that Judy reminded him of most. His mother, always holier than thou, always standing on her narrow reading of the Bible back in the cramped hills of Carolina. He had learned clever ways to get around her, to conceal, to make light of; and as these ways had offered him escape from her domination as an adolescent, they had stood him in good stead dodging the toughest questions as a politician. And now, at perhaps the most critical moment of his marriage, her wording had played right into his hands, offering him yet another providential escape.

"Judy," he said, coming to stand directly over her at the table. "I swear to you—from my heart—that I am not sleeping with Colette Daniels."

He could see that she believed him. Almost. And why not?

In God's truth, he was not sleeping with Colette Daniels. He was merely having evening trysts with her in the inner sanctum of campaign headquarters.

Judy stared up at him, at disconcertingly close range. "Why should I believe you?" she asked.

"Because it's true," he replied. A lie, he knew from years of experience, grew less painful the longer you drew it out. As if embellishment made it true. "Judy, I know you don't like it. But the fact is that Colette is an asset to the campaign. And even if I wanted to—which I don't—I would no longer sleep with that woman. Do you think I'm so blinded by passion for anyone that I would risk ruining what I have?" He bent to kiss her forehead. "What *we* have?"

Judy rose, coolly brushing past him with her plate. She rinsed it in the sink, loaded it in the dishwasher, and turned to him, her arms folded defensively. "Even if what you say is true, it's more than a matter of a physical, sexual affair, isn't it Ben?"

"I don't follow you."

"It's the fact . . ." Her voice broke. She recovered. "It's the fact that your heart is no longer with me."

He came forward, standing in front of her awkwardly before laying his hands on her stiff shoulders. "That isn't true, Judy," he said. "We just need to spend more time with each other. Which we'll do—I promise you—when this campaign is over."

For a moment, it seemed that she believed him, the stone in her jaw crumbling. Then, sliding out from beneath his hands, she moved away and turned, her face hard, unforgiving. "I'll give you the benefit of the doubt, Ben. One more time. But if you ever violate my trust again . . ." Her eyes flashed. And Ben felt the anger of her footsteps as they echoed from the stairs.

Hellfire, he thought. She means it this time.

That same evening, Sylvia was settling in at her desk at the *Trib*, deciding which of Kokoh's leads showed the most promise. The phone rang.

"Sylvia," B. D. said. "How's my favorite workaholic?"

"You mean other than yourself?" The line was out before she had time to censure it.

"Look," he said, "I have something extremely important to discuss with you."

"B. D. . . ." She twisted in her seat. "Look, if it's about the roses you sent . . ."

"It's not about the roses. I have something that may be of interest to your Hookergate story."

Sylvia hesitated.

"It won't keep," he said, a note of spitefulness in his tone. "If you don't want it, I'll very happily call the *Post*."

Sylvia Loring did not like herself just now. Why did she do it, she wondered, leaving the cold night air on Capitol Hill and entering the cavernous Hart Senate Office Building. She had let B. D. manipulate her into driving the long way to the Hill, where he claimed he would be all night, at work in Ben's office.

At nine-thirty P.M., the building was all but deserted. She took the elevator, then walked down the long, deserted corridor, her footsteps echoing eerily, to the door number he had given her, one of a number of rooms in Senator Fincastle's corner suite. Recalling her lack of attention toward B. D. in recent weeks—turning him down when he'd called from Iowa, failing to acknowledge the roses—Sylvia felt a vague uneasiness as she confronted the huge closed door. Probably it was guilt over using the man and then discarding him that brought her here, that along with a desire to leave things between them on good terms.

B. D. was nowhere in sight. She had entered a reception room, with chairs for visitors, American and North Carolina flags, a huge map of the Tarheel state on the wall, a rack of brochures about Washington attractions for the folks who'd come from back home. At the far end of the room, a door was half open, affording a glimpse of another huge room.

She heard B. D.'s voice, his words slightly slurred, and realized it was dictation, something about the campaign. Approaching the sound, Sylvia swung the door open wide and saw him, seated in the red leather swivel chair behind a massive desk. His sleeves rolled up, his tie loosened, he drank an amber liquid from a glass and didn't see her. She took in the black marble fireplace, the plush couches and chairs, the photos on the walls of the senator with prominent politicians. This had to be Fincastle's private office. Sylvia could not suppress a smile; here was B. D. playing senator at Fincastle's own desk.

Then B. D. looked up. There was no question he'd been drinking. "Sylvia Loring, I presume." He gestured with his hand. "Sit down. Sit down. We have urgent matters to discuss!"

He made no effort to rise, instead leaning back in Ben's chair. "Let's get a look at you," he said, appraising her across the desk as she sat down opposite. "Been so long, I want to be sure it's you. Is that a frown I see?"

It was a frown, all right. This was all Sylvia needed, B. D. drunk and on some power trip behind Fincastle's desk. "This better be good," she said curtly, slipping out of her coat.

He reached for a crystal decanter. "Bourbon?" She merely looked at him. B. D. poured himself another hit and set the decanter down beside the dictaphone.

"I want a story," B. D. started.

Sylvia tensed. "Story? What are you talking about?"

"You're going to do a story."

Sylvia stared at him. "What's going on here? You asked me to come over here because you were going to tell me something about—"

A derisive laugh cut her short. "How else was I to get a chance to talk to you? You're not exactly Miss Accessibility of late."

This wasn't happening. Sylvia told herself to rise, to leave right now before things got worse. But the perversity of his performance held her spellbound. It was the most incredible power play she'd ever witnessed.

Almost as if she weren't even there, as if B. D. were dictating instructions to a subordinate into his dictaphone, he laid out in precise detail the story he wanted about Ben and Judy—their long marriage, their devotion to their children, their many adversities, their commitment to strengthening the marriage despite the ordeal of the campaign. Sylvia grew increasingly wooden in her chair, shocked not only by B. D.'s manner, like that of some unbelievably arrogant editor, but by the nerve of him, telling her how to write a story that reeked of deception. Was this the man she'd seen fit to go out with, to whom on occasion she'd given her body? Could she have been so blind?

"Make it real enough to be believable while at the same time dispelling doubts," he concluded, and waited for her reaction.

"You've outdone yourself."

He glanced at her darkly, then drank his bourbon. "Explain."

"No explanation necessary. Do you think I'm a plant for Elect Fincastle?"

He glowered from behind the acre of desk. "Of course not. However, when the stakes are this high, Sylvia, I do expect to cash in some old chips."

She was incredulous. "You mean I owe you?"

His fingers squeezed the bourbon glass. "You think that the nights out, dinner at the White House, the whole enchilada was a free ride?"

Sylvia stared at him, throat tightening. She could feel it in the very air between them: one more negative word from her would be the match in a gas can. Everything about him was primed to explode.

He poured himself more bourbon. She wanted to tell him to stop, but fear blocked her throat. "What does it take with you, Sylvia?" he asked, leaning toward her across the desk. "I show you a good time. Then, poof! Where are you? So time goes by. I decide to ask you out. Nothing. I send flowers." He drank. "So what happens? Nothing." Another drink. "Now I make a simple request. Will you do this for me or not, Sylvia?"

She rose, unsteady on her feet. "No."

His glass slammed on the desk. Remarkably, it didn't break, only spewed bourbon in every direction, spraying Sylvia's cheek. B. D. was on his feet in virtually the same

motion, his shouts filling the room. "Who the hell do you
think you are? You're not the goddamned *New York Times*.
You're a two-bit rag!"

Sylvia turned to leave.

His feet pounded the carpet; she could feel his body rushing
through the air toward hers. Frightened out of her wits, she
wheeled on him, hoping to back him down. But B. D. grabbed
her wide belt, his red face contorted with rage.

"Let go of me!" she screamed.

He yanked her toward him with her belt. "You journalists
think you're above the rest of us, huh? It's all the same game,
manipulation."

"I said let go!"

With ferocious strength, B. D. got both her arms in his
grip, then slung her onto the couch. Before Sylvia could fight
back, her arms were pinned and the bear was above her,
tearing at her blouse, ripping it open, savagely hiking her
skirt and grabbing for her panties. It was happening, she was
being raped, and by B. D.

"You bastard!" she called out.

He slapped her hard across the cheek. His hand reached
for his crotch.

But suddenly, before he'd even opened his fly, B. D. froze.
A look of horror—as if the storm had blown through and just
as quickly departed—overtook his face. He dropped to the
floor. "Sylvia," he said. "My God, I'm sorry, I'm sorry."

She stood quickly. B. D. was down on his knees, his hands
pressed together as if in prayer, tears tugging at his eyes. "I
don't know what happened. I . . . Please, talk to me. . . ."

Sylvia ran from the office. She was on the bottom floor,
almost out in the cold again, before she realized she'd left
her coat. It was B. D.'s now. So, too, was the assault charge
she would file as soon as she called the police.

Sylvia jumped inside her Nova, her crossed arms hugging
her chest to cover the rips in her blouse, and warmed her
body with the heater. Twenty minutes later she was home,
not quite as sure that she would call the police. Nightmarish
as it was, B. D. had been drunk, and when he sobered up to

the full import of what he'd done, not even B. D. Cole would dare barge into her life again. Filing charges would mean continued dealings with the man, would mean a major distraction from her story. It was time to focus all her energies on Hookergate, the way B. D., in his own demented way, focused all of his on electing Fincastle president. What astonished her most was her judgment—having ever considered any future with him.

Sleep was out of the question. The best way to put the incident behind her was to go back to the *Trib* and resume work. Right now. She showered quickly and changed clothes, found an old red coat that would do, and climbed back into the Nova.

The night-side shift was on duty at the *Tribune* when Sylvia hurried in. Copy editors, working busily on the morning edition, offered her no more than the usual, perfunctory courtesies. They had become used to her erratic hours, so no one bothered to inquire what story was so important as to bring her in at 10:55 at night.

She went immediately to the shelf of phone books from around the country—placed conspicuously near the coffee machine as a standing hint that reporters check here first rather than dialing directory assistance at sixty cents a pop. Pulling out the yellow pages for the metropolitan D.C. area, she headed for her desk.

She turned to the listing "Photographic Studios," scanned the columns for businesses with a female name. It was a long shot. It was entirely possible that the madam could be working for someone else or under a name not her own. Sylvia jotted down the names of the three apparent women-owned listings, including an Eleanor Gardiner. The name caught on her pen: Eleanor Gardiner—Hale's cousin. That ruled one out.

So-called escort services, Sylvia knew from earlier research, were businesses that flourished on the "impulse buy" in the twilight hours when men most wanted sex and companionship. Therefore, phone lines would have to be open at this hour for customers' calls. She dialed the numbers on the prayer that the madam used a studio as a front for her escort service; if that was correct and if she'd listed the number, someone who booked appointments just might answer. She dialed the two businesses with female names. No answer.

She counted the photographic studios listed in the book: thirty-seven. What the heck, she'd call them all. As she plodded down the list, dialing and getting no answers or answering machines, she came again upon the name of Eleanor Gardiner.

As much to wake herself as to satisfy her curiosity, Sylvia approached Hale's office. The morgue would be locked at this hour; they didn't like reporters using it when the librarians weren't around to check you in and out. Reporters were known to play fast and loose with files. But you had to be able to get into the morgue at night for emergencies. The night editor had a key, but she'd rather not call attention to herself.

There was another key in Luanne's desk. Sylvia shot a glance toward the few remaining copy editors plugging away at their terminals. Opening the drawer, she slipped the key, which hung on a long string, into her pocket and walked down the long hall to the large, dark morgue. Here, by day, librarians clipped and filed into manila envelopes every item and article that appeared in the *Tribune*. And when they could, those from the *Washington Post* as well. There were subject files, people files, and byline files. A file for aviation accidents; for Chuck Robb; for stories by Pam Tursi.

She pulled the drawer for "GA" and thumbed through the giant manila envelopes until she reached the name Gardiner. There it was, right in front of the thick pad of stories about the accomplishments of Hale Gardiner: Eleanor Gardiner. Eleanor had been featured in the paper three times, the most recent appearance being a Society Sketch profile by Colette Daniels that Sylvia and Pam had joked about but had never bothered to read.

Only one blinking fluorescent light was illuminated, which made it hard for Sylvia to see. She glanced over the piece, with its fawning phrases about how extraordinary were Eleanor's shots, how singular was her talent. The classic fluff piece.

What she was looking for, she couldn't say. An article was

peeking up over the Hale Gardiner file. Sylvia pulled it out. There was Hale collecting a plaque at some awards banquet, flanked by cousin Eleanor.

Quickly, Sylvia read the piece. A sentence stopped her: ". . . Eleanor Gardiner, escorted by Rich Kurtz."

Rich Kurtz. Rich. She read the name again. Rich and Eleanor. Rich and Ellen. Those were the two names Kokoh had given her. Coincidence? Maybe not.

Bang! A loud thud screamed out from the far end of the morgue, and Sylvia cried out. Someone was in here with her. She ran to the long panel of light switches and flipped up every light in the house. She flung open the door to the hallway.

"Everything okay in here, miss?" said one of the night janitors.

"I heard a noise, over there."

A broad grin crossed his weathered face. "It's only mice coming out at night."

When he'd left, Sylvia inserted the glossy black-and-white photo from the piece about Hale into the Eleanor Gardiner file and brought it with her as she exited the library. By instinct, she stepped over to the Xerox machine and made copies of the clips as backups to tuck away in safety. For the first time, some pieces of the puzzle were starting to fall together. It was just possible that the Hookergate story reached into the inner sanctums of the *Washington Tribune*.

Kokoh was asleep on the couch, *Late Night With David Letterman* blaring on the TV beside her, when Sylvia got home. Sylvia shook Kokoh awake. "I want you to look at something."

"I'm asleep," Kokoh protested.

"No, you're not." Sylvia turned on the overhead light and sat down beside her. She held up the glossy of Hale and Eleanor. "Look at this photograph."

Kokoh gave it a groggy glance. "What about it?"

"Look at it very closely."

Kokoh rubbed her eyes and examined the photo of Hale and her cousin Eleanor at the awards banquet. "So?"

Sylvia tapped Eleanor with her finger. "Do you recognize this woman?"

Kokoh took another look. "No. Why? Am I supposed to?"

Sylvia sighed. Apparently, this wasn't to be. "I have a newspaper story that describes an Eleanor Gardiner—this woman here—being escorted by a Rich Kurtz to this banquet. Eleanor—Ellen—and Rich: those were the names you gave me."

Again, Kokoh studied the photo. "This lady has short hair. It looks dark in this picture. Boss Lady has long blond hair, down past her shoulders. She's got long eyelashes—you can't even see 'em on this lady here. She always wears, like, heavy mascara and stuff."

"Okay," Sylvia said wearily.

Then, as she started to rise with the photo, Kokoh seized it. "Hold it. This lady does look kind of familiar."

Sylvia sat down, feeling a rush of adrenaline. "What about her?" When Kokoh didn't reply, she prodded her. "You said the madam was tall. Eleanor Gardiner is tall—look how much taller she is than the other woman."

"Yeah, right." Then Kokoh brought her face close to the photo. "Something about her."

"Her eyes?"

"Yeah, kind of."

"Her nose?"

"I don't know. Boss Lady's got like, uh, I don't know, like her nose is crooked or something."

Sylvia peered with Kokoh at the photo. It was a frontal shot of Eleanor—she couldn't tell much about the nose. Then it hit her: That time she'd seen Hale and Eleanor together at the paper, she remembered noticing how the cousins had that same bend in the nose!

"Kokoh, look at this woman very carefully. Is it possible that she is the woman we're looking for?"

"Sure it's possible," Kokoh said after a moment. But Sylvia detected the note of doubt in her voice.

"Is it the woman you know?"

Kokoh rose with the photograph, walking, cocking her

head at it, walking some more, keeping Sylvia in suspense. "I wish I could say yes for sure," she said finally. "Boss Lady looks like her—kind of. And kind of not—you know what I mean? I mean, they could be sisters or something."

Sylvia was close, oh, so close, but not close enough. Kokoh was not giving her positive identification, certainly nothing conclusive enough to write a story. Yet there did seem to be a very good chance—a tantalizingly good chance—that Eleanor Gardiner was the madam!

The next morning, Sylvia drove Kokoh to her bank, where she had persuaded Kokoh to convert her cash into traveler's checks, then on to Washington National. Though Sylvia's sanctuary offer still stood, Kokoh had made up her mind she wanted to take her $5,000 and go to New York. She had a plan—a very vague plan, Sylvia worried—to launch her modeling career by finding a room somewhere and walking into modeling agencies. She promised to call Sylvia with her new phone number and address when she got established; Sylvia figured she would, to collect her five grand on the other end, to parlay Sylvia's story into overnight fame.

# CHAPTER
## 33

Late the following Monday morning, Hale Gardiner came into work a happy woman. She had paid an unannounced visit to Digby's home over the weekend. And while it was impossible at the moment to revoke Sylvia K. Loring's senior-writer status or her raise, Digby had agreed last night to allow Hale to make her start producing again—under Hale's supervision. Digby told her that he'd given Sylvia a week to wrap up the Hookergate follow-up, or give it up; and he'd

admitted he was pessimistic about her coming up with anything at all. When Hale had suggested she put Sylvia on
something else immediately, he'd offered no objection.

Sylvia, for once, was in. Smiling, Hale approached the
desk of the reporter whom she'd come to regard as her own
nemesis, whose intractability and resolve had proved greater
than she'd ever calculated. Hale had avoided her too long.
This time, she was going to be diplomatic. This time, she
would prevail.

"Good morning, Sylvia. Do you have a moment?" she
asked with utmost politeness.

Sylvia blinked away her incredulity. They had not spoken
since the *Post* had reported Colette's fabricated story, and
Hale had correctly guessed its source.

"Yeah, sure," Sylvia said, remembering the Eleanor Gardiner file on her desk, which she quickly covered over with
a press release meant for the trash can. Luckily, her desk
was messy enough that Hale hadn't noticed it.

Hale pulled up a stray chair and sat herself down next to
Sylvia's desk. "I know you care about conservation, the
outdoors, and wildlife, as do I. You write with conviction
and concern. A case in point, your fine story about Ridgway
Farm."

A compliment from Hale Gardiner. It did not compute.
This from the woman who had fired her. "Thank you," said
Sylvia, guarded.

"On your year-end report, you mentioned an interest in
covering more environmental issues. Do you still feel that
way?"

Sylvia couldn't believe this suddenly sensitive Hale, concerned about her needs and goals.

"Yes, eventually."

"Sylvia, I'd like for you to begin work on a series on the
future of the National Park Service. Three parts, possibly
five, depending on what you find. I'd like you to be in touch
with me once you've done initial research, and we can decide
then whether it merits three or five parts. Of course, in the
first part you would deal with its history and goals."

"Sounds good," said Sylvia without enthusiasm.

Hale pulled a silver Cross pencil from her Filofax date book. "Let's try to set up a reasonable due date. Say, a week from Monday."

Sylvia furrowed her brow.

"That shouldn't be any sweat, an investigative pro like you?" In this last line, Sylvia detected a trace of a barb.

"You know I can't start till end of next week at earliest. I'm still working on Hookergate."

"Digby and I have talked," Hale said, "and we think it's high time to call closure on that."

"Digby gave me a week," Sylvia said.

"We can all change our minds from time to time."

As Hale walked away, Sylvia was left with the realization that Hale had pulled off what might be her biggest triumph —she was pulling the plug on her story. As the full implications sank in, Sylvia's anger began to verge on the murderous—if there was ever a human being she could just strangle with her bare hands, there she was, strolling in that haughty, self-satisfied gait toward her office.

But why? Sylvia wondered. Was Hale killing the story because she despised Sylvia? Or was it something even more damning? For the first time, Sylvia wondered if there was well-disguised desperation under Hale's saccharine act. Could she somehow know of Sylvia's suspicions? Could she be trying to cover up for her cousin?

Discreetly, Sylvia returned the Eleanor Gardiner file to the library. Then she stepped into Digby's office, where she would make her appeal.

His jaw was set, his mind made up.

"We never had a story here, did we, Sylvia?"

"Digby, I'm really onto something. Let me run—"

Digby cut her off with a hand gesture. "That story's finished, Sylvia."

She considered for a moment confiding in Digby her suspicions about Eleanor Gardiner, but thought better of it. He might pass them along to Hale, who seemed to work her magic on him, and she would certainly tip off Eleanor. The prospect of beginning on another story at a time when she needed every ounce of energy for this one was more than she could handle.

Sylvia decided to play another card. "I'm burnt out," she said, and asked for a two-week vacation.

That much, Digby could do for her. Having waited this long, the *Trib*'s readers would certainly not object to being a few more weeks in the dark about the National Park Service.

Ben Fincastle was lying on the plush sectional couch of the entertainment and conference suite on the third floor of Elect Fincastle Headquarters. It was eight o'clock in the evening. Hiring Colette had been the canniest move of his campaign, he thought as she ran her delightful fingers from his forehead to his nose, tracing his profile, and then worked her way into his royal-blue velour bathrobe and moved down his chest. Now they could make love like newlyweds any time they chose and damned if any Michael Paradyne—or any other reporter or busybody—could stake them out. Nobody could find them, because they were doing it under their own roof.

Then Colette, suddenly serious, interrupted his self-congratulatory reverie. "Have you talked to your lawyer yet?"

Ben got up, stepped into his trousers, and moved over to a closet from which he selected a freshly laundered shirt. "Can this discussion wait?" he asked, tearing off the plastic skin.

There was little Ben liked less than spoiling a good time with sober talk. Even with this setup, good times were hard enough to steal these days. So he milked them for every bit of pleasure. He was having a wonderful time with Washington's sexiest woman, who happened to possess not only an incredible body but equally wizardly political instincts. She gave good advice, and she came up with clever lines.

Ben had wowed network television's toughest late-night political host with his response to the "Judy Factor" question he'd known was coming. The words were Colette's, and they proved perfectly disarming when he delivered them.

"Judy's entitled to keep an open mind about the election,"

he'd said with a glint in his eye that seemed to charm even the tough interviewer. "But then, I haven't decided if my wife's cooking is better than Julia Child's, either."

But Colette, donning her clothes, was not as easily appeased as the interviewer. She wanted dates and plans. She had this dangerous idea of making it permanent. She told him that she was falling in love for the first time, what happened to other people in high school. Here she was thirty-one.

What was even more alarming was that he was beginning to feel that way too. He had come to count on Colette and their time together. The woman was his soul mate. She saw politics as he did, as a great wonderful game, in which if you played your cards right and moved your players you could win the grand prize. She was as clearheaded and realistic about the way things worked as Judy was idealistic and obtuse. Not only that, the woman adored him and would seem to do anything to further his interests.

"You know, we really make a sensational team," she said.

"Yes," he mused.

Colette slipped into her dress. "Zip, please." Ben obeyed, kissing the nape of her neck for good measure. "Now that you see what I can do for your campaign, just imagine what I can do for the Ben Fincastle White House."

He spun her around in his arms. "Meaning what?"

She traced a finger along his lips. "Eight long years in the White House, leading our nation. Eight long, dutiful years with Judy. Wake up with Judy. Go to bed with Judy. And you know, Ben, a president just can't make it with anyone he pleases. The golden days of JFK are over."

"Subtle, aren't you?" He grinned. His eyes fell to her bosom, heaving against his chest. He was tempted to have a quick second go-round.

"You like, don't you?"

His head lowered, his lips nibbled a clothed breast. "Mmmmmmm . . . I like."

"Imagine what your life would be like without it."

His head rose, and he peered down at her with amusement. "You're growing subtler by the moment."

"Oh, I'm never subtle, Ben. I believe in being very direct when the time comes. The time has come. You need to divorce her now—before reaching the White House."

"Do I?" he said with a hint of facetiousness.

"Yes. Once you're the president, divorcing Judy would be much more difficult. First ladies are elected, too, you know." Her voice became a mother's, explaining it in simple English to a small child. "Divorcing Judy in the White House would make the president a very naughty boy."

Ben was still playing along in a facetious undertone. "Yes. But so would divorcing Judy now make Ben a very naughty boy—would it not?"

"No," she corrected him. "Divorcing Judy now would make you even more admired than you are now. A president couldn't get more popular than Ronald Reagan. Besides," she said, "America loves nothing more than a royal wedding!"

Ben was transfixed. Colette was awesome. With a few bold words, she had the power to paint a vision before his eyes, a promised land of power and bliss. Here was the very concern that had been gnawing at him most: Judy's threat to destroy him if she caught him once more in adultery. And what did Colette do with it? She took Judy's ultimate weapon right out of her hands. In one bold stroke, if he followed Colette's urging, he could do unto Judy what she threatened to do unto him. Beat her at her own game by divorcing her first.

But it was impossible to share Colette's certainty on the matter. There were those who would say that divorcing Judy in the middle of the campaign would be political suicide, as it would run the risk of antagonizing that large, family-worshiping segment of the electorate that every candidate needed to win over.

B. D., of course, would be the loudest shriek in that chorus. He would be quick to point out that, in response to the "Judy Factor" crisis, their ad agency had just launched a new campaign in the vitally important arena of TV advertising. Running throughout the new TV spots was the idea that Ben was a model family man. For one ad, a camera crew had filmed him in his Senate office, picturing him smiling fondly beside photographs of Judy, Glenda, and Arthur. For another, Ben was pictured walking and talking with Glenda in front of the Lincoln Memorial, a strong image of involved fatherhood. Divorcing Judy, B. D. would argue, would destroy this carefully crafted and unbelievably expensive TV image.

True enough, Ben realized. But as Colette had pointed out, B. D. had been responsible for the "Judy Factor" crisis in the first place by contriving that unnecessary interview with the *Post*. Then he'd failed to deliver the Sylvia Loring story he'd promised. In their last tryst, Colette had even gone so far as to suggest that Ben fire B.D. "What good is he doing you?" she'd asked. "He's very divisive. He makes mistakes and never admits he's wrong. And the few times he happens to be right, all he does is take credit for what you would have done anyway."

Ben would have to think long and hard before firing B. D., he knew. There was something to be said for loyalty. And the two men had been friends a long time. But he had to admit to himself that Colette was right. She was a shrewd judge of character, and B. D. was certainly no god. In the end, a man had to rely on his own instincts.

Those very instincts were what made this one a surprisingly tough call. What had gotten him this far was having complete faith in them, faith in himself. And Ben had to admit that every time he'd ever taken a big risk—from going heavily into debt to run against a popular incumbent senator in North Carolina, to declaring his candidacy for president at a time when the odds looked impossible—extraordinary things had happened. If he hadn't had what a political pundit for the *Charlotte Observer* had called a "compulsion" for taking risks, Ben was well aware that he would still be a tinhorn local politician. Instead he was knocking on the front door of the White House. The willingness to take risks had made a giant out of just another man in the crowd.

Looking down now at Colette's upturned face, Ben could feel the truth in what she'd said. Since their affair had begun, nothing but good things had happened, and not only in bed. This woman made him a better campaigner, gave him strength to endure the rigors of the campaign and the prospect of sexual

as well as political reward at the end of the trail. With Judy
there was none of that. Colette had hit home with the image
of Judy in the White House. Eight years of bedroom torture,
eight years of Peace Links. Eight of what ought to be the
great years of his life.

It was tempting to imagine a permanent life with Colette.
Sometimes making a clean fast break was the best way to
go. He wouldn't live a lie, the writers might say. He was
honest enough to marry the woman he loved.

"What color would the princess wear? Shocking pink?"
With that, Ben kissed his lady good-bye. He took the elevator
to the second floor, the private staff floor, and stepped into
the large men's room, where he bumped into B. D.

"Where's Colette?" B. D. asked with some bite in his
voice.

"Upstairs, taking a shower."

B. D. grunted. "Listen. Paradyne is prowling around the
building. Says he won't go away till he speaks to you."

"Should I?"

"Yeah, but watch out for that prune. He's got something
up his sleeve."

Coconspirators, the men read each other's expressions in
the long mirror that hung over the row of sinks.

What they didn't know was that Michael Paradyne—who
had just spent two minutes admiring his mediocre features in
the same mirror—was crouched hidden in a toilet stall, noting
every word.

# CHAPTER
## 34

Sylvia was parked in her Nova in the lot of the "Social
Safeway," as it was called, where Washington's elite had

groceries loaded into limos, Mercedes-Benzes, Volvos, and Porsches. But Sylvia had purchased no groceries, had not rubbed elbows in the aisles with the chic wives of European ambassadors and American politicians, the suave foreign diplomats stopping for a bottle of imported wine on their way home from work. Across Wisconsin Avenue, the sun was setting behind the brick building that housed Eleanor Gardiner's third-floor photography studio, making Sylvia squint into a liquid red blaze. Knowing she could never go in, as Eleanor would recognize her and suspect her mission, Sylvia had kept her vigil for over an hour. Since Kokoh knew of no "headquarters" for the operation, Sylvia wasn't sure what was here, if anything, to stake out. But something was keeping her: a need to get a sense of Eleanor's workplace, maybe to see the woman in a different context.

Maybe, Sylvia told herself, she was just here to try to change her luck. Things had reached a pretty pass. With Hale killing the story again, Kokoh at a loss for substantive information and no good way she could think of to follow up on her suspicions about Eleanor directly, she had to do something. Anything. And it had occurred to Sylvia that maybe Eleanor wore a blond wig around her girls as a precaution against this very kind of identification Sylvia had hoped to get. There were too many other similarities between the Eleanor of the photo and Kokoh's description of the madam.

It would also be nice to get a look at this guy Rich Kurtz, to see if a man entering Eleanor's building answered Kokoh's description of the short, muscular guy with dark, curly hair. But it wasn't happening. Sylvia glanced at her watch—5:20—and decided to pack it in. She eased the Nova into the rush-hour traffic on Wisconsin.

Then she saw them. It was Eleanor, all right, bundled up in a scarf and coat, with that bend in her nose; and the man, a good three inches shorter, his hand on her back, his face a scowl against the wind that tousled his dark, curly hair, had to be Kurtz. Instinctively, Sylvia hunched lower behind the wheel, cruising past them slowly for a closer look as they exited the building. Kurtz strutted along, low-slung with wide, powerful-looking shoulders under a brown leather bomber jacket. He had a blade for a nose, a square jaw, a restless glance that darted up and down the street like a searchlight as they turned the corner behind Eleanor's building and disappeared.

Sylvia raised her head, feeling a chill shoot down her spine. He was not the kind of man you wanted looking at you. Luckily, he had not appeared to see her. She veered off Wisconsin, angled through the quaint cobblestone streets, and crossed Rock Creek Park, trying to sort out what she'd just witnessed. That had to be Kurtz; and if it was him, then, surely, Eleanor was the madam! But this only confirmed what she'd already suspected. The problem remained: she had nothing on the woman. If only she'd thought to keep Kokoh in town a few more days, to have Kokoh watch the place with her and verify the madam's associate. Too late, the idea struck her like a sudden rock on the windshield. Had Kokoh just been with her, Sylvia would have had verification on both the madam and her associate. Then what would she have done? Well, just maybe, she would have brought Kokoh in with her into the paper and sat her down in Digby Reeve's office with the most sensational story a publisher would ever have: his editor's first cousin was at the very heart of Hookergate!

Sylvia swung around Sheridan Circle, a little dazed, more than a little lost as she steered toward Adams-Morgan. It was a big, big story in the world's most important city—but it was all on her shoulders, and she had no idea what to do next. The thought of dealing with Kurtz all by herself—the man who had all but murdered Kokoh—made her feel small, small and frighteningly alone. Kokoh, it seemed to her now, was one incredibly brave woman.

Then she remembered Max Ridgway.

When Sylvia called him, Max was on his way out the door. Double Reverse was about to foal, he told her. If she wanted to talk, she could come along with him to the farm.

How strange, she thought as she settled into his car, that she'd happened to call at this moment. Neither of them spoke.

Max's Ford Taurus seemed to float down the road behind the headlights, Sylvia riding a wave of strange and blissful feelings, sensing from time to time Max's curious gaze in her direction. In his jeans, boots, and denim jacket, Max had an air of expectancy about him that words would violate, that pointed him home with a white-hot urgency as if a wall of fire were advancing on Ridgway Farm.

They arrived without benefit of conversation. It astounded Sylvia that so many miles could pass without it, each person alone in a private whirl of thoughts. She knew, in this golden capsule of silence and darkness, that she was powerfully drawn to him. The closer they got to the farm, the harder it was for her to stay away from him.

He zoomed up the driveway, slammed the brakes at the stables, and sprang from the car.

The clock on the wall in the tack room read ten P.M. Lounging on a cot, the nightwatchman was sipping on coffee and doughnuts, watching TV on the little black-and-white portable.

Double Reverse was an enormous black mass in the bright light, about to explode with new life. Moaning, braying, standing on one leg, she seemed to be concentrating her energies on the big job ahead. A bucket of water stood in the corner with a pile of newly laundered rags ready for swabbing. The stall smelled of fresh hay and was swarming with midwives: the farm manager; a veterinarian in case something went wrong; and Colin Ridgway.

Max approached Double Reverse, cradling his face into the length of her neck, stroking the forelock away from her eyes. Sylvia saw the caring and love in his manner and felt almost jealous. "Ready, girl?" he said.

Double Reverse was not her usual responsive self. She lay down. An old pro, the farm manager was pulling out the foal in sync with Double Reverse's hard breathing and heaving. The brood mare ignored the small crowd gathered around her. Her head was down, as if studying the configuration of the hay beneath.

There was tension in the room. Sylvia knew the risks, that

the foal could be born dead, as occasionally happened, the umbilical cord wrapped around its neck, strangling it to death before birth. She reached out, unthinking, for Max's hand.

Two legs, sticklike masses of bone and flesh, popped out first. A good sign, thought Sylvia, watching them twitch. These legs might be capable of saving the fortunes of Ridgway Farm, of someday clocking the final lengths of the Belmont Stakes in record-breaking time, capable of bringing home the Triple Crown.

Then out it came: its head, its whole spindly body. A chestnut foal bursting with the manic energy of new life. A white star in the center of its forehead seemed an omen, a whiteness matched by two backsocks on its hind legs. She heard Max breathe in relief.

The manager ripped off the tattered, commodious birth sac, which he tossed over against the stall wall, where it sat like an enormous heap of dirty bed linens, stiffening in the cold air. It was unbelievably fast and simple, a sleek delivery. Double Reverse looked exhausted, relieved to be through her ordeal and somewhat proud of herself.

Max moved in to inspect the foal.

"A colt!" he cried out, miracle in his voice. Sylvia was beside him, and he was at her lips. A kiss, a communion of joy. A spontaneous act, but all the feelings inside her surged up, and she was flushed with joy and expectancy. He might have kissed a fence post in the excitement of that moment, she thought. But no, it was no coincidence that he had brought her here once, now twice. He had brought her here because he wanted the two of them to be reborn together.

The colt lay on the hay near the legs of its mother, as the veterinarian painted the brood mare and then the foal with thick coatings of iodine. The foal was all legs, legs that seemed as delicate and spindly as outsized chicken bones. And head, which Max molded into place with his strong, firm hands like a sculptor. Within fifteen minutes, the colt was up on his legs, exploring his mother's nipples.

Puffing nervously on his cigar, Colin Ridgway called out, "He's a winner! And the size, look at the size!" he exclaimed. "This one's going to be seventeen hands, maybe more."

"So where does this leave you?" Sylvia said. It was two in the morning, and the nightwatchman was on his way home, the next brood mare not due for another week. The veterinarian had left, joking that he'd never been of less use. And Colin Ridgway had packed it up and headed back to the house to bed.

"Me, meaning Ridgway Farm?" said Max. It was chilly, and he put his arm around her, draping his roomy wool coat protectively around her—there was enough of it to share— as they used to back at UVA. She wished she hadn't asked. With their bodies so close together, conversation was an intrusion.

They walked to his car, and Max opened the door for her.

"It's a damn good sign, a damn good sign," he said, starting up the engine. Like her, he seemed suspended in some fantasy place, not grounded in reality. He reached over toward her, his hand landing on the glove compartment. From inside, he extracted two celebratory cigars, lighting one up.

"Smoke?" he said, irony on his face. She had never seen him smoke, and had, in fact, never smoked herself. She looked into his twinkling eyes.

"Why not!" she said, to throw him off.

He took her unlit cigar to the fiery tip of his, transferring the spark. When he handed it over, she thought she might die, he looked so unspeakably handsome in the dark of the night.

He made no effort to speak. Just as they had come, they returned to Washington in silence. A silence interrupted by her feeble attempts to puff at the cigar without coughing. She realized it had finally happened. She had crossed over from her world into his. This was where she wanted to be.

Somehow it seemed to violate the sacredness of the moment to bring up her work. But there was no other time. When would they next speak? Their reacquaintance had formed a strange pattern of closeness and distance, of past commingled with the mysterious present.

"Max, do you know a woman named Eleanor Gardiner?"

"Eleanor, sure," he said. "She's your Hale Gardiner's cousin."

"Max, on this story . . ."

He looked over at her, appraising her. "Is that why you called—a story?"

"Well, initially, yes," she said, and then seeing a fierce turbulence in his eyes, she added, "I wanted to see you. This has been the most . . ."—and suddenly she could find no words to describe her feelings about watching the birth, about their excursion—"wonderful thing, seeing that foal born."

He said nothing for a while, and then in a voice that was calm, caring, but somewhat distant, he asked, "How can I help you?"

She poured out her story to him. All of it: from the first time she met Kokoh at the French ambassador's party, to her sighting of Eleanor Gardiner and Rich Kurtz outside the Georgetown studio. Max listened with rapt attention, making no comment except to say that he'd read Colette's fake story and the *Post*'s revelations about it. From time to time, as Sylvia told him about having tipped off the *Post*, about how scary Kurtz looked and what she believed he'd done to Kokoh, he glanced at her sharply as the deserted road rushed under the car. When she was finished, he mused a few moments, then said, as if the two words were some kind of talisman that conjured up his memory of the woman, "Eleanor Gardiner."

"You know her, don't you?"

"How would you know about that?" he said testily.

"Because after I wrote the story about Ridgway Farm, Eleanor was at the paper and told me, quote, 'You obviously don't know Maxwell Ridgway very well.' She accused me of doing a 'hatchet job on Maxwell Ridgway.' "

His eyes smiled. "Didn't you?"

"How would you know?" she shot back. "For all I know, you never read it."

"All I know," he needled, "is that you said if you forgot to tell me when the story was coming out, you'd save me a copy."

All true, Sylvia remembered with a pang. Then he grinned. "Don't worry. I read your story." He paused, sobering. "It was a hell of a good story, Sylvia. It made a difference. Just like the one you're going to write next."

An electric thrill flashed through her body—his praise, the implicit offer of help. She tried to find the right words.

Max's came first. "I know your research seems to incriminate Eleanor, but I just can't see her being a madam. We're talking about a woman from one of the stuffiest families this side of the Potomac. Girls like Hale and Eleanor are bred from age three like harness horses. They're groomed, they're trained, they're dressed and shod in the proper way: for show. The problem with most of them is that they never break out."

"Right," she said, quickly trying to suppress any doubt, "and maybe that's why this one did—in a big way."

"So I'm Woodward to your Bernstein," he said with a touch of irony. "So what would you like me to do for you?" They were crossing the Potomac, approaching the city of lies, the moment of truth.

"Go see her. Find out what you can, any way you can."

A minute passed, a minute of city lights rushing toward the windshield like shooting stars, of Max's jaw set like a granite slab. She could sense his whole body locking tight like a closing fist.

"Just don't hold your breath for what I find."


"Hello, Eleanor," Max said. He stood just inside the entrance to her studio, taking in the face he had never seen in its handsome adult form. "Been a year or two."

Eleanor rose from her desk. She smoothed her plaid skirt. "A year or two!" Quickly she stepped toward him, and Max kissed her cheek. "Maxwell Ridgway, it's been at least ten, maybe fifteen, years."

"You look terrific."

Eleanor basked in the compliment, licked her lips, and drank in this Adonis in an overcoat. "Maxwell, you're the one who looks terrific. Take off your coat!" She was tugging at the sleeves before he could reply. "What brings you here, for heaven's sake?"

Max glanced at the walls hung with portraits, some of them prominent Washingtonians. "I heard you take a mean photograph. Now I know it for a fact."

She hung up his coat. "Should I be flattered or devastated? You mean to tell me you haven't come out of a burning desire to see me once again?"

Max laughed. Already it seemed that Eleanor, for all her verbal flair, was falling into that old aggressive, adolescent one-upsmanship she'd shown way back when. "I came to see you *and* get my picture taken by the best photographer in town."

"Flattery will get you everywhere, Maxwell. Do sit down," she said, laughing heartily and indicating a couch. She sat down ahead of him. "A million things to catch up on. I did, however, know you were in town." She smiled coyly. "Word does get around."

Max sobered. "I'm sorry, I don't have much time. Can I take a quick look at your studio? I'm sort of an amateur photographer myself. And," he added hastily, "I want to make an appointment."

There was just a moment, Max thought, when he thought he saw hesitation in her face. Maybe it was just surprise. Then, "Of course," she said, and taking him by the arm, she ushered him past her desk into a room with a couple of chairs and all kinds of fancy lighting and photographic equipment. "This is where I'll shoot you. That's it, actually," she said. "Nothing fancy."

The whole place appeared quite small; he'd spotted only one other door off the front room.

"Eleanor, may I use your rest room?"

Again, what seemed a moment of hesitation. "This way."

She opened the other door and snapped on a light that revealed a narrow hallway with three closed doors. "End of the hall."

Max closed the door behind him and considered his next move. So far, nothing but those just slightly odd reactions to his requests and questions. Which could have been anything. And nothing suspicious in the bathroom.

He flushed the toilet for Eleanor to hear, came out into the hall and didn't see her. Two doors left. Keeping one eye on the open door into the front room, he slowly opened the first. A darkroom, as she'd said. Just standard equipment and chemicals. He closed the door softly. Opened the other one after a stealthy glance in her direction. Inside, the large closet was stacked with cardboard boxes.

"Maxwell?"

He shut the door frantically, just ahead of Eleanor coming around the corner of the front room. From her expression, he could tell she might have heard him shutting the door. "Nice place."

"Thank you," she said.

With all his cards played but one, Max joined her in the front room, his heart pounding at the thought of it. He saw the couch and figured it was as good a place as any. "Eleanor, sit down with me a minute, will you? You know I've, uh, been in town a few months now, and . . ." He could hardly believe he was going through with this. "Well, a guy does start getting lonely for female companionship."

Eleanor beamed, and leaned closer to him on the couch.

"The word is that you're something of a matchmaker these days."

Eleanor pulled back. "What are you talking about?"

Max leaned closer. "I think we understand each other. Men get lonely sometimes, and there are traditional ways of addressing that problem."

"Maxwell," she said huffily, "I have no idea what you mean."

Max rose from the couch. Her face betrayed nothing but a painfully obvious indignation. "I'm sorry, I didn't mean to . . ." He felt like a fool, as if his fly were open and she were staring at him. "I guess I . . ."

"I guess you did," she said coldly.

Max headed for the door.

"Don't forget your coat." She rose, and as she handed it to him, her expression suddenly thawed, her voice becoming almost coquettish. "I don't know about matchmaking, but call me, and we'll have a drink."

\* \* \*

"Sylvia," he said brusquely. "I didn't look in the boxes, okay? But that doesn't mean—"

"But she must have had something in them," she interrupted.

"Sylvia!" He stopped himself, staring at her, then paced to the edge of her kitchen. "Of course she had something in them. Paper towels, maybe. Old books. Who knows what? They could have been filled with paintbrushes for all I know."

"Or condoms."

"Condoms?"

"For her girls. Maybe photographs of the girls. Client files. Who knows what."

"Right. Who knows what. Seems to me," he shot out, pacing straight toward her on the couch, "you're grasping at straws. You've convinced yourself and no one but yourself. You have absolutely no positive evidence." He threw her a keen, appraising glance. "Are you sure you're not on a vendetta against the Gardiners?"

Sylvia brushed aside this charge. "Max, will you hear me out? I—"

He cut her off. "I know. But maybe what you don't know, Sylvia, is what it feels like to sit down on the woman's couch and tell her you want to buy—"

She cut him off. "Don't tell me what it feels like, Max." Suddenly, she was spinning out of control. "You have no idea. You have no idea what it feels like to be chasing this story for months, giving up everything else, borrowing money from my mother, losing my job and"—she sprang from the couch, pacing like a woman in a madhouse—"scared out of my wits I'm gonna throw my whole life away. You have no idea, Max!"

They stood, staring at each other. He spoke quietly but firmly, as if reasoning with a child. "True. I didn't look in the boxes. Maybe that would have established whatever it is you're looking for. Maybe it wouldn't have."

"Max, I know, I just know—she's the one. If you're not behind me, I'll just do it alone."

The moment those words came out, she knew she'd gone over the line. His face told it all. It was a face that forgot nothing—the way she'd left him, the way her obsessions left no room for him to walk into her life.

He walked toward her door.

"Max?"

"Do it alone," he said, eerily quiet. "That's Sylvia Loring."

"Max . . . I'm so sorry." This story was killing everything, even what she wanted most. She started toward him, saw his look and stopped. "You're the last person on earth I'd want to . . ."

He stood coldly as she fumbled for the words, then opened the door. "Good luck, Sylvia."

# CHAPTER 35

So now there was no one. No one but her. No one but her and the woman she had to become to prove to Max, to herself, to the whole damn world that Eleanor Gardiner and her prostitution ring was the hottest Washington story since Watergate.

It had taken Sylvia all night to discover that other woman, that woman very much like her, but different. That woman with guts and sex appeal—like her. That woman a little like Kokoh, whose manner she'd had plenty of time to study. That underground woman who, if all went well, would soon be in the employ of Eleanor Gardiner and Rich Kurtz. One of their girls. Sylvia Loring, aka Sonya Rees.

On this first day of March, a new month, a new start, a plan of action formed in Sylvia's mind. She would go into work, as if making final arrangements before her "vacation." She would tell Dennis. Pam already knew, knew every development as she'd gone along. But Sylvia wanted two trusted confidants, witnesses who knew her suspicions and plan of action in case something went wrong, in case she met with the same fate as had Kokoh King. Or worse.

She told Dennis of her decision to go underground, and stressed the importance of secrecy. After all, Hale might know something she shouldn't—or at the very least, have a conflict of interest when the exact story revealed itself.

Dennis protested her plan, saying that her safety was worth more than any story. "I don't care if the President of the United States is getting nookie on the side. Your well-being is more important."

But when he saw that her mind was made up, that she had put too much into this investigation to back out now, he said, "I haven't heard any of this." He winked. "And I've heard every word."

Sylvia lied artfully to colleagues and friends at the paper about her upcoming vacation in Fort Lauderdale.

"The way I see it," B. D. was telling Ben as they lounged in their Tallahassee hotel, "we're going to have to cut some new ads before going into the convention, so we can come out of the gate hard and running. I see something that makes a frontal attack on the President's weaknesses."

With the next campaign appearance several hours away, Ben poured first B. D. and then himself a shot of Kentucky whiskey. B. D. needed to relax, Ben thought. He'd become incredibly intense of late, working long hours on position papers, turning issues over and over in his mind, as if possessed by some newfound demon that would not rest until it had hurtled them both into the White House. It amazed Ben how the man could summon up out of thin air energy for future work when it was all he could do sometimes just to stay a step ahead of himself.

The phone rang, and B. D. jumped for it. "He's not available right now," he barked.

"Who is it?" Ben asked. B. D. hung up the receiver as if not hearing.

"Who was it?" Ben persisted.

"That woman," B. D. said finally.

"What the hell?" Ben said, rising out of his chair. "I would have taken it. Why'd you go and do that?"

"Because," B. D. answered curtly, "you and I are busy right now."

Ben scowled at his adviser and pointedly walked to the telephone. "Look, I make the decisions on this campaign," he said, dialing Colette's number.

B. D. slapped his hand on the receiver to cut off the call before it was completed. "You're foolish to make that call out of this hotel," he said, glaring at the man. "I'm not going to let you."

"Goddammit, B. D.," Ben exploded, "you're trying to boss me, and I won't be bossed."

"This is not the time or the place to be getting a little something on the side," B. D. persisted. "Staffers are talking; everyone's talking. I'm not going to let you ruin your career."

"Colette Daniels is not 'a little something on the side.' She's an astute and capable political adviser, who"—Ben shot his political wunderkind a pointed glance—"helped us out of at least one major scrape. Furthermore, my reputation is not the only one subject to scrutiny. Your own record is not exactly flawless. You had Sylvia Loring in the bag, did you?"

B. D.'s voice broke into a shout. "Listen to me! I'm not going to take low blows from you or anyone. And if you know what's good for you, you'll knock it off with this Daniels woman. If you don't, I'm going to bail out. I swear I will."

The gaze Ben returned was every bit as heated. "I had not noticed that my ship was in any danger of sinking." Significantly, he picked up the telephone receiver again and began dialing Colette's number. "Now, clear out of here. I'm making a call. And don't inflate your importance to this campaign. If you leave, fine. The campaign will go on without you."

At her apartment, Sylvia taped a message on her answering machine saying that she was out of town but would check the machine periodically. She purchased just the right outfit—something to put her in character—then plunked herself down with a hairdresser whom she'd never used before and had her blond hair dyed brown with auburn streaks and her straight locks permed curly. When the outraged hairdresser demanded an explanation for covering natural blond hair that most women would kill for, Sylvia replied, "Let's just say I'm doing it for kicks."

Back home, Sylvia Loring, aka Sonya Rees, made herself up heavily and disguised her blue eyes by applying the green contact lenses her mother had given her last Christmas. Her hair and eye color were different, as were her clothing, cosmetics, and gait. It was an odd sensation, feeling like another woman. She tried talking differently, as she had to the hairdresser: ungrammatically, peppering her phrases with obscenities, thrusting sex to the front of her remarks.

Night was falling as Sylvia arrived by cab fifteen minutes early at the Connecticut Avenue entrance to the "grande dame" of Washington hotels, the Mayflower. This is where Jacqueline Kennedy, dressed in a white chiffon sheath, had danced with her husband at one of his inaugural balls, where Hollywood celebrities and heads of state were regular guests, where every president from Calvin Coolidge to Ronald Reagan had danced in the Grand Ballroom and dined on the city's most celebrated cuisine. And where, Sylvia knew from Colette's columns, the annual debutante Christmas ball was held, a proud tradition of the city's elite.

"How you doing?" a balding, middle-aged man in a gray trench coat asked as Sylvia approached the hotel. He was parked in a Mercedes at the curb.

"Fine."

He looked her over appreciatively. "Are you free?"

When she realized what he was asking, Sylvia had to suppress her normal indignation. This was exactly the result she had hoped for.

Flushed with her first triumph, Sylvia sauntered into the main lobby. This was her first visit. Remarkable, after all these years in Washington, that she'd never once set foot here in this place. And how ironic, now that she was finally here, to be dressed in red high heels and a matching suede miniskirt that were totally inappropriate in this majestic 1920s showcase. Her eyes lifted inevitably to the rose marble frieze, the elegant wall murals, the two-story marble columns crowned by an illuminated ceiling patterned in ornate gold squares. Her high heels sank into the plush greens and golds of the carpet, and she strolled down the famous Promenade, lit by huge crystal chandeliers, the walls decorated with capitals of twenty-four-karat gold and classical marble friezes and hung with rich tapestries, with paintings of the ship *Mayflower* and its pilgrims. From the corner of her eye, Sylvia was aware of the glances coming her way from men in dark suits.

Well, she would soon learn how good an actress she actually was. Sylvia entered the Town and Country Lounge, taking a deep breath, as if about to take a long dive underwater. A slim, elegant young black man in a tuxedo played the piano, a soft, tinkling, bluesy sound. The spacious lounge wrapped around an elegant bar, and in the dim light, Sylvia was escorted to a plush leather chair near a tall window with sumptuous draperies and a tinted view of Connecticut Avenue.

She ordered a Bloody Mary, nibbled on a nut from a bowl on the table. Her eyes remained fixed on the entrance, so as not to miss Eleanor if she came in.

Then, with a slowly dawning realization, Sylvia realized she was hearing a conversation two tables over. Familiar voices, in low yet intelligible tones, were discussing Ben Fincastle. Her glance swung ponderously, with a reluctance verging on panic, to the two men nursing their drinks: Max Ridgway and his dark-suited uncle Ernest.

It was the sort of coincidence that was not supposed to happen—not in a town the size of Washington, not even in the sort of hotel that seemed perfectly suited for a rendezvous of two members of an old Virginia family. Only fate, Sylvia thought, could have brought Max into such proximity, after their bitter words, now that she was Sonya Rees. But fate toward what end?

"You were right about Fincastle," Max was saying. "The more I see of him, the more I realize the man has no position that will last beyond the election, no real conviction about anything. Just charisma. How do you run the country on charisma?''

"Reagan did it," Ernest Ridgway replied. "I suppose Fincastle may well do it too."

"Well, he'll do it without me. I've raised my share of his war chest. God knows why. I'm quitting next week."

"Back to the horse business?"

"I think we've got a shot. It's going to take a full-time effort, and then some."

"That little gal Nicole isn't going to like your leaving, I suspect," Ernest said. What a nosy remark, Sylvia thought, straining her ears to hear his response.

"She's already history," Max said. "As soon as I moved to town, she started putting the squeeze on me to move in. It was fun while it lasted," Max added, then his voice turned meditative, "but when you're so obviously mismatched, the fun rarely lasts."

Here Ernest Ridgway paused a moment, as if to say something important. "You never cared for the girls you grew up with."

"I couldn't give you an argument on that. I never wanted to marry a lifestyle."

Ernest rose. "Excuse me. I'll be back in a minute."

Sylvia watched as Max's eyes tracked his uncle toward the rest rooms. What to do? She tried to think. But wait! The idea was so nervy that it gave her cold chills. If she could pull it off, nothing could give her more confidence in dealing with Gardiner and Kurtz.

Sylvia turned her head directly toward Max. At the table in between them, a man and a woman in their mid-thirties were talking about the stock market. Max, Sylvia realized, was up to one of his old tricks—his head was turned another way, but he was eavesdropping, picking up any stock tips he could, or tuning in just for amusement. Sylvia had to smile; same old Max. How to get him to look her way? Many times it had seemed to Sylvia that Max could pick up her thoughts telepathically; in the excitement of this moment, she sent him one: "Look at me, Max."

*Dear God*, Sylvia thought. *He's looking at me.*

He was. Without looking at him directly, Sylvia was aware that she was drawing his full and confused attention. Did he recognize her? Their eyes met, and she knew—he didn't know her! She wasn't Sylvia Loring.

Sylvia smiled. He seemed to hesitate, then returned the smile faintly.

Sylvia rose, and with an air of nonchalance—though her heart was pounding—strolled to his table. "You wouldn't mind if I kept you company, would you?" she said, disguising her voice in a husky, suggestive drawl.

"Well, actually . . ."

She sat down in Uncle Ernest's chair. "I didn't think so."

"Look . . ." But he stopped, staring at her. Something about her was familiar—yet Sylvia could tell he still hadn't broken through. She crossed her legs seductively and sensed his excitement. The smashing success of her disguise gave her a surge of confidence, and, with no warning, she touched her finger to his cheek.

He drew back.

Her hand dipped for a moment to his muscular thigh and glided down it lightly before it was airborne again.

"Look. You'd better take your business elsewhere," he commanded. But stern as it was, his face betrayed another wish, or so she thought. And somewhere inside her, the touch of his thigh still in her nerve ends, Sylvia had that wish too.

"Oh, a married man?"

Max glared at the man and woman at the next table, who had halted their discussion of stocks when they became aware of the goings-on at his table. Sylvia gave the man a coy smile. Clearing his throat in embarrassment, he glanced away quickly.

Then Max saw Uncle Ernest approaching rapidly. Panic crossed his face, an expression so comically contorted that Sylvia laughed out loud.

It gave her away. "Sylvia!" Max said.

"Max," Sylvia quipped, "we have to stop meeting like this."

"Damn it, Sylvia. What the hell are you doing?"

"Going underground. Trying out my act."

His look of outrage, she sensed, was tempered with both amazement and admiration.

Then Ernest was there, looking from Max to Sylvia and back to his nephew with a silent demand for explanation.

Max rose. "Uh . . . Uncle Ernest, this is . . ."

Sylvia rose. "We've met. Sylvia Loring."

Ernest narrowed his eyes. "We've met?"

"Yes, uh . . ." Before she could think of a way to explain, her eyes lighted on a couple strongly resembling Eleanor and Rich. Could it be they? Momentarily panicked, she reminded herself it wasn't too late to abandon her disguise and bolt the place. She looked closer, and there seemed to be no mistaking it. This was her chance. She would have to act quickly.

"Excuse me," Sylvia said. She rose, catching a glimpse of Max's eyes, which appeared more amazed than angry.

Gardiner and Kurtz had not yet seen her. Sylvia strutted to the bar and sat herself down conspicuously. She ordered another seltzer with lime and sat there nursing it, her long legs in black stockings dangling seductively for all to see. Her eyes began working the room, the independent working girl on the scout for her next customer.

She didn't have to wait long to catch their attention. Rich approached her. "Can I buy you a drink?" he asked, squiring her to his table when she accepted. "My partner, Ellen."

"Hi," Sylvia said, looking into her eyes. There was no doubt; it was Hale's cousin, Eleanor Gardiner, in a blond wig. "I'm Sonya."

Never taking his eyes off Sylvia, Max stirred his drink. A man answering Sylvia's description of Rich Kurtz brought her back to his table. And there was a blond Eleanor Gardiner sitting with him. He'd been dead wrong. It was all as Sylvia had suspected.

Drink in hand, Max approached the edge of their table.

Eleanor's glance was frosty, as if to say "I'm busy now"—a message Max deliberately ignored.

"Eleanor, twice in one week," he said, pulling up a chair.

"Small world," she said coldly. "Maxwell, I'm sorry we can't invite you to join us."

"Oh?" He feigned surprise. "I like what you've done to your hair," he said.

Eleanor was staring daggers. And he noted that Sylvia's expression was artfully blank. Was she really going through with this? Damn it all, she had a hell of a lot more guts than she did sense. But he had to be careful not to tip his concern.

Then he saw Kurtz, his neck tense, his shoulders and arms powerful under his white silk jacket, and it was all Max could do not to grab Sylvia right now and get her out of here before it was too late. You could see it in his eyes. This son of a bitch would as soon shoot you as look at you.

"The lady is busy," Kurtz said.

It was all churning in Max's brain. If he got her out of here now—especially if he blew her cover—she'd never forgive him. If she went through with this and got hurt, he'd never forgive himself.

Kurtz rose slowly, his body making his statement: beat it now, or there's going to be trouble.

Max stood to leave. "Well, see you around then, Eleanor." He glanced at Sylvia: his last chance to act. Something in the way he looked at her almost gave him away.

"You know this girl, Maxwell?" Eleanor asked suspiciously.

"I'd like to have the chance."

After the last round, Rich paid the check. "It's very important that we keep our operation secret," he said to Sylvia, as if by way of explanation.

Ten minutes later, they climbed out of a cab and into a booth in an after-hours club on K Street, dark and smoky—the antithesis of the sedate Mayflower. Eleanor did the talking, most of it. Kurtz was there to nod his big, rocklike head and take care of trouble.

In a level voice, Ellen made her two-minute pitch, giving hours, method of payment. She, too, stressed the element of secrecy. Without inflection, she noted there'd been a few breakdowns lately, breakdowns that had almost been fatal.

"Yeah," Sylvia drawled, "I read something about that."

They both tensed a moment, watching her guardedly. Damn, why did she say that? She wondered if she'd made a crucial mistake.

Then Rich smiled a crooked smile. Sylvia sensed that he liked her style—and by the way his eye kept roving over her, her body as well. She wondered with a shudder if part of the job description was servicing this guy.

They asked a few questions. Sylvia had been expecting them and had her story ready. The liquor she'd downed helped enormously with not feeling self-conscious about making all this up. She'd been in town only two weeks, she informed them. She'd been living in Atlanta, where she broke up with her boyfriend. Yes, she'd had experience, but not at a service. Mostly doing it with her old man's friends. Sylvia sensed they were listening closely for anything suspicious.

Then Eleanor glanced at her watch. She looked exhausted, ready to get some sleep. Must be tough, Sylvia thought, keeping two lives going.

"So do you want it or not?" Eleanor said crisply.

Sylvia hesitated. Particularly after their problems with Ko-koh, she was surprised they weren't doing a more careful background check. But she had heard that truly beautiful women in this profession were hard to find, that outfits like Eleanor's snapped them up at the first opportunity. And to-night she felt like a stunningly beautiful woman.

She had to remind herself not to bite too easily, to remain a bit skeptical. "Why should I share with you over working for myself?"

Rich moved in for the closer. "Two reasons. We prescreen all our clients, and we take care of you. Number two, you'll see men you'd never meet in a bar. No way. Top people. Power brokers. I'm not naming any names, but you know who I mean."

"Any girl in this town in the business should be so lucky," Eleanor said haughtily, tiring of the sales pitch.

"So why me?" Sylvia said, as if greatly flattered.

Kurtz glanced at Eleanor. "Big party coming up," he told Sylvia. "Some of the girls are sick. We need bodies."

"That's none of her business," Eleanor said sharply.

"Take it easy, will ya?" Kurtz snapped back. He turned to Sylvia and smiled. "Your body looks like it can hold its own. Of course," he added significantly, "Eleanor will have to give you a lookover."

Eleanor sighed. "Let's get this over with." She rose, beckoning Sylvia to follow.

Inside the women's room, Eleanor hooked the latch. "Okay, strip," she said curtly.

Sylvia could feel every muscle tensing in her body. Having to show her "goods" to Hale's cousin Eleanor was almost too much. She had a momentary impulse just to tell Eleanor she wasn't interested.

"What's the problem?" Eleanor barked. "Just do it."

"Look, why don't we both forget this part," Sylvia drawled. "Honey, you'll get no complaints with what I've got."

Eleanor's reply was a scowl and a finger pointing into a stall.

Sylvia had no choice. She closed the door behind her and stripped naked. Then she opened the door and felt Eleanor's eyes move up and down every inch of her body as if she were at auction. The eyes lingered at Sylvia's breasts, at her genitals, and it was all Sylvia could do to find some breath, any breath at all.

"Have you ever thought of going blond?" Eleanor asked.

"Yeah," she said.

"Might want to think about it," she said. "Turn around."

Sylvia obeyed. She felt the eyes burning into her flesh, felt them taking command of her. This was Eleanor's way of seizing power in the relationship with each of her girls, she thought. Of putting her brand on their flesh.

"Turn around."

When she did, she looked into hard, unflinching eyes. "When's your period?"

"Last week." It was the truth.

"Good. Get dressed and meet us back at the table."

As she dressed, Sylvia's body felt weak, as if she had been fasting for days. Maybe it was the shock. No amount of mental preparation could have braced Sylvia for what had just happened to her. Wolf whistles were one thing. Certainly no experience she'd ever had with a man—not even B. D.'s assault—had felt quite like this. Like she'd just been coldly, dispassionately evaluated and bought as a piece of meat.

She told herself this was part of the job. She told herself to put on her "game face," as she'd heard Max describing his preparation for football combat. Max—he might as well be on the moon for all the help he was to her now.

She could sense they'd been talking about her as she approached the booth. It gave her an eerie feeling, but she shrugged it off and went to work. Quickly, they came to terms. Sylvia stressed her interest in earning "lots of money" and agreed to become "one of the girls." She shook hands with them both.

Eleanor laid out the ground rules, emphasizing this was a "strictly high-class operation. Our girls are never raunchy. Pretend you're having dinner with Prince Charles—and open your mouth only when you have to."

With that, Rich let out a crude chortle.

"Usually," Eleanor went on, "we break our girls in, but in this case, since the party's coming up on Sunday—and you seem to have experience—we'll skip the formalities." She cast a disapproving eye on Sylvia's outfit. "We are going to need to get you some clothes; our clients like something tasteful. Where can I reach you so we can go out?"

Sylvia was prepared. Her own address was out of the question, as it might blow her cover. "I'm at the Travel Lodge. Just call the switchboard and ask for Sonya Rees."

As they got up to go, Rich's expression turned almost cruel. He put a vise grip on Sylvia's arm. "There's gonna be a lot of big shots at this party." He sent her a long, silent stare. "If anybody finds out about this. . . ." He slowly drew his forefinger across his throat.

Sylvia checked in at the Travel Lodge—luckily for her story, there were still some vacant rooms. Then she called Dennis Berman at home.

She told him where she was and that she'd confirmed that Eleanor Gardiner was the madam. And she told him about

Kurtz's threat. "Dennis, in case something happens, I just want you to know what's going on."

Dennis was silent a moment. "Sylvia, you may not want to hear this, but it seems to me Digby Reeve ought to know about this development."

He was right—she didn't want to hear it. "But what if he tells Hale? That woman could be dangerous in this situation."

"I know. But I still think Digby needs to know. You don't want to put yourself in this kind of jeopardy for naught. If he's not going to run the story, why go through with it?"

"So what does telling him get us?"

"It prepares him, Sylvia. It greases the wheel so it's ready to roll—if and when you come in with the story."

Sylvia thought that one over. "Can you promise me he won't tip off Hale?"

"This is a very delicate situation. I'll do my best. In something as big as this, it's in the interest of his newspaper to keep his mouth shut. I'll get that across to him."

Sylvia wasn't so sure. But telling Dennis he could reach her from now on only at the Travel Lodge, she let it go.

"Sylvia," Dennis said. "I'm going to be worrying about you."

"I know."

She took a cab back to Adams-Morgan. Of all the things that had happened on this eventful evening, the thing that had shaken her most was Eleanor's examination of her body. Even now, in the rear of the cab, trying to think positive thoughts about the encounter with Max, she couldn't expel those restroom images from her mind. They made her burn with shame, made her feel much more vulnerable than she wanted to feel about the work at Sunday's party, about the risk of discovery. What would Kurtz do to that body, she wondered, that Eleanor had only examined? What would Kurtz do to a reporter trying to wreck his business that he hadn't done to Kokoh?

Sylvia asked the cabdriver to wait and moved urgently in her apartment, filling a suitcase with clothes. The frightening thought had occurred to her that they had elaborately masked their suspicions, that even now they might come by the apartment and see that Sonya Rees was Sylvia Loring. She kept imagining the doorbell ringing and Kurtz standing menacingly at the door, and hurried her packing even more. Perhaps she should have picked a first name that didn't sound so much like "Sylvia."

And there was another thing that worried her. Everything else had gone well—her southern drawl was credible, her story about coming from Atlanta and being new in town seemed reasonable. But that stupid line about reading something in the papers. There were two things wrong with it, she realized. The first was that it might make them suspect she was Sylvia Loring, particularly if there were other incriminating clues. The second one might even be worse: she'd been in town only two weeks, she'd told them, and there hadn't been anything in the papers about Hookergate in that time. Maybe a subtle point, but Eleanor Gardiner was no dummy. If she started putting two and two together, Eleanor might just realize she was being had.

With a shudder, Sylvia closed her suitcase, turned off the lights, locked her door, and descended to the taxi. She was taking a huge risk, compounded by her own dumb mistake. But it had to be done—she'd come too far to turn back now. As she watched her apartment building recede in the night, she felt the way she did as a child when she'd first gone up to dive from the high board at the pool in Silver Spring. It was a long way to fall. And once you stepped off the board—as she was doing now—there was no going back.

Fifteen minutes later, Max Ridgway was ringing her doorbell, pounding her door in frustration.

He sat down heavily against her door, deciding that the thing to do was park himself here until she returned—if it took all night.

*If* she returned, he thought after a few chilly minutes had passed in the March night air.

He hoped to God he hadn't blown her cover. What he'd done was instinctive—the same as the sudden change of direction you make when a 250-pound body comes flying at you on a football field. Pure instinct. He'd wanted to scope the thing out. To send her a message that he was there, that he would help, that if she wanted to turn back at that moment she could count on him to get her out alive.

But something had roused Eleanor's suspicion. That was obvious. She never would have said, "Do you know this girl, Maxwell?" And that worried him. Not so much because of Eleanor, but because of Kurtz.

Max remembered Sylvia's story about what Kurtz had done to Kokoh, and it made his body stir restlessly in the cold. Suppose he was doing it to Sylvia now—or worse. Suppose Kurtz didn't take to the idea of a *Trib* reporter playing games.

Max stood up against the door. He wanted to tell her to call it off now. He wanted to kidnap her himself, as Kurtz had kidnapped Kokoh, if that's what it took to keep her out of trouble.

But Sylvia wasn't here. Max glanced down the street. She wasn't here, and something told him she wasn't coming back.

# CHAPTER
## 36

When Colette had broached the idea of a benefit event for Ben Fincastle that weekend—organized by the two of them but hosted by Mr. and Mrs. Robert Gardiner—Hale had jumped at the idea. Only later, after she'd accepted, did Hale begin agonizing over helping Ben Fincastle.

He was a glib, superficial operator who—although he was a southerner—was not, after all, a Virginian. And his only claim to family was that he had married well. Nonetheless, Hale saw benefit in positioning herself well with the country's probable next president, to whom she already had excellent access. This had been the line of reasoning she'd used to convince her parents to act as hosts.

The benefit had thus far provided a wonderful opportunity for time alone with Colette: lunches to compose the guest list, refreshments and entertainment, a joint trip to the caterers. Spending time with Colette made her realize just how much she'd missed her at work. The place seemed empty without her.

Not long after Colette pulled up to the Gardiner estate at three o'clock—not one for lunch as promised—delivery trucks started arriving with cases of liquor and other supplies for tomorrow's party. The catered event for the exclusive guest list of 150 members of the First Families of Virginia would be held inside in the Gardiner dining room, drawing room, and glass-paneled sun porch. Spotting the overnight bag in the back seat, Hale was gratified that Colette really meant to spend the night.

"Come on inside," she called to Colette, who was around the side, carrying on with the delivery boy, of all people.

Colette was in great spirits, laughing and joking. The campaign was going great. Ben had just gotten his second cover of *Newsweek*—"Fincastle, the Front-runner"—and there was a flattering mention of her work in the sidebar on campaign insiders. Now her fabricated story was a mere footnote in her colorful past!

Hale stepped toward Colette and placed a hand on her arm. "There's much to do!"

As she turned, Colette's heel caught on the edge of a cart pushed by another delivery boy headed for the kitchen's service entrance around the rear. It was loaded with boxes stacked five high. Thrown to the ground, Colette lay motionless, straddling the sidewalk and ground.

Hale was at her side. "Look what you've done," she barked at the speechless boy. With his assistance, Hale hoisted Colette to her feet.

Luckily, nothing was broken. Colette stood up and dusted herself off. "Oooh," she moaned, discovering she'd been bruised and cut on one leg.

In Colette's bedroom, Hale poured them both generous shots of brandy, and they drank. Then Hale turned her attention to Colette's wounds. This was the child she would never have, Hale thought as she swabbed her with a hot washrag and rubbed in first-aid cream.

The brandy took hold. Slowly, methodically, hypnotically, almost like a masseuse, Hale worked Colette's skin, moving from the wounds on her calf to the white flesh of her thigh. She could tell Colette was enjoying the massage as much as she was. And who wouldn't? Warmth, love, and pleasure flowing through her fingertips, flooding the room.

As she drank, Hale accidentally slopped some brandy on Colette's blouse. "Oh dear! Let me get that," Hale said, pulling the garment up off her, revealing the contours of Colette's breasts. Colette raised her arm to shield herself.

"Don't do that. You're beautiful," Hale said, pulling back her hand. Without thinking, Hale's fingers went to work, reaching out and unhooking Colette's bra, liberating the milky breasts.

"Beautiful," Hale murmured. She gazed into Colette's eyes, wide, translucent, not saying no.

Slowly, Hale buried her head in Colette's bosom and tenderly kissed each breast. Then, once more, she met Colette's eyes, which were beginning to smile, Hale thought, beginning to say yes.

"Colette . . . ?" Hale murmured.

Colette was silent. Serene. Waiting.

The feeling inside Hale was overwhelming, delirious, pushing her down toward Colette like the force of water rushing downhill, making her fingers want to touch, to skim, to sail, to fly around Colette's Botticelli body.

Hale couldn't stop herself, and didn't try. Colette lay beneath her touch, and new sensations, glorious sensations, raced from Hale's fingertips into her blood, making her warm in every corner of her body, making her liquid.

"Colette," Hale heard herself say. "Dear Colette." The words sang from her lips. "I love you."

Hale's hands cupped Colette's cheeks; slowly, she brought her lips to Colette's and kissed her, a sweet, lingering, brandy kiss. Nothing had ever felt so right.

"May I?" Hale whispered.

Colette's eyes gazed into hers. Only waiting.

Hale's kisses rained down her body. Slow, gentle rain, tap, tap, tap, into the warm belly button, a quick dip of the tongue; then trembling hands unhitching the skirt, Colette arching underneath, the skirt sliding off, then the panties.

Hale's lips parted, her breath quickened. Her head landed softly, her tongue probed, touched dampness, sweetness. A streak of fire torched Hale's body, singed every nerve end. She gasped. It was too much, too fast, but now that it was here she only wanted more, she wanted to ride the wave. *I'm in love*, she thought. *I'm in love, I'm in love, I'm in love.* But the words were a tiny lifeboat, the frail voice of thought lost in an ocean of sensation. The wave was coming, the swell rocking her body, Colette's fingers unhitching her clothes, beginning to find her, making her shudder, making her shout. The wave was breaking. Hale was drowning.

Colette had never been with a woman. But somehow it didn't surprise her, Hale coming on to her like this. On occasion, she'd wondered if Hale's preoccupation with her was more than strictly professional. Colette had always had a hard time saying no, rejecting any lover who had worked so hard to position himself for intimacy. But this, this was something new, something different, something unexpected.

Dizzy drunk, Colette allowed Hale to make love to her. And it wasn't half bad. It was naughty; it was forbidden to give and receive pleasure from another woman. She could hardly wait to tell Ben. Hale's passion made her beautiful to watch, delicious to touch. Colette couldn't quite believe it. She even had an orgasm.

Hale watched from the veranda as the cream of Virginia aristocracy turned out on this splendid, sunny, unseasonably warm March Sunday. They drove the long gravel driveway into the circle at the front entrance, handing their car keys to the parking attendants, who drove them to a nearby field.

Inside the mansion, long, linen-clothed tables were dressed for the occasion with the Gardiner Spode china. Enormous dishes of Virginia barbecue, dainty finger food, ham biscuits, watercress sandwiches. White-coated waiters circulated, serving drinks.

Ben had spoken—a brief, twenty-minute speech hitting just the right note, Hale had to admit, reining in his folksiness for this particular audience, substituting four-syllable words for two-, dazzling them all with his presidential charm and wit.

Three fund-raising staffers, Colette's assistants, were working the room, handing out cards and taking down names and numbers on small leather notebooks.

Euphoric from her encounter the previous evening with Colette, certain that Colette—who'd obviously enjoyed herself too—shared her own feelings now that they were out, Hale made her way over to the candidate.

"I must admit," she said in a tone suggesting that this rarely happened, "I was impressed."

Turning on his most engaging smile, Ben extended his hand. "And you are?"

"Obviously, Senator," Hale said icily, "you haven't done your homework. I'm the youngest female editor of an East Coast daily, and I happen to be—"

"Ah, but I have, Hale Gardiner," he said, cutting her short while savoring his little prank.

"I think we have a mutual friend," she said. "Who appears to be playing a more important role in your campaign with each passing day."

"Colette Daniels, one of the best."

"Tell me, Senator, is there any chance she has a solid future with Ben Fincastle?" Hale gave him a look signaling that she knew precisely the footing on which the clandestine couple stood.

But Ben Fincastle was not easily cornered. He returned her volley with a deft stroke. "My dear Miss Gardiner, just about any sort of alliance is possible in this world." Then, spotting the chairman of Kensington Industries, Ben took Hale's hand and shook it. "Thank you for your continued support."

Colette left the event with the Fincastle party, gushing to Hale over how much it had meant to her, what a debt of gratitude she now owed. She gave Hale a little squeeze and a peck on the cheek that left Hale floating on air.

When Hale returned that evening to her house in McLean, Digby Reeve was standing at her door, his shoulders hunched against a chill wind off the Potomac.

"I tried to reach you at your parents' house," he said urgently. "Your father said you were on your way home."

"What is it?" she asked in alarm. Getting only a Cheshire grin, she said at a higher pitch, "What on earth, Digby?"

"It seems that Hookergate is alive and well."

"What do you mean?" she demanded.

Digby smiled coyly, but what he had to relate was too ripe inside him not to burst. And something about Hale's manner, her perpetually superior air, made him want to get it out without further delay. "Well, for one thing, our Sylvia Loring has gone underground on the story."

"What!"

Digby chortled at her reaction. "Oh, yes. There's one other thing." He paused, extending the suspense, savoring Hale's inferior position of ignorance as long as he could.

"Spit it out, Digby," she snapped.

"Yes, well, it seems that the ringleader is someone you know very well. Even love."

"Colette?" she gasped.

Flushed with excitement, Colette's name didn't even register on him. "It seems that a Gardiner is at the helm."

It took a minute. Maybe two. But when it finally penetrated Hale's consciousness that there was hard evidence implicating Eleanor Gardiner, her Eleanor, as a madam, Hale grew indignant. She couldn't believe it. She wouldn't. There had to be some mistake, she said.

But then, she thought, turning it over in her mind, maybe it was true. Maybe this explained Eleanor's mysterious life —why she never came for holidays, why she always insisted on meeting for lunch, not dinner, saying that nighttime was her prime work period. But even so, who did they think they were? Sylvia Loring and Dennis Berman, working in collusion, going around her, even managing to enlist Digby Reeve. Who did they think they were, going after a Gardiner? Hale demanded to know why she wasn't consulted sooner. "I suppose you've given Sylvia the word through Dennis that the *Tribune* won't have anything to do with a story gained by misrepresentation."

"No, I hadn't," Digby said, weighing this ethical consideration for the first time.

She had him on this one, but didn't know when to let up. "And why not? Why didn't you think of it?" she accused, as if he were an idiot for not seeing what she saw immediately.

Once again, she was setting herself up as omniscient. "The ethics in this type of undercover investigation are not clear-cut," he said, marshaling the resources inside him. "A case can certainly be made that journalists have every right to go under cover if that's the only way to get a story."

Hale remained silent.

"This story happens to represent a conflict of interest," he continued. "Not for the *Tribune*, but for Hale Gardiner. Perhaps I shouldn't have told you until we had the story in hand. But I did. And let me make one thing perfectly clear. This is confidential information. You are not to breathe a word of it. Not until the copy is set in type."

Hale saw that once again she'd pushed him too far. So she must mask her impatience. She needed more information from him. Where did Sylvia stand with the story this minute? She paused, feigning respect for his line of reasoning.

"I see," she said. "And when would we be going to press on this story?"

"As soon as Sylvia has gained conclusive evidence against the operation."

When Digby was gone, Hale wasted not a moment before picking up her telephone to call Eleanor. No answer. She grabbed her keys and rushed back out the door. It hit Hale as she stepped out of her Sterling in front of her cousin's apartment building: if Eleanor was a madam, perhaps that explained Rich Kurtz.

At Eleanor's building, Hale convinced the superintendent to give her a key to her cousin's apartment. She flashed her press card and identification, and she saw him get an eyeful of her fine vehicle out front.

"There's been a family emergency," Hale lied. Once inside, she would find out for sure.

Inside the apartment, the first thing Hale did was play back the messages on the answering machine. One was from Misty, telling Eleanor she wouldn't be able to "work the party." She had her period and was "bummed."

On another call, a foreign-accented caterer confirmed the address of "the party tonight."

The third call, from Cheri, reported that "this asshole slapped me around last night. Don't ever give me that turkey again. I'm really PO'ed."

Slipping into a spare bedroom—which had always, come to think of it, been locked on Hale's few visits—she found the key to the file cabinet, which held incriminating evidence: Polaroid photos of the girls and their measurements; a list of clients and their sexual preferences. For a moment, Hale stood there in disbelief. How could Eleanor have pulled this off without her knowing? Then another thought struck: this was the woman that bloodhound Sylvia Loring had been tracking all these months.

Regaining her composure, Hale replayed the message from the caterer and jotted down the party's address. Now the stakes were even higher. She'd have to head Sylvia Loring off at the pass.

# CHAPTER
## 37

There are a thousand ways to cope with nervousness, Eleanor Gardiner thought as she surveyed the elegant penthouse where tonight's party would soon get underway. Her father, the Episcopal priest, always said a silent prayer before ascending to the pulpit. A way of forgetting himself, he said. Forgetting himself was the key to preaching a powerful sermon, to delivering an eloquent eulogy at a parishioner's funeral.

Eleanor considered herself a chip off the old block in more ways than anyone had ever suspected. Every Sunday without fail, she attended St. Alban's Episcopal Church on Wisconsin Avenue, and frequently she walked quietly, reverentially through the National Cathedral next door, or sat down in a pew to breathe in its grandeur and peace. These ritualistic visits to holy places were more than a way of connecting her present with her past, of expressing her kinship with her father. Her attendance at St. Albans this morning had been a way of calming herself, of taking brief sanctuary from the relentless stress of leading a double life. As her father might have done in her place, Eleanor had said a silent prayer. Hers had been for the success of this, the biggest and by far the most lucrative event of her career as a madam. And it had served to calm her.

But not for long. With the party almost ready to start, Eleanor was feeling as nervous as she had during the first few weeks of launching the business with Rich Kurtz. Those were hairy days, days when the exhilaration of doing something taboo had been more than offset by the anxieties of being detected, of finding enough money to keep going, of working with a man whose bedroom habits thrilled her but whose working habits were not always reliable. So now, hovering over the caterer, Eleanor was conducting a hard-nosed inspection of his work.

"I'd like you to try that again," she said, indicating the arrangement of the hors d'oeuvres on the tray. "I'd like something more poetic."

"They were set out the right way to begin with," he said, resisting her attempt to direct him.

"I've asked you once," she started, "and I'm not going to ask you again." She stood staring at him until, reluctantly, he began rearranging the tray.

This was the thing about most people—they were lazy. Too lazy to start a new business, too lazy even to keep a job. It was crazy that Hale had had her photography business written up in the Society Sketch when the real genius of Eleanor Gardiner was her flaming success at an even higher-risk entrepreneurial venture. Unlike Hale, whose career had been charmed, whose family money and connections had propelled her into position, Eleanor had always had to fend for herself. She was the archetypal preacher's kid who went from one scrape to another. Sure, she was a Gardiner, but a fine old name didn't pay the rent. Because Dwight Gardiner had been all but cut out of his inheritance—for something as petty and bigoted as his sexual preference—she felt driven to earn money, to prove that the Gardiners of Middleburg had no lock and key on wealth and status. The Gardiners—who remained pillars of the church—saw nothing inconsistent in their behavior. They'd robbed her father blind, then acted hurt when he refused their invitations to Easter dinner and Sunday brunch.

Success was sweet. Perhaps no city in the world was more lucrative for a woman of her profession than Washington, D.C. Last year, Eleanor had netted $150,000, because she was the very best in the business.

Eleanor moved on to the bar, giving the bartender a hard appraisal before inspecting his liquor stock. Eleanor had a reputation to protect: only the finest for her distinguished clients.

She'd thought long and hard before consenting to this party. It was one thing to arrange a rendezvous with a client and a girl. But it was quite another to bring twenty people—ten guests, ten girls, and the two guests of honor—together under one roof. The more people who knew, the greater the chance of a security leak—although, knock on wood, they'd never had any problem with the police. Things were tense enough already, what with that loose cannon, Kokoh King, still at large and saying God knows what to whom.

But her VIP client had offered so much money and so much reassurance that every guest had been prescreened. And Rich had argued they'd be "insane" to turn down a chance like this—not only the money, but the chance to hook in wealthy new customers who might become regular clients. Reluctantly, Eleanor had agreed. And she'd rested a little easier since Hale had told her the *Trib* had closed the book on its Hookergate investigation. But not much. And there was also the new girl.

Eleanor had been so rushed this weekend, nailing down all the last-minute details. If it had been any other time, she would have conducted a much more thorough background check. There was something about this girl. For one thing, she seemed so much more intelligent than the others, not only her face, but in the way she talked. And that business about reading about a Washington madam—that was peculiar. None of her other girls ever read anything more profound than her horoscope. And that moment with Maxwell. Eleanor had replayed that scene in her mind several times: the way he'd made such a point of coming to their table, the way he'd looked at Sonya as if he knew her.

This afternoon, Eleanor had met Sonya at Hecht's and bought her a designer cocktail dress, a sea-green silk that set off Sonya's slim figure and green eyes. Sonya would pay her back from her earnings. Eleanor had to admit that none of the other girls looked quite as stunning as Sonya. Rich had said they were "damn lucky" to get her, and he was right. The bottom line was having the best—that's what kept the clients coming back for more.

Still, there was something that kept nagging in the back of Eleanor's mind. At Hecht's, after paying for the dress and a pair of shoes with her American Express Gold Card, Eleanor had asked Sonya about Maxwell. "That man at the Mayflower acted as if he knew you," she said. "You sure you've never seen him before?"

"He just had the hots for me, that's all," Sonya had replied. But there was something about the way she said it—a difference between her brash voice and a sensitive look in her eye—that Eleanor hadn't missed. She prided herself on having a sixth sense about her girls. When a girl wasn't telling the whole truth, she could almost always pick it up.

All there was was a feeling. Driving over here to the party, Eleanor had asked Rich to keep an eye on Sonya. Look for anything strange.

"You got it," Rich had said.

Sylvia's cab dropped her at an impressive, glass-fronted, postmodern, cooperative apartment complex off Massachusetts Avenue, overlooking Rock Creek Park. She'd been in-

structed to come to the penthouse of the twenty-story
building. As the elevator gained in altitude, Sylvia's heart
thumped madly with dread. What if she were forced to make
a choice between blowing her cover and getting the story?
What if she found herself in a situation in which she couldn't
talk her way out?

The first person Sylvia saw inside was Eleanor, wearing a
full-length chiffon chemise printed in a gold-and-turquoise
paisley pattern.

"You're fifteen minutes late," Eleanor snapped.

"I'm sorry," Sylvia drawled. "The cabbie didn't know
the city that good." It was true. The driver had thrown her
into a virtual panic by taking a series of wrong turns that
Sylvia had to correct.

"That's no excuse," Eleanor said, guiding Sylvia by the
small of her back and moving her along down the hallway.

The other nine girls had arrived, sitting and standing in a
spacious, elegant room with a spectacular night view of the
city. Sylvia had never seen so much exposed female flesh in
one spot—shoulders, cleavage, thighs—all seductively set
off in shimmering garments. Sylvia introduced herself and
felt the girls' appraising glances, like men's eyes roving over
the goods. Good God, there was Shana. But there was no
hint that Kokoh's ex-roommate recognized her.

A stunning redhead walked straight up to Sylvia and said,
"Those aren't falsies are they, honey?" When the laughter
subsided, the woman offered her hand. "Just breaking the
ice. My name's Kitty. We're all getting a little jumpy; we
thought you might be the first guest."

Sylvia shook Kitty's hand and settled into conversation, at
the same time trying to eavesdrop on as many others as she
could. This would all be part of the story, and her mind would
have to do the notetaking.

Sylvia was so nervous that she felt nauseous. Like stage
fright in high school, when she'd played Laura in *The Glass
Menagerie*. It was good trying out her lines with Kitty: what
she'd done in Atlanta, how she'd started in cocktail waitressing and found the real money was elsewhere. But they
weren't helping much. The butterflies were so bad that she

could feel them fluttering all the way up in her throat, making her voice sound breathless. She was going to have to calm herself.

Then Eleanor walked in with Kurtz. The sight of him in his tuxedo, his red bow tie, his hard face, made her blood curdle. He searched the faces of the girls until he found hers. Yes, he was lingering on her. Sylvia lowered her eyes a moment, and when she looked back up, Kurtz was still looking at her keenly and Eleanor was talking.

"Most of the night, you'll just be standing around stroking their egos," she was saying. "And by the way, don't stuff yourselves. And, girls, there is a one-drink limit."

As Eleanor marched over to the bar, Sylvia could still feel Kurtz's glance as he strutted around the room inspecting the girls one by one. Was he onto her? A dark cloud crossed Sylvia's mind, and she stared out the window, realizing there was no exit that way, a long, long way to fall. The only way out was the way she'd come in.

At the bar she heard Eleanor snap at the idle bartender, "Don't just stand there. Polish those glasses."

Then Kurtz was a foot away, looking right through her silk dress as if she were naked. His steely eyes lifted slowly to her face. "At ease, soldier," he said, playing out his military fantasy. Giving her one more glance, he reached and very slightly readjusted the hang of her dress. Sylvia shuddered.

"Something wrong?" Kurtz said.

Sylvia shook her head no.

Then there were footsteps in the hall, and the burly doorman, whose tuxedo barely housed his musculature, squired in two self-important gentlemen in their fifties. Their eyes ignited at sight of the roomful of luscious girls.

"Would you gentlemen care for a drink?" Eleanor inquired. Escorting them to the bar, she graciously made small talk and told them that the other guests would be arriving shortly. "May I introduce you to the girls?"

A brusque New York sentence, then a Texas drawl, answered in the affirmative. Summoning the girls, Eleanor introduced each of them by name. "And this is Sonya, our new girl."

"So nice to see you this evenin'," drawled the Texan, his beefy hand not letting go of hers. "Tell me about yourself, darlin'." He drew her into a dimly lit corner, his hand brushing her breast. "Everybody has a life story."

"You're the man that's got the real story," Sylvia said. "What's your name, cowboy?"

More guests were arriving. Eleanor escorted each guest to the bar, where drinks and girls beckoned.

"I can't wait to get better acquainted," Tex said, lowering his voice for the word 'better.' "In fact, I'm not gonna wait." Tugging Sylvia's hand, Tex made his way to Eleanor. "Tell me something, ma'am. Where's the bedroom?"

"Bedroom?" Eleanor said, taken aback. She had invited one girl for each man—except for the guests of honor— planning they would each take one home for party favors. "Oh, yes. We had planned that each guest would have a private evening after the party."

"Looks like my private evenin's startin' right now," he said, pulling Sylvia toward the door.

"Oh, but you must wait till the man of the hour arrives," Eleanor stalled. "He told me this afternoon he wanted to talk to you personally."

Glancing at his Rolex—it was nine-thirty—he fumed, "Where the hell is he? In Texas, a good man's always on time."

Sylvia excused herself for the powder room. It was elegant, with twin basins, the shape of shells, set in marble. A Princess phone was mounted on the wall. Latching the door, she wrote his name in tiny letters on the sheet of paper that she'd hidden under the insole of her shoe, like a crib sheet. "Tex" was, in fact, John Haskell, an Odessa oil baron. She jotted a few key details of the look and feel of the party.

When she emerged, she saw Eleanor steering Haskell toward Kitty. Praise the stars!

As Sylvia approached the bar, a silver-headed man in his early sixties lightly touched Sylvia's elbow. "Can I buy you a drink?"

"Yes, thank you, but I think they're on the house," she quipped.

Correcting himself, he laughed, "I knew that."

Sylvia felt at ease with this man. He reminded her of a favorite college professor. Before long, he was telling her his life story. Born in Indiana, Ralph Tyler now made his home in Chicago, where he chaired a Fortune 500 corporation. Divorced, he had one son who made block prints. Nowadays, Ralph lived for his golf game.

"How long have you known Ellen?" she asked.

"Ellen, the hostess? Never met her before."

Unbeknownst to Sylvia, Eleanor was within earshot.

"Gee, how'd you find out about this party?"

Before he could answer, Eleanor stepped into the conversation, smiling sweetly at Ralph Tyler. Sylvia tensed, sensing that she was in for it. But before the party, she'd rehearsed her every move: she was to play dumb.

"If you'll excuse us a moment," Eleanor said, drawing Sylvia into another room.

"Sonya," she said in a fierce whisper. "You don't ask them what they do. You don't ask them where they're from. You don't even ask their names."

It occurred to Sylvia that she'd heard this tone before from Hale, telling her she was out of line. She'd better be more careful.

"I thought we were supposed to be friendly," Sylvia said, feigning hurt feelings.

"Friendly yes, nosy no."

Back at the party, Sylvia positioned herself alluringly on the couch, figuring that alone she could extend her radar in all directions. She heard snatches of conversation, several mentions of Ben Fincastle, Dan Tison, and the election. Not unusual for this time of year—but somehow, here, it seemed out of place. Why so much political talk? she wondered.

One remark in particular riveted her: "This is some kind of return for raising all that money!"

Seeing Eleanor was engaged in conversation across the room, Sylvia made a beeline for the talkative man. "I'm Sonya. Who're you?"

Handsome, fortyish, and impeccably dressed, the man turned playfully from his tête-à-tête with Shana. "Good to know you, Sonya,'' he said with a southern accent. ''The name's Clint. Whew, they said you girls were something else, but I've never seen anything like this.''

Shana, an accomplished performer, nibbled on his ear.

''I'm just so impressed with all you important men,'' Sylvia said.

''Honey,'' he said, his voice growing confidential. ''Let me tell you something about the men in this room. We're talking movers and shakers, guys who can shake the money tree. Maybe we like to gamble, but in my estimation, we're putting our money on a damn good horse.''

Sylvia smiled, urging him to continue.

''Men like us get together every few years and decide who's going to play president.'' As he took a sip of Jack Daniel's, his eyes lit on the newest guests to arrive. ''Speak of the devil . . .''

# CHAPTER
## 38

For a moment, a hush descended on the party. The doorman had just escorted in Senator Benedict Fincastle of North Carolina. With him was his chief political adviser, Barry Dinsmore Cole.

This couldn't be. Sylvia had to tell herself not to stare. She glanced away in disbelief, then back to the two men who had to have walked into the wrong party.

Spontaneously, the guests broke into a welcoming applause and raucous cheers, with the girls following suit. Ben threw up his hand gleefully, responding to this show of support. B. D. scowled; he wasn't hard to read. Ben's adviser was here under protest.

John Haskell, closest to the door, raised his glass. ''To the

next president of these great United States, Ben Fincastle.''
At that, Haskell threw his crystal whiskey glass into the
fireplace, the glass shattering into the fire. He pulled Kitty
to his hip. "Hell of a way to thank us, Ben, ole boy!"

Sylvia could not believe the scene unfolding in front of
her. In a flash, it all came together. Incredibly, she had
stumbled into Fincastle's own private party. The ten men
were his guests, men he was evidently rewarding for helping
to finance his campaign. Her story would ruin him.

For confirmation, Sylvia sidled over to Ralph Tyler. "I
can't believe it," she said, once again affecting the dumb
girl. "Ben Fincastle! Is he the mystery host?"

"Oh, yes," said Ralph, swept up in the drama. "Ben called
me personally to invite me to this shindig."

B. D.'s eyes met Sylvia's. For an instant, it seemed that
he'd recognized her. Then he shifted to the other girls, roving
the room. There was no mistaking what these women were.

B. D. turned to Ben. "Goddammit, Fincastle," he muttered in a barely audible voice. "You said there'd be girls
here, not a bunch of damn hookers. You really did it this
time."

Unperturbed, Ben clapped B. D. on the back. "Just a little
healthy fun."

"Like hell it is," said B. D., calming his voice but still
fuming. His voice lowered to a whisper. "You're self-de-
structing right before my eyes."

Flashing his signature charismatic smile, Fincastle steered
B. D. to a female with a come-hither look in her eyes.
"Loosen this boy up, will you?"

A telephone rang somewhere in the background.

A few moments later, out of the corner of her eye, Sylvia
saw Rich Kurtz emerge from a back room and tap Eleanor's
shoulder. Together, they disappeared into the kitchen.

Something was wrong. She knew it. Sylvia had all she
needed for the story—everything but a photograph of Fincastle in a compromising position. She approached Haskell,
suggesting they go off together now. Several of the girls had
already disappeared with their "dates" into back rooms.

"Plenty of room here," Haskell said.

"No, let's go somewhere else where we can really be alone."

She saw B. D. approaching behind Haskell's shoulder. "You look very familiar," he said.

"Sonya? She's a living doll," Haskell said proprietorially. "And if you haven't seen her before, you wish you had. I hate to break it to you, fellah, but I've got first dibs on this one."

Sylvia turned her eyes adoringly to Haskell, as if to say, "Let's go."

"No, really," B. D. persisted, scanning his memory bank for her identity. "I'm positive I've seen you before somewhere."

"Tall, blond, some would call her stunning, but watch out, she's cold as ice," Hale was saying on the other end of the line.

"Not here at the party," Eleanor interrupted.

"She's gone underground to infiltrate your operation. Have you hired any new girls lately?"

Eleanor froze. Sonya Rees. Tall. Stunning. And blond hair can easily be dyed brown.

"I couldn't stop this, because I didn't know about it until this very evening." Hale's voice was strained. "That woman went behind my back. You know I'm going to do everything I can, but I can't promise you anything. This thing has grown beyond what anyone could have imagined."

Hanging up the receiver, Eleanor looked into Rich's face in fear.

Sylvia was arm-in-arm with John Haskell at the elevator when Eleanor stormed up to them. In her most official tone, Eleanor informed Haskell that none of the girls was to leave quite yet. "We have a delightful surprise in store for all our guests."

"I'm sure this one here is all the surprise I'm needing."

"Mr. Haskell," Eleanor retorted, "a gentleman from Texas would never disappoint his hostess."

Sylvia's heart raced. Was this a legitimate party plan, or

were they onto her? Eleanor was assiduously avoiding eye contact.

Then her eyes dug into Sylvia's. Venom. Sylvia saw her answer. She flashed on Rich Kurtz's warning: his finger slashing his throat.

The elevator doors parted, and Sylvia made a dash for it. "I'll be waiting for you in the lobby," she said to Haskell, punching the Door Close button.

"She's not to go!" Eleanor commanded.

The startled doorman shot his thick body between the closing doors. There was no way out. Sylvia let him guide her back into the hall.

"Now, you lovebirds go back in and have a good time," Eleanor cooed. As she watched them move down the hall, she told the doorman not to let any guests leave without permission—especially that comely brunette.

Sylvia tried the powder room, but finding its door locked, darted into a bedroom, in search of a phone.

There was a phone, all right. There was also Clint and Shana, ensconced on a king-sized bed. Shana appeared to be dousing Clint from a bottle of Jack Daniel's.

Seeing Sylvia at the door, Clint managed, "Care to join us?"

Finding the powder room free as she retreated, Sylvia locked the door and grabbed the phone. Who could she call?

Max.

She dialed his number from memory. One ring. Two rings. His voice on the answering machine. Damn it, she thought as she considered hanging up and dialing Berman. She waited twenty seconds for the beep and left her emergency message, including the address of the party. "Send for the police. Immediately."

She hung up and dialed Dennis Berman's home number. Before she could finish, a voice came on the line. "Sylvia Loring, too bad you're not in Florida like you're supposed to be." The voice came from an in-house extension. Rich Kurtz.

Her mind leaped to B. D. An egomaniac, yes, but a murderer he wasn't. It was the only way out.

As she stepped out of the powder room, Kurtz seized her arm so sharply that she felt a stab of pain. He hustled her toward the back.

"B. D.!" she called out so loudly that heads turned. "B. D.!"

Recognizing a familiar voice, B. D. stepped forward, then stopped in his tracks.

"B. D., it's me, Sylvia," she said urgently, almost hysterically.

"My God," he said, seeing that it was so. There was Sylvia Loring, in brown hair and some kind of disguise. His worst fear was reality. He had to act fast. None of the guests must know a reporter was present.

"What some women won't do to get attention," he quipped for the benefit of the startled guests.

Ben Fincastle joined in the laughter.

With a fuming Kurtz at his elbow, B. D. escorted Sylvia into a back room and shut the door.

"What the hell do you think you're doing here?" B. D. demanded, knowing the answer all too well.

"I had no idea you were mixed up with this," Sylvia said.

The door opened. It was Eleanor.

"So what are we going to do with her?" Kurtz said.

The door opened again. It was Ben Fincastle, a grin on his lips. Somber faces wiped it off. "What's going on here?"

"Close the door, Senator," B. D. said. He nodded toward Sylvia. "We have a reporter in our midst."

"Eleanor," the senator said quietly. "How could you have let this happen?"

Eleanor and Kurtz exchanged furious glances. There was no good answer.

"I know her," B. D. said. "I'll talk to her alone." He nodded toward another room.

Once inside, B. D. shut the door behind him. He collected his thoughts carefully.

"It is of utmost importance that you forget everything you've seen and heard tonight."

Sylvia said nothing.

"Do you follow?"

"I'm not dropping this story."

B. D. paced the room, pulling at his hair. Never in his life had his fate been so largely in someone else's hands. A woman's. It was a position he'd vowed never to put himself in. But now, there it was. He stood beside Sylvia, who seemed to tower over him in her high heels. He'd always been a power person, and she had it now.

He finally spat it out, a word that had never had a home in his vocabulary. "Please."

For a moment, he had touched her. Finally, she said, "B. D., you know I can't."

He looked at her a long time. Without another word, he took his leave, closing the door behind him.

Kurtz was waiting outside the door. As B. D. exited, he turned and locked it. His powerful body stood motionless, his eyes smoldered, as he addressed B. D. "It's my ass too. I'll take care of this."

"And do what?" B. D. said sarcastically.

Taking his time, Kurtz glanced commandingly from B. D. to Eleanor to Ben. Then he drew his hand across his own mouth. There was an audible gasp in the room as the gesture sank in.

"Senator," Kurtz said, "when you get to be president, you'll owe me one."

"Owe you for what?" Ben said. "Look, pal. I don't intend to get in any deeper than I already am."

"Oh, it's not what you think, Senator," Kurtz said in a low voice.

The door handle twisted as Sylvia tried to get out. "Damn it, let me out of here!"

A smile played on Kurtz's lips.

"Gentlemen," Eleanor said to the guests at the party, striking a crystal highball glass with a teaspoon. "I see that some of you are still here, while others have gone on to more intimate encounters. The senator will be coming out in just a moment to say good-night. Now we must end this phase of the party. Thank you for a lovely evening. And, uh, for those of you who haven't yet selected your date, please do so now.''

The remaining guests chose their partners. An inebriated John Haskell was left standing alone.

"Where's mine?" he slurred, his body swaying with booze.

"Unfortunately, Sonya is indisposed," Eleanor said.

"Indisposed? There's no such thing as an indisposed woman. Not with John Haskell, there isn't. I'm gettin' her!''

Before Eleanor could reply, Haskell lunged toward the back of the penthouse. But his legs buckled and he sprawled to the floor. Despite themselves, the guests roared with laughter.

Ben Fincastle appeared. Joining conspicuously in the merriment, he bent low for an inspection. "Poor ole Haskell," he said. "He's going to miss the good stuff. He's out cold."

Instructing Eleanor to call a cab for the Texan, Ben thanked each guest personally.

"Good night, boys," he said. "Better enjoy it while it lasts. I can't do this for you in the White House."

The door opened. For a moment, Rich Kurtz was plainly visible in the light, his frame filling the doorway. She saw his eyes narrow on her in her alluring, sea-green silk.

"I don't scare easily," she said, her voice sounding funny to herself. "If that's what you're trying to do."

He switched off the light and closed the door behind him. All was dark, the room silent but for the sound of his breathing.

She felt better having exposed her cover to Ben and B. D. Surely no harm could come to her—not with all these witnesses around. Surely this man would not try anything dangerous. Surely Ben and B. D. weren't so ambitious as to do away with her. But why were they keeping her locked in here?

A match flame tore the darkness. It lit a cigarette, which glowed in the dark. Sylvia heard an exhaled breath and smelled the acrid smoke.

"The cops are going to be here any minute," she said coldly, trying to mask her fear. "In case you don't know it, I told a friend to call them."

No answer.

"Where are all *your* friends, Kurtz?" she asked. Anything to break up the terrifying stone of silence in the room.

His only response was the in and out, in and out of his breathing. Slowly, the glow of the cigarette traveled toward his unseen lips.


B. D. should have been angry, had every reason to be. He'd never even been consulted about this party, and his own reputation would suffer by the association. But there was no anger in him, only remorse, as if this were a long-awaited death, one he'd known was coming. He should have left Ben in Tallahassee, as he'd threatened when they'd had words. But in the end, he'd faltered; he'd let his hopefulness about the campaign get the better of his judgment. He'd never come so close before, never ridden so high.

Ben and B. D. stood silently on a windblown street corner. The cab would be here any minute. The streetlight cast a strange silver glow on Ben's face.

"I have a feeling about Kurtz," Ben said. "He can take care of a situation."

Grimly, B. D. inhaled the night air. The man was grasping at straws, trying to wish the story away. B. D. could have blown him away. Instead, he said calmly, "I wouldn't count on it."

"We have to take the chance. It's all we've got."

Ben's eyes searched B. D.'s for a response but came up wanting.

The cab pulled to the curb.


First there was the doorman. "Are you a guest?"

"No," Max said, stepping out of the elevator and past him.

"Hey! You can't go in there!"

Football's a tough sport. If you're good at the game, you learn how to unleash quick bursts of devastating violence, to turn destruction on and off at the sound of a whistle. Long after you've quit the sport, your body hasn't forgotten. It still knows how to hurt or be hurt.

Max moved toward the door. The doorman grabbed him. Max froze, the burly man's fingers curling around his arm.

Then, in an instant, he ducked and slammed his body full force into the doorman's belly, knocking the wind out of him and driving him with powerful legs into a knockout collision with the wall.

The doorman slumped to the floor, gasping for breath, and Max flung open the door into the penthouse.

Eleanor stood at the entrance, pocketbook in hand. A coat draped over her shoulders. She took a draw on a cigarette.

"Where's Sylvia?"

"What makes you think—" A piercing scream from the back cut short her denial.

Max stiff-armed Eleanor aside and bolted toward the sound. Another scream, and he saw the closed door between them. "Sylvia!"

He shoved open the door, breaking the lock. Darkness. The air choked with cigarette smoke. And Sylvia's muffled sobs.

Then he saw them, dimly outlined against the wall. One of Kurtz's hands held a burning cigarette. The other gripped her arm.

Her arm. Bruised with red grip marks. And a round, black burn—from a cigarette—burrowed into her white flesh. "You son of a bitch."

Kurtz stuck the cigarette in his mouth and reached inside his jacket. "Who the fuck are you?"

Below, from the street, they heard the wail of a siren. Another siren close behind. Approaching fast.

Kurtz drew a pistol. "Look, creep, if you know what's good for you, you're gonna disappear." Brandishing his weapon, he twisted Sylvia's arm, shoved her toward the door, and trained the gun on Max's face as they brushed past.

They disappeared beyond the next doorway.

* * *

The madam was making her descent. In the elevator, where she could no longer hear them, the sirens still screamed in her inner ear. She was hoping against hope to win this race.

The elevator opened, and she rushed into the lobby. Still time. The glass doors showed only the street.

Then uniformed men filled the space behind them. Four cops. All staring at her.

The doors swung open. Large male bodies closed in and formed a wall between the madam and her escape. The questions began.

Max had never been lighter on his feet. Not even dancing down the chalk sideline on his toes, trying like all hell to stay in bounds while some 250-pound body took a shot at him, had come close to this. He tiptoed around the last corner.

"Freeze!" Kurtz said at the elevator, the breathless doorman still on the floor. The gun was trained on Max's head. Kurtz's other hand lay flat across Sylvia's mouth.

Her eyes, never more beautiful, squeezed all the life they still had into Max. He looked down the barrel of Kurtz's pistol and knew he would get it done. Somehow. You just did it.

"On your knees," Kurtz barked.

Max had no choice. Down on all fours. Kurtz loomed above him. It could end this way. A quick bullet to the brain.

Max sucked a breath. The corner of his eye caught Kurtz turning the pistol around in his hand. Going to hit him on the head. Anticipation was the name of this game. After that, pure instinct. Max's toes bit into the floor.

He felt the slashing motion of Kurtz's arm. But Max was quicker. He sprang from his toes. The blow missed his head, landed heavily on his back as Kurtz lost his balance and their bodies fell together, grappling. The gun was on the floor.

"Sylvia, the gun!"

She scrambled toward it as the elevator doors opened and three cops stormed the hall.

Kurtz shook Max loose and grabbed the gun.

"Drop it," a cop screamed.

Kurtz came up firing.

"Sylvia!"

But she was already hitting the floor. Max's body dived protectively across hers as a hailstorm of bullets punched Kurtz against the wall.

A long pause followed, and then "Are you all right?" they both said at the same time.

Whatever shape they were in, Rich Kurtz had it worse. He sat bathed on the floor in his own shiny blood.

# CHAPTER 39

Right there in the lobby of the penthouse of the crime, Sylvia and Digby conferred on a pay phone, weighing the lateness of the hour (it was closing in on eleven P.M.) against the chance that the *Post* would get the story if they were to wait until tomorrow to run with it.

Operating on pure adrenaline, Sylvia felt no fatigue. The story had to get out. It was pure instinct, her feeling that if they waited a single day, it might vanish into thin air. This time, there could be no doubt about accuracy. A man had been shot, a woman arrested, a prostitution ring exposed. And the man who would be president was one of the customers.

"I'm up to it," Sylvia insisted. "You'll have my story an hour from when I get to the VDT."

Digby agreed, but she would have to rush. The absolute last deadline was one-thirty A.M., and every extra minute was costing the newspaper money.

Possibly because of her intense focus on getting the story written, or because of sensory overload, Sylvia didn't at first see a new player appear on the scene. Not until she was with Max in his car did Sylvia notice Michael Paradyne of the *Washington Post* pull up to the building, hot on the trail.

Max sliced through the dark Washington streets like an expectant father on the brink of his wife's delivery, stopping only momentarily at a twenty-four-hour pharmacy for a burn ointment to treat Sylvia's wound. On the drive, neither mentioned what had happened, or how close they had come to what might have been, or how this crucible of events had forged them together.

At the *Tribune*'s rear parking lot, Max watched Sylvia get out. "Don't tell me," he said. "You'll save me a copy—if you remember."

What could she say to the man who might have saved her life, who was sitting there letting her off so easily with a funny line when real feelings were too overwhelming for either of them to handle? Just play along.

She fished in her pocketbook and handed him a quarter. "Here, Max." She laughed. "Just in case I forget."

A nervous Digby Reeve, who'd come in to meet her, settled Sylvia to work at the computer terminal in the same private room where Colette had written her fabrication. The room had doors connecting on one side with Hale's and the other side with Digby's offices.

Sylvia pulled the notes out of her shoe and jotted her thoughts on a yellow notepad. She tried not to think about the impact of the story, but simply to focus on writing it.

Once she started, it was a dead sprint against the clock. Periodically, Digby hovered over her shoulder, checking on her progress. "Terrific," he muttered, scanning her screen. "Unbelievable!"

It was well after midnight when Hale got the word from Eleanor by phone. Just back from a preliminary questioning at the police station (she wouldn't tell them a thing without her attorney present), Eleanor railed on about Sylvia Loring's duplicity in penetrating her operation.

Then, as if an afterthought, she added, "It's not only me, you know, but Ben Fincastle's in for it. He paid for the party and made up the guest list."

"Ben Fincastle was there?" Hale asked, incredulous. "Did Sylvia see him?"

"You couldn't miss him. There were only twenty people present. Well, twenty-four counting Ben, B. D., Rich, and me."

Hale Gardiner quickly formed a plan of action. Although she would have been delighted under any other circumstances for Fincastle's political star to be snuffed out, in this case her cousin came first. And the Gardiner name.

"Rest easy, Eleanor. I'll have this story killed within the hour."

As soon as Hale hung up the phone, she dialed Colette. "I have some very bad news. . . ."

It was 1:08 A.M. when Sylvia dialed Judy Fincastle's number. After seven rings, an irritated voice answered the phone.

"Judy, this is Sylvia Loring. Sorry to call at this hour, but there's something you have to know. . . ."

It was 1:22 A.M. when the two women marched into Digby's office together. Hale and Colette. In the next room, Sylvia was scanning her story for the last time. Digby had already read and approved it.

Confident of her mission, Hale began a high-toned pitch about how Ben Fincastle was "good for the nation."

Colette chimed in in her little-girl voice. "I know for a fact, Digby, that Ben thinks highly of you. And with Hale here and me there, you can be sure that the *Tribune* will have the inside track to the Fincastle administration."

From the next room, Sylvia heard their unmistakable voices and immediately grasped their purpose: to kill the story. The lines had been drawn long ago. Sylvia pushed the keyboard command to film the story and, uninvited, stepped into the room.

Hale glanced at Sylvia and continued, seemingly unfazed. "If we run this story about him, there's his political scalp.

Leaders are fallible. They have feet of clay. If the *Tribune* had exposed John Kennedy and Martin Luther King's sexual antics, we would have lost two great leaders.''

Almost against his will, Digby was caught up in the magic of her rhetoric, and a part of him had to agree with her. Had he not himself succumbed to the occasional extramarital adventure when Nancy was living?

''What business is it of the public,'' Hale continued, stepping smartly around his office as if it were her own, ''what public men do in private?'' It seemed she was voicing his very doubts.

''You're right, Hale,'' Digby said quietly, scratching his chin.

''You're forgetting one thing,'' said Sylvia, watching Digby dangerously teetering on the edge.

Hale brushed aside this intrusion. ''And here's the clincher, Digby. No self-respecting paper publishes a story gained through misrepresentation.'' She cast Sylvia a contemptuous look.

Sylvia could not believe what she was hearing. She'd always been better with the written than the spoken word. But, in this case, she must rise to the occasion. She stationed herself in front of Digby's desk and folded her arms in front of her like building blocks. Hale had counted her out too soon.

''First point,'' Sylvia began. ''Going underground was not my first choice, it was my only recourse. Many other journalists have done the same. In this case, there was no other way to get the story.

''Number two. Neither of these women has any business in this editorial decision.'' Sylvia turned toward Colette. ''You are, shall we say, intimately involved with someone implicated in a major scandal, the biggest story this paper has ever had. I ought to be questioning you right now—instead of you questioning me. I resent it.''

Then Sylvia stepped toward Hale. Always before, she had crooked a knee to downplay the difference in their heights, to give them rough parity. Not this time. This time she would stand tall, underscoring every inch's advantage over her boss.

"And Hale, in case you haven't put it together, you have a conflict of interest that precludes your having any involvement with this story."

Sylvia wheeled and aimed her final shot at Digby. "And if we discuss this for even one more minute, I'll leave this paper never to return. And you can bet your bottom dollar that you'll see every inch of this story in the *Washington Post*."

The three women were on their feet, their attention riveted to a seated Digby Reeve. Saying nothing, he picked up the telephone and dialed the security desk. "Escort needed in the publisher's office. On the double."

No one uttered a word as they waited to see whom the guard was coming for. When he arrived, Digby nodded his head toward Hale and Colette. "Walk these women to their cars, please."

The two women trudged along with the escort toward their cars in the dark parking lot.

"Thank you," Hale said, dismissing the guard. "Damn Sylvia Loring," she started, her voice flaring up. Then she sobered. "At least—at least we were in this together."

Colette did not seem moved. In fact, she seemed almost to recoil from Hale. "Nothing we can do at this point," Colette said distantly.

Hale moved toward her, seeking an embrace, comfort, reassurance that at least their friendship would stand in light of this new, troubling turn of events. "Now we're both out of the *Tribune*. I plan to resign tomorrow. I don't see how I can stay on given how my leadership has been ignored."

But there was no response—no sisterhood, no solidarity, no commiseration. It was as if Colette hadn't heard her, couldn't feel her loss. But then, Colette probably viewed her as everyone else did: strong, confident, always able to cope. She would tell her friend the truth. "Colette, I need your help."

Colette eyed her warily. "I've got to get going."

Hale pondered this turn of events, indignation stabbing her in the chest like a shooting pain. She'd put her own neck on the line for Colette in her hour of need. Where was Colette now? She already knew the answer. Her mind was on Ben.

"At least Ben has shown his true colors," Hale said, trying to conceal her bitterness. "And you'll be free of him."

"I'm with Ben now more than ever," Colette flashed back, angry.

It was hard to believe that Colette could talk to her this way. And leave her all-alone, without a friend. "But is Ben with you?"

"Of course he's with me! He's going to marry me now."

Colette was deluding herself, and Hale would never again be an accessory to her self-delusions. "It will never happen," Hale said definitively. "Never."

Colette's face grew red, as if Hale had shaken something loose inside her. She took in a deep breath and let it out. "I don't ever want to have anything to do with you again."

There for him in his hour of need, Colette slept fitfully that night, awaiting Ben's call. It never came.

Never before an early bird, at six A.M. she was at the newsstand for the first edition of the *Tribune*, which arrived twenty minutes late. Standing out on a cold sidewalk, she read Sylvia's story word for word. It was more damaging than she could have guessed, more vivid than anything she could have invented. It was a mortal blow. Colette tried to imagine how people would forgive and forget. But even Colette Daniels could see that after this story Ben Fincastle would never reach 1600 Pennsylvania Avenue.

Back in her car, Colette headed for the house she'd driven past and studied so often, the house that had become mythical in her imagination, the house from which she wanted to spring him loose: the Ben Fincastle residence.

As she approached the imposing home in the early-morning light, she was overwhelmed with a surprising joy. In limbo for so long, now, finally, she could call Ben her own. This awful story and Hale's vicious words of last night were all meaningless against what would now happen. With the White House no longer in reach, his marriage on matchsticks could only collapse.

A female voice—Glenda's—called through the closed door, "If you're a reporter, get lost!"

"Campaign staff," she said. "Colette Daniels."

A crack opened, and a red-eyed Glenda peered out. "We know all about you and Daddy. He doesn't want to see you."

Colette smiled at the misunderstanding. "Honey, I know you're upset. We all are. But your father does want to see me."

Still in yesterday's suit, dark circles under his eyes, Ben came to the door, instructing Glenda to step aside. "What did you come here for?" he said, not inviting her in. "To my wife's house? My Glenda is here. Don't you respect anything?"

The phone rang inside. Through the opening in the door, Colette saw B. D. Cole grab for it. At a nearby table, Judy Fincastle and Lyons Smith grimly sipped coffee.

Ben turned toward the phone. His only concern now was how he was going to meet the press at noon. B. D. and Lyons had urged him—and so had key party leaders contacted within the last half hour—to cut his losses and withdraw from the race. Democratic support must now be consolidated behind Dan Tison.

"Don't you know what this means, Ben?" Colette pressed, her voice low and urgent. "We can start over together. We can finally become a real couple."

It was as if she had not even spoken. Ben began to step back inside.

"Ben," Colette said, searching his eyes. "I love you. *You*," she repeated.

He heard her, but it was as if she was gone, like a TV actor you just turn off. She had been part of the giant fantasy, the amazing, Ferris-wheel ride of his projected presidency. When that died, so had she.

"It's over," he told her. "It's all over."

# CHAPTER
## 40

Hale combed her hair back and stepped from her tasteful suite, done in the Williamsburg colors, toward the drawing room where tea was being served this Wednesday. It was April Fools' Day, little more than three weeks since Sylvia K. Loring, in one fell swoop, had managed to depose both Ben Fincastle and the Gardiner cousins. Yes, she had resigned. She'd had no choice really, after that dreadful, eleventh-hour showdown in Digby's office. Dennis Berman had been named acting editor, but Digby would soon realize that the man was not suited for an executive position. He was a plodder and a moralist, without panache. Every day, Hale looked for the telegram to come, summoning her back to the *Tribune*, or the telephone call from Digby suggesting that bygones be bygones. She had even rehearsed her response. She would have to think it over. If he called at the beginning of the week, she'd be back to him by week's end; if he called at the end of the week, she'd tell him at the beginning of the next.

In the meantime, Hale would bide her time here in the nurturing environment of Sweetbriar College, surrounded by girls from Virginia's finest families, girls who recognized her professional stature and admired her success. It was not lost on either Hale or her maternal uncle, the school's academic dean, who'd invited her as a guest lecturer-in-residence, that she'd created something of a stir on campus. He said it was good for the girls to be exposed to the realities of the working woman, the realities of the world.

"Did you even suspect at the time," one of the girls was

asking her while munching on a Swedish cracker, "that Colette Daniels was making up the story?"

"I did," said Hale, "but our publisher wanted to increase sales, so he pressured me to run the story before we had the chance to check it out."

"What about Sylvia Loring?" another girl asked. "Did you ever realize how far she'd go to get the story?"

Hale's eyes narrowed at her questioner. "Young woman, I trust you're not naïve enough to believe everything you hear about Sylvia Loring."

"Oh, no," said the student in alarm.

"Good. Let me tell you. Sylvia Loring is the sort of woman who would have climbed into any bed to get that story if need be. I trust my meaning is not lost."

"No," the girl said, flushing.

It was possibly the bitterest pill she'd had to swallow. Having to watch Sylvia bask in her ill-gotten glory. A girl who'd grown up in a duplex in Takoma Park. A subordinate who'd once tried so hard to please.

But when Hale returned to the *Trib*, she would put Sylvia back in her place. No, a woman of that sort could not ultimately be the bitterest pill of all. That distinction must be reserved for the failure of her friends. They had forgotten her when she had worked so hard for them.

Colette had been true to her words that night in the parking lot and had never returned her phone calls. And then, her phone had gone dead. And Eleanor, with whom she'd at least had lunch, had never once said thank you. Instead, she'd monopolized the conversation, talking about Rich's critical condition and dreadful hospital bills and the D. A.'s probable case against her.

When she'd chastised her cousin—"If only you'd confided in me, none of this would have happened; I would have suppressed the story in the beginning"—Eleanor had retorted rather rudely. She'd had the gall to suggest Hale needed to go into therapy. "That's always been the problem with the Gardiners. Repression, suppression. Double lives," Eleanor added, eyeing her significantly.

One of the girls, in a lovely English print jumper, came in to find her. "Miss Gardiner," she said. "Phone call for you."

Colette Daniels's bags were packed, her apartment cleared. The few big items she'd planned to keep had been shipped ahead of her to Los Angeles. The rental company had retrieved its furniture. Everything she didn't want she'd given to Goodwill. It had always amazed her how quickly you can enter an affair or call it quits.

It was incredible what had happened. In all of her years, this was the first time she'd ever been left. No man had ever done it. Not one. She still loved Ben. If he were to arrive here this moment to retrieve her, she'd call it all off, but somehow, his dumping her had been freeing. She finally knew what it meant to love someone. She knew what it meant to hurt and cry. To care. To be just a woman who loved a man and slept with him and tried her damndest to get him. She was a loser, just like everyone else. Now, she had lost once, just like that janitor who was sweeping cigarette butts into a metal ashbin right underneath the phone booth she had settled into.

Colette Daniels had not seen nor spoken to Ben Fincastle since that morning twenty-three days ago when the story had appeared that had effectively ended his candidacy. Apparently, he'd meant every word. It was over. He did not want to see her ever again. She'd watched his withdrawal from the race on television, tears streaming down her face. And she'd realized in her pain that Colette and Ben, the two of them, had been connected in his mind to a rising star, not a falling one. Out of loyalty to Ben, the first man she'd ever loved, Colette had turned down every interview request that had come through, including one that gave her some small satisfaction from Sylvia Loring.

One request, though, had been providential. It had come through the day she was having her phone disconnected. A job offer from a famous Australian publishing tycoon to head up the society section of the new tabloid newspaper he was starting in Los Angeles. He'd considered purchasing the venerable but floundering *Los Angeles Herald-Examiner* before it folded, but decided the better to start his own. Start anew.

The tycoon had taken a personal interest in her story, he'd said over the phone. "Hollywood is the place where your past isn't held against you. Fame and infamy are virtually synonymous here. One prominent young writer," he'd noted playfully, "who plagiarized most of his first novel, is now the head writer for a hit TV series." Colette didn't have the foggiest idea who he was talking about, but she'd find out. He'd offered to pay her moving expenses and put her up for a month at one of his company suites while she found a place. She'd accepted immediately.

Thirty minutes remained until she had to board her flight to Los Angeles. It was the first time she could remember having shown up for a flight on time.

Colette dialed the number at Sweetbriar that Hale had left repeatedly on her answering machine.

"I'm calling to say good-bye," Colette said to Hale. She told her about the job offer she'd accepted in L.A. She thought about how she'd "lost it" that night in the parking lot, and how, as it turned out, Hale had been right about Ben. "You've been a real friend to me."

Hale could hardly believe it. The woman who had set the ball rolling to the chain of events that had brought them each to these places was on the phone now. Thanking her. The debacle was almost worth just this.

"Colette, I love you."

"I do you, too," Colette said. The words felt funny when she said them. Remarkably, for Colette Daniels, a confirmed liar, they conveyed a fraction of the truth.

It was a balmy Friday evening, the third of April. Ben himself, for the first time in years, was browning an old downhome specialty—barbecued ribs—on the outdoor grill. And the flowers were something new. Never in all their years at this house had Ben picked daffodils from the yard, put them in a vase, and set them on the dining-room table.

He had resolved to make a new start, to put Ben and Judy

Fincastle back on the road to a decent life together. It was the year of Dan Tison, not of his own grand ambition, but all was not lost. Grimly, Judy had marched with him through the political firestorm without one word against him. But from her refusal to talk, her coldness that never thawed, he knew their marriage was in deep trouble. As in the days of their courtship, he wanted again to prove himself worthy of her.

The problem was, he'd let himself get drunk. Damn near it, anyway. It seemed he couldn't pull this off without just one more shot of liquor. As soon as Judy walked into the house, surprised to see the flowers, amazed to see him cooking in the backyard, Ben would have to do his damndest to pull himself together.

Now he had seen it all. Now he had seen what the advisers who had hitched their wagons to his star, the reporters who had touted him as the southern JFK, would do when the lights went out. B. D. Cole had not been back since that morning when he'd taken himself out of the race. Ben had read in the paper that B. D. had tried—and failed—to get a job with Tison. And the same reporters that had sucked up to him when they thought he was going all the way were now chopping him up into little pieces. They'd laid old Fincastle on a cutting board and dissected every conceivable aspect of his personality to explain why he'd taken such a huge risk.

None of them really knew. Ben himself didn't know for sure; there was never one reason for anything. But he'd had plenty of time to think about it. And he knew he had a clue that none of these experts in the media would ever learn about.

It was a half hour later, the ribs were burnt, and Ben was good and drunk when Judy came in from an engagement for Peace Links. She was surprised to see the daffodils. Then she spotted her husband, standing miserably in the yard, black smoke rising from the grill.

"Judy," he said when she approached, "there's something I want to tell you."

The slurred words. His breath. The half-empty whiskey glass. With more disgust than shock, Judy started for the house.

Ben seized her arm. "Please, Judy."

The air chilled, the sky darkened as he told her about Billy Britt. About the guilt he'd carried for Billy's death since high school. Billy was his best friend, the son of the owner of the plant where his dad worked, who'd died in a single-car accident on the Blue Ridge Parkway near Asheville. The truth was that he and Billy had been racing each other, and Ben had whipped his own car too fast around a curve. Billy had tried to keep up with him. Instead, he'd plunged through a guardrail and sailed five hundred feet before his Ford smashed against the mountain.

"It was my fault," he said. Only, no one ever knew. "I was never punished," he confessed to Judy. And maybe punishment, he said, can help to free a man of his sins. Maybe he didn't really feel he deserved to be president. Maybe, without even knowing it, he'd set up the now infamous Rock Creek party because he wanted at long last to accept his punishment.

"Now you know," he said. "You and me—and Billy."

Judy's words were sympathetic, yet at a curious distance. "I wish you'd told me this years ago," she said. "When I loved you so much."

Ben watched her return to the house. Why was it that Judy's detachment made her all the more attractive? He wanted to grab her before she got to the door, lift her up in his arms and carry her to the bedroom like a honeymooner.

For some reason, perhaps the booze, he began to cry.

When he came into the kitchen, his eyes were red. "Don't worry, I'll get dinner," she said, her back to him as she opened the refrigerator.

"Judy . . ."

She turned. "Ben, I . . ." He'd been crying. She saw her old flame, now a red-eyed, tender drunk, and knew this was going to be tough. "Ben, I want you to know I filed for divorce this afternoon. I, uh . . ." He was gawking at her now, a plastic spatula in his hand. "My mind's made up. I have to go it alone."

Her words were filtering slowly into his head. So slowly he did not yet fully comprehend. "Judy," he said. "I'm sorry I burnt the ribs."

# CHAPTER
## 41

Sylvia Loring walked slowly across the lawn toward Jefferson's white-domed Rotunda. On impulse, she had driven down from Washington this first Saturday in April to attend the late-afternoon alumni gathering honoring the University of Virginia's newly appointed president. In a few minutes, he was to speak in the famous Dome Room, what the *New York Times* had once called "the most beautiful room in America," on the third and highest floor in the Rotunda. Sylvia knew she should hurry, should claim a seat before they were all taken. But the spring day was gorgeous—a deep blue sky and flowers blooming everywhere—and Sylvia paused to watch the students with envy. In T-shirts and shorts, they sailed Frisbees or spiraled footballs across the Lawn, digging bare toes into the lush green turf. She wanted nothing more than to slip out of her cashmere sweater dress and Pappagallo pumps and soak up the rays in something casual and turn it loose. Just enjoy herself for a change.

Pleasure had been in short supply the past few weeks. That in itself was perhaps the most striking aspect of her success. Becoming famous, Sylvia had learned, did not guarantee an internal glow. Sure, there had been a certain satisfaction, a feeling of vindication after all the obstacles, all the doubt, all the risk. She felt undeniable pride in bringing down Eleanor Gardiner, who had so exploited Kokoh and the other girls, and to a lesser extent Ben Fincastle, who, after all, had treated Judy cruelly. But through it all remained a strangely hollow feeling.

Sylvia's story, that Monday morning in March, had hit the

stands and sold out the *Trib* in record time. All the wire services—Reuters, AP, UPI—and the radio and television press had picked it up immediately. Not only had the story spelled out Fincastle's connection with the party and unmasked the madam, but it had quoted Kokoh in identifying other Gardiner clients. Among them was the majority whip and the secretary of defense. Sylvia's story had uncorked the biggest scandal in Washington since Watergate.

That Monday morning, Sylvia had found herself in the eye of a hurricane. First had been her ten A.M. arrival at the *Trib*. Nothing like it had ever been seen before at the grand old paper—a madhouse of swarming colleagues, the phones ringing off the hook, reporters waiting to interview her! Of course, she had given Frank Glover the scoop and had the distinct satisfaction of waiting till late in the afternoon to return Michael Paradyne's calls. She had answered questions for as long as she could, and then had isolated herself in Digby's side office to write the follow-up story of her own undercover adventure.

It had not taken Kokoh King long to collect her money. Hearing the news that very morning on a New York radio station, she'd managed to reach Sylvia at the paper. Knowing it was the right thing to do, Digby had reluctantly agreed to pay Kokoh the additional $5,000 and to reimburse Sylvia for the same amount. Kokoh had been ecstatic: as a former "Gardiner girl"—the very one who had blown the whistle —she knew she was destined for all the publicity she'd been craving.

By late that Monday morning, the first of what Dennis had called a "media chain reaction of explosions" had occurred: the top network nightly news anchor had requested a live, personal interview. For three weeks, the requests had not stopped: the other news anchors, the morning shows. Sylvia had turned none of them down. Overnight she had become the most famous print journalist in America, again and again telling her story and offering her opinions in front of studio cameras. At first, the experience had been nerve-racking; later, with more experience under her belt, she had become more at home on-camera, and no less than three top network executives had offered her the job her mother had long coveted for her: that of television journalist. Sylvia had not yet given them an answer.

And, of course, there had been the book offers. No one was better equipped than Sylvia Loring to write the book about Hookergate. A bidding war and big bucks were in store. Yet on that question, too, Sylvia had hesitated.

There were others beside herself, Sylvia knew, who had been less than utterly thrilled by her triumphs. Hale Gardiner had resigned—never, Sylvia hoped, to return to the *Trib*. She hoped to God that she would never have to deal with that woman again.

Sylvia had parted with Colette on relatively friendly terms. Though Colette had turned down her request for an interview, she had told Sylvia, "You did what you had to do, and I respect that. So I'm doing what I have to do—I'm not giving any interviews concerning Ben." Which Sylvia, when she'd thought about it, had in fact respected.

It seemed that no one had enjoyed her success more than Jan Loring. "Now you can have any man you want," she'd told her daughter one night at dinner.

There had been no point that evening in arguing with her mother—Jan Loring was set in her thinking. But if her success had taught her anything, it was that she could *not* have any man she wanted. Not when the man she wanted had a three-letter name. Not when that man had not called, had not spoken to her once since that parting exchange in the *Trib* parking lot.

That evening before her journey to Charlottesville, Sylvia had taken Pam Tursi to dinner. Pam had just tendered her resignation at the *Trib* to start her own fantasy-toy store. "Your courage inspired me, made me think you should go for what you really want."

"Why are you waiting for Max to call?" Pam had wanted to know, abruptly changing the subject. "Why can't you just call him up and tell him you're nuts about him?"

"I don't know."

"So you're angry at him; you think he owes it to you to pick up the phone first, right?"

"No, that's not it." Then she'd thought about it. "I don't know. Maybe there is some truth to that."

"Why does he owe it to you?"

At that moment, Sylvia had not been able to think of a reason.

Pam had given her a long look. "You do love him?"

Sylvia, finally, had nodded.

"Why are you nodding? Why can't you say the word 'love' out loud?"

"Pam," Sylvia had snapped, "since when are you my therapist?"

"Maybe you need one."

Maybe, Sylvia had realized, she did. Why had it been so hard to admit to her friend that she loved this man? Why couldn't she do what Pam suggested and just pick up the phone?

Later that night, the simplest answer had come to her: Alec Loring. No doubt a therapist would work overtime with that one—how her father had abandoned her, how she couldn't trust any man, how maybe she was filling the void with her work.

"At least you've admitted you love him," Pam had said. "That's a big step."

"A big step," Sylvia had said. "But not the biggest one."

Now here she was in the old haunts. Feeling old, watching these kids. Feeling, for all her success since college, that life had left her behind.

Sylvia started toward the Rotunda. She was here, she supposed, because the spirit of Max was here. The spirit of Max and her together. How else could she explain the impulse this morning, after that dinner last night with Pam, to drive down here for some stiff alumni event?

Dodging a Frisbee, she walked up the west side of the Lawn. She had lived here that senior year. Room number 15. There it was, the ancient window, the faded brick. And there beside it was number 13. Edgar Allan Poe had lived in that room as a student. And so, as he had planned, had Max Ridgway. Max always loved that sort of thing.

She remembered a night in that room. Ironically, though the most prestigious, they were also the most primitive rooms on campus. There were no toilets, no showers in these rooms, you had to go outside and down the quad for facilities. She had been in Max's room studying. She remembered the sight of him coming in from a snowstorm, dressed only in a towel wrapped around his waist. Max was wild in those days. "Just another jock," he'd say teasingly, knowing she hated football. He'd just taken a shower. His hair was feathered with snow. He looked both gorgeous and ridiculous.

They'd sat beside the fire in his room, that wonderful old brick fireplace, Max drying under his towel, the manly smell of him as he wrapped his arm around her and she pretended to read. Her mind wasn't on the book.

Later that night, as was her custom, Sylvia had left for her dorm, one of the modern, antiseptic ones.

Now she lingered at room 13. It wasn't the first time she'd wondered what it would have been like to spend the night with Max Ridgway. Then she entered the Rotunda.

Her pumps touched rich, white carpet, then Sylvia climbed the stairs. The Dome Room, large and round and fringed with stately columns, admitted the spring sunshine through tall windows. A lectern had been set up and chairs brought in for a capacity audience. All the men, it seemed, wore blue blazers, red ties, and khaki slacks; all the women, long, body-concealing skirts or dresses. Sylvia recognized no one—almost everyone here was much older than she, or much younger. Taking one of the last vacant seats, she told herself she wouldn't stay long. Certainly not for the reception afterward in the President's Acceptance Room a floor below.

When the new president arrived, escorted by high-ranking university officials, he was greeted with a standing ovation. Just as Sylvia was ready to sit down, she saw through a wall of bodies one body in the rear, the familiar eyes searching for a seat. Instead, they landed on her.

Max Ridgway did a double take. He wore a gray tweed coat, a blue tie that matched his eyes, khaki slacks, and, yes, his signature cowboy boots. A smile began to etch itself into his face as Sylvia, catching her breath, sat down and made a point of keeping her eyes on the new president.

They didn't stay there forever. No doubt a fine administrator, the new president left something to be desired as an orator. It wouldn't have mattered if he'd been Julius Caesar. Sylvia's mind ablaze, she soon urged her eyes back for a quick glance at Max. He caught her in the act. He stood against the rear wall, disdaining the one empty seat in the room, with that teasing smile. Sylvia turned away quickly. But, after several more wooden paragraphs from the president, when Sylvia next turned to look, Max held his gaze on her, then turned, inviting her to follow, and walked casually down the stairs.

This was the moment, she knew.

He was waiting at the foot of the stairs. "Want a snack?" he said as if they had been talking together all day.

Beckoning, Max led a baffled Sylvia down the hall into the President's Acceptance Room. Long tables with white tablecloths were even now being decked with heavenly hors d'oeuvres. With a grin at a young man in a bow tie and white jacket, Max made straight for a tray of puff shells stuffed with crabmeat. He seized two handfuls.

"Excuse me, sir?" the man said. "Are you a—Hey, aren't you that football player? Uh . . . Max Ridgway!"

"You got it."

"All right!" he exclaimed. "I used to watch you play, man!"

Max nodded toward Sylvia. "You should talk to her. She's much more famous than I am."

"Oh, yeah?" The man turned quizzically to Sylvia. "Do I know you?"

Max and Sylvia laughed together. "Sylvia K. Loring," Max informed him, handing Sylvia her hors d'oeuvres. "This has got to be the only place in the country where Max Ridgway is as famous as Sylvia Loring."

Sylvia wondered what he meant by that. She took a bite of the crabmeat and watched Max's face as he thanked the man for the food and swung his attention back to her. He held his eyes on her with such clear and sudden yearning that Sylvia had to look away.

"You look beautiful," he said.

The man cleared his throat and made a show of going back to work.

"Want to walk?"

Sylvia swallowed the lump in her throat. "That's the first thing we ever did together, Max."

"No," he said, his eyes catching the reddish rays of the setting sun that slanted through the window. "The first thing we ever did together, Sylvia, was dance."

It was the same fraternity. Night had not quite fallen, but already the party was in full swing, the music booming out onto the street.

"Nothing ever changes, does it?" Max said, opening the huge front door for her, ever the gentleman.

Sylvia nodded. But he was wrong, she thought. These 1990s kids looked different—something about the hair. And she, Sylvia Loring, had changed. The heart had changed inside her.

She felt the eyes of these kids upon them, wondering what these old people were doing here as they danced to the blaring music. She wanted to go. Then she looked up at Max, tall above her, and saw that he wanted to be here. That he could somehow make it work.

She slipped her hand into his. By the way his hand reacted, she knew that she had startled him. But she only tightened her grip. "Want to dance?"

He only looked at her. Then, tugging her strongly into the crowd of kids, he waited the few moments till the song had ended and said in a strong voice, "Anybody got a Stones tape around here?"

"Who wants to know?" a jockish-looking guy said, approaching.

"Max Ridgway."

The young man stared at Max, incredulous. "You're Max Ridgway?" He examined Max more closely. "It is! You look just like your picture, man. Hey,'' he sang out to his football brethren, ''we got a legend in our midst! Where's that Stones tape?''

They danced until they dropped. Sylvia slipped off her pumps and rode in Max's arms until the night swam in front of her eyes. Sweat had never smelled so good. The kids brought them beer, and in the end the kids fell aside, watching intently, caught up in the spell of romance as Max and Sylvia danced on, alone on the floor. At last the music ran out, and Max and Sylvia leaned against the wall, tight in each other's arms.

''Want to get some air?''

''I think you said that, too. The last time.''

''I guess I just repeat myself.''

She laid her finger on his lips. ''I guess if I didn't remember it so well, there wouldn't be a problem, would there?''

They were aware that the kids were still watching them. But it didn't matter. It was almost a thrill to be watched.

''I was talking about poetry, I remember that much.''

''You were always talking about poetry.''

Max gazed into her eyes. Then his hand reached, stroked a damp lock of her hair high onto her forehead. ''Did I say that T. S. Eliot was wrong? April is not the cruelest month.''

''So where do we go from here?'' They were out on University Avenue, the night was starry and mild, and Sylvia was looking up into Max's eyes.

He tightened his arm around her shoulders. ''Are we talking about life? Or love? Or what?''

''All of it.''

''I don't know.'' His grin was radiant in the streetlight. ''We better decide fast. We're getting old.''

''No, we're not. We're getting smart.''

A car passed and then the street was dark, save for the streetlight. They were looking at each other, bodies knitted tight, both thinking the same thing.

''I know a place,'' he said, speaking for them both.

She said nothing. She let him take her up past the Rotunda, down onto the Yard. ''Wait here,'' he said.

It took faith. Almost all the faith she had. It was fifteen minutes in the quiet night before he returned. "Max, where are we going?" she said.

He walked her to the door. Number 13. "Our lucky night." He fished into his pocket, pulled out a key, and inserted it into the lock.

"Max, what are you doing?"

He swung open the door. Then he grabbed a few sticks of leftover firewood from outside room number 15. His free arm swung around her and steered her gently into the darkness.

"Max, there's somebody in here!"

He dropped the firewood, pulled her tight against his chest. "I told the security guy who I was. He remembered me."

"So?"

"I told them I wanted to take a look at my old room."

She stared at him. "So?"

"They said no problem. The student who lived in number 13 this year left school last month."

Sylvia looked up at him. This man who could always do anything. A miracle, this time. An omen. She had never seen more light in his eyes.

He smiled down at her. "What do you think? Do you think it's bad luck?"

Then he kissed her. A slow, maddening, delirious kiss.

She watched him take off his coat. Loosen his tie. She watched his muscles stretch against his slacks and shirt as he bent at the fireplace, lighting the fire. He blew on the flames and slowly the wood caught.

Sylvia shut the door and locked it. Not for another million years was she going to open that door again and face the world. Face the rest of her life. The hard choices.

"No, Max," Sylvia said. "Not bad luck at all."

There was only the firelight now. The firelight and Max Ridgway.

It was her own official secret.